CONTENTS

Preface and Acknowledgements

PART ONE: *Festivals* 1

PART TWO: *Worship* 63

PART THREE: *Rites of Passage* 131

PART FOUR: *Christian Beliefs and their meaning for Christians* 175

PART FIVE: *Christianity in a non-Christian World* 221

Glossary 273

PREFACE AND ACKNOWLEDGEMENTS

This is no ordinary textbook. It contains quite a lot of information, but perhaps more significant is the approach to each topic. The earliest Christians had a deep knowledge of Jewish religious rituals and sacred scripture, but the most significant thing for them was their own experience. Christianity has grown out of the encounter with Jesus Christ, whether this was with the disciples in Galilee or in countless different ways for later generations. So personal experience is fundamental.

The students who will be using this book, however, will not themselves have had these kinds of experiences. It may be quite foreign to them. Instead they have had a lot of valid experience in other contexts, and these have been drawn upon to introduce the topics in this book — or in some cases to help make them meaningful and memorable.

Some of the activities or exercises here are of a fairly normal type and have been designed to help students explore a topic, to make it understandable. But many others of the suggested activities are not like this at all. They are experiential. The purpose of these exercises is either to help students recall experiences they have already had which ought to be relevant to the topic, or in a few cases to present new experiences. Some of the experiences (of both kinds) are communal ones, so there is a certain amount of working in groups. The idea is that lively minds stimulate each other.

At the same time there are a very few actual questions from past GCSE papers. There are rather more activities which could be made into course work or at least form the basis for course work. Each of the five parts also has a number of '**One Line Answers**' which can be used at any time.

Because of the emphasis on experience, the general approach in this book goes much deeper than a body of fact to be learned. It goes deeper even than what is normally meant by understanding and makes some appeal to the feelings and gut reactions. This has been done for two reasons: first because it gives plenty of scope for less academic pupils to take part in what is going on and to display perhaps little–known talents; and second because religion is of its nature like that. Christianity appeals to all aspects of the human being, not just to the intellect.

Throughout the book, there are suggestions that Christianity has deep roots. Although the stress is on Christianity today, there are references to the generations between the first and the twentieth century. Christianity is also highly symbolic, and it has been necessary to explain some of the many layers of meaning which lie behind or under some of the rituals and beliefs. This in turn should show the more ambitious students that there is a lot more to be studied, felt and appreciated. Some suggestions for further development are made for those who would like to take them up.

In this way it is intended that the approach adopted will fulfil the main aims of the GCSE. Every aspect of the course will be rooted in experience, even though the experience of modern day students is very different from that of the first Christians. The first Christians also included a wide range of ability and interests and it is hoped that this book will, in a rather different way, also appeal to wide variety of people.

I feel that I have put a lot more of myself into this work than is usual with books of this kind. But it would not have even begun to take shape without the help of teaching and other colleagues. Foremost among these is Maureen Potter, the l.e.a. Adviser for R E in Durham County, who started me off in the right direction. Among the many teachers and pupils who have read or used parts of the text and given me helpful feedback, I would especially like to thank Lesley Wood, who read every word and helped me simplify and improve much of what I drafted.

Ideas for exercises and activities came from too many sources to mention, and most of them have anyway been so modified over time as by now to be scarcely recognisable to their original authors. My wife had many enterprising ideas, and also put me in touch with Donna Brandes from whose books *Gamesters' Handbook* (with Howard Phillips) and *Gamesters' Handbook Two* (both published by Hutchinson) the activities Gripes Market and versions of the Value-Continuum come.

Of the other material, much is public knowledge, for instance about Bruce Kent and Steve Biko. The story of Father Pavel comes from *A Samizdat manuscript translated by Marite Sapiets* and published by A.R. Mowbray in 1978 with the title *The Unknown Homeland*. Jean Vanier has published several books about the work of *l'Arche*. There is a lot of published material about St Elisabeth as well as the ornate but empty shrine and pictorial windows of stained glass in the Elisabethkirche in Marburg. Some other sources are mentioned in the text.

The idea of writing on the subject 'What I believe' came from Mary Spain's book *What Do I Believe?* published by Shepheard–Walwyn in 1978, together with some of the pupils' comments.

I am specially indebted to friends for some of the pictures which they either suggested or lent to me. Ginny Straugheir took the pictures of Baptism in the Jordan and of the Coptic Bible, and the Rev. Philip Lambert of Alston in Cumbria took the picture of the Easter sheep roast in Greece. My wife snapped the family picture (in Turkey), and my son Richard took one or two others which have been used.

Other pictures for which I am grateful come from the following:

Allsport 22, 23(a,b), 64, 146; Andes 24, 31, 41, 58, 84, 86, 100, 102, 107, 111, 119(a,b,c), 135, 149, 162, 195, 223; Associated Press 231; Hazel Bartlett 56, 69; BBC Hulton Picture Library 271; Bible Society 102; British and Foreign Bible Society 127; Camera Press 167, 227; Central Office of Information 49; Christmas Archives 5, 17; Giles Conacher 193; Country Life 229; Dean and Chapter of Durham 254; Darton, Longman, Todd 254; Department of Environment 57; Elisabethkirche Marburg 232; Keith Ellis 6, 8, 12, 13, 26, 30, 53, 59, 66, 77, 86, 91, 138, 158, 161, 164, 206, 248, 250, 261; Mary Evans 200, 213, 232; Gina Glover Photo Co-op 236; Greenhills 95; Sonia Halliday 89, 139, 140, 198, 153; Brian Hodgson 182; Japan National Tourist Organisation 87, 136; Keston College 94, 163, 186; Robert Lenz 246; Littlewoods Pools 228; Mansell Collection 11, 19, 82, 142, 190, 201, 214, 215; Ministry of Defence 264; Robin Minney 36, 103, 132; National Tourist Organisation of Greece 248; Bill O'Connor 161; Oxfam 202, 235, 259; Oxford Crematorium 171; Oxford County Newspapers 47; 135; Paul

Popper 154, 164, 226; Popperfoto 12, 19, 85, 88, 195, 199, 265; Radio Times Hulton Picture Library 178, 179; Rugby Advertiser 145; Brian Shuel 52; Spectrum 243; Katy Squire 204; Louise Stewart 47, 73, 147; Surrey County Council 183; Graham Topping 91, 95, 97, 113, 133, 171, 192, 216; John Twinning 33, 44, 86, 103, 157, 165; Ukranian Museum, New York 241; World Council of Churches 266; WCC: Peter Williams 177.

Finally, it remains to thank those who have put up with my rush and pressure over the two years it took to put this book together. My wife and family have been exceptionally patient and kind, and I must also thank many colleagues who have waited for me by the photocopier when there was a rush to get material off to the publisher. Last but not least, thanks are due to the publishers, who suggested the book in the first place, and to their reader. They have given me every kind of patient encouragement, not least when I have disagreed with them.

Part One

FESTIVALS

Chapter One

SPECIAL TIMES

Make a list on a piece of paper headed '**Things I am looking forward to**', and keep it for reference a little later in this section.

$\Large\mathrm{T}$ake a few moments to think what events you are looking forward to in the course, say, of the next few months. A list of things might include your birthday, Christmas, a holiday you are planning, the passing of exams, or maybe having a load of work behind you.

To mark these occasions you will probably do something special, something different from the routine of ordinary life. This is likely to include a rest from work and a meal, or at least something special to eat and drink. And even if giving a party does in fact mean quite a lot of work, it is enjoyable and quite a bit different from working for pay or for examinations. These two ideas, eating with friends and taking a day off, seem to figure with most festivals, whether it is a public festival like Christmas or something more personal like celebrating your success in exams.

SOMETHING TO CELEBRATE

ACTIVITY: as a group

Now is a good time to do some shared thinking on this.

Get together with four or five others and jointly make up a list of things you think you would like to celebrate.

Head your list '**What's worth celebrating**?'

One person writes down all the ideas and suggestions from all the members of the group without argument or discussion.

Only when you have got a list should you start to talk it over and decide on the things that seem most worthwhile to you all.

Now get a second sheet of paper and write the heading, '**What's the best way to celebrate**?'

After you have got ideas from your group, look again at your first list headed '**What's worth celebrating**'.

- Are some ways of celebrating more suitable for certain types of occasion?
- Can you say why?

Brainstorming

What you have just done is an exercise in exploring an idea fairly thoroughly. The idea you worked on is 'celebrate' and 'celebration'. Brainstorming is a group activity. It is used quite a lot on this course because it is a good way of getting ideas from everyone, and particularly from people who maybe do not say very much normally. When you have got a good number of ideas, the group works together to arrange them, sort them out, and perhaps improve them.

ALL members of group give their ideas and suggestions.	'Secretary' writes down all the ideas, as they come.

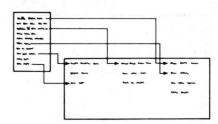

Then the WHOLE group looks at the list of ideas in silence.	Any duplicates are crossed off, then on a clean sheet of paper ideas with something in common are grouped together.

The best size of group is from five to twelve. You will need a big piece of paper or a blackboard and someone to write down all the suggestions. There are some basic rules in brainstorming which you must observe, and they are:

1 Members of the group speak out their ideas connected with the word or topic and these are written quickly and briefly for all to see. This part should be more or less off the tops of your heads.
2 No–one may comment or interrupt when someone else is speaking.
3 Everyone in the group should contribute something, unless really unwilling to do so.
4 People need to feel they can trust each other within the group, and say what they think about the topic being discussed.

Only after you have together made your first list do you go through it again and try and get some order or system into the various suggestions. This list now belongs to the group. Individuals do not own the suggestions they may have put forward originally.

Now you get a new board or piece of paper to organise the ideas on the first one. Rewrite the suggestions, putting into a column ideas that seem to be linked. Give each column a title if you can. You can revise some of the ideas, add new things if they really seem important, and cross out anything that now does not seem to make much sense.

By going about it in this way you have as a group explored the idea of '**celebration**' fairly thoroughly.

MARKING THE PASSAGE OF TIME

Find out what the letters A.D. and B.C. stand for, if you do not already know. Some people like to use C.E. and B.C.E. instead. Try to find out why, but only after you have found out about A.D. and B.C.

People talk about doing things 'before Christmas' or 'after Christmas', 'before the wedding' or 'after the wedding.' Special occasions help us to measure the passing of time. We begin the calendar each year with New Year's Day, and we number the years as A.D. or B.C.

Think whether there is any big event in your life which has made a difference to the way you see things. This might be moving house, especially if you moved a long way, changing schools, a new friendship or a new member of the family. This change was not just a special occasion or a point in time, but it has had a lasting effect, and as a result of it your outlook on life is now different. This is certainly true for religious festivals. Christians celebrate Easter and other festivals not just as a convenient point in time, but because for them Easter has made a big difference to the way they see life.

Religious festivals are also used to measure time. Almost all Christian festivals occur once a year, except of course Sunday which is every week. At one time lots of things in ordinary life were timed to happen round religious festivals. Rent was paid on Quarter Days, three of which were Christian festivals, and all the holidays (holy days) were also Christian festivals in this country. Some of our public holidays are still linked to the Christian calendar.

But even events which only happened once can be recalled with a special celebration. Birthdays are like this, as you were only born once, but you can have a party every year. Other celebrations like this would include a wedding anniversary. Some of these are big occasions like a Silver Wedding (how many years?) or a Golden Wedding (how long?).

After the 1870 Education Act a lot of new schools were built, and in the 1970s quite a lot of village primary schools were celebrating their centenary. A typical occasion would be a sit–down supper in the main hall one evening, a few speeches, and reminiscences from the oldest person present, who had been a pupil in the school maybe eighty years before. To prepare for the party, the room would have been decorated with curtains and flowers, and photographs of the school, the pupils and teachers in bygone years.

ACTIVITY: on your own

Find your list of 'Things I am looking forward to'.
Divide these items up under separate headings, such as public things, personal things, things that you can look forward to every year, and things that will only happen once or twice in your life.
You may want to add one or two things to your first list.

Symbols and Celebrations

Two special things apply to celebrating. The first is that something has happened that you want to remember or enjoy or emphasise, and the second is that you want to remind other people of it too. You want to share it with people who were not even there perhaps when it happened. Not many people were present when you were born, yet you throw a party for your friends on your birthday.

Religious festivals help people to remember something important which may have happened long ago. The ways in which they do this need to be studied, and these include two sorts of things: marks and

In this book Christmas, Easter and other public holidays are going to be studied as Christian festivals. But you need to remember that other people keep them too, and this means that some of the symbols (like the Christmas tree) have got little to do with Christian faith and practice.

signs which seem to have a special meaning (**symbols**), and special things that people say and do (**symbolic acts**).

You will be thinking more about Christmas a little later, but because it is so popular it is useful to think now about how Christmas is celebrated. Many people who are not Christians, people of other religions or of no religion, know the outline of the story — the baby born in a stable, the bright star in the sky, the shepherds, angels and wise men, and they know that people buy presents at Christmas and have parties.

So if you have a Christmas tree, the star on it is a reminder of the star of Bethlehem. Jesus is often called the '**light of the world**', and so the star on the Christmas tree is both a symbol of the star of Bethlehem and of Jesus himself. Of course there are also symbols which are not Christian, like the tree itself, evergreen to remind us that life is there even in the depths of winter.

CHRISTMAS DECORATIONS

ACTIVITY: on your own

Look at this picture and notice the things which are special for Christmas at home.

Make two lists and call one '**Christian symbols**' and the other '**Other symbols**': if these are not Christian symbols, what do you think they are?

ACTIVITY: as a group

When you have made your own lists, get your small group together and **compare lists**. Discuss any things that are different.

Street Decorations

ACTIVITY: as a group

Now look at this picture together.
This picture shows a street decorated for Christmas.

- Can you find any things in these decorations which could be called **Christian symbols**?

Although Christmas sounds like a Christian festival, it is also celebrated by lots of people who would not call themselves Christians, or not very often, perhaps only when very ill or dying.

Celebrating Special Events — Joy and Sadness

Almost everyone who is likely to read this book has been away on holiday at some time or other. This might have been a family holiday or a school trip in Britain or abroad, an expedition or a camping holiday. Maybe someone took some photographs. It can be fun to get together again, to have a meal or a drink, to look once more at the pictures, and to talk about the things you did. The friendships made seem specially important. It does not seem to matter somehow if some of the things you remember doing together were not really quite like that. They were good times, and if there were also problems and hardships, you got over them, and can now look back. Friendships seem to make an occasion like this.

If you belong to a sports club or team, think of some of the really big moments, maybe a victory, or a successful expedition. The success of the team sometimes seems to depend on a single person, who may be the coach, or the captain. If this person suddenly announces he or she is leaving, your excitement can be turned to something near despair. This announcement may be made in the middle of a party or celebration when it seems incredible that the person who has done so much to make the club a success should now be wanting to go away.

This is what the first Christians felt like, the disciples of Jesus and other men and women who knew him best. He kept the festivals of the Jewish people with them, and then he was arrested. Yet they knew that he could easily have gone away and so have escaped being put to death by the authorities who wanted to stop what he was doing.

The First Christians

It is hard to say whether the disciples of Jesus thought their time spent with him had been successful or not. There had been good times and times of great wonder, but they had faced many difficulties and had been opposed by some of the most important people in the country. They had travelled about with Jesus and done a lot of things together, including fishing, which had been normal work for some of them. They had had times of great happiness, but also times of sadness and disappointment. In spite of all this, however, they wanted to be with Jesus and could not accept the idea that he was going to leave them.

When he did go, it was to be arrested and to die, after only a sham of a trial. The disciples were so upset and frightened that they all ran away. They could not help it. It meant that they were not just disappointed that Jesus had been taken prisoner and put to death, but also they were angry with themselves, frustrated and unable to make up their minds what to do. If you have ever felt both badly treated and at the same time disappointed by your own reactions, you will feel some sympathy for the disciples.

After two days, the news of Jesus coming to them again seemed unbelievable. He had told them several times, but they were just not ready to understand. When at last they did get the message, they were transformed with joy and excitement.

ACTIVITY: as a group

Although this course is about Christianity and not about the gospels, you should know at least the outline of the life of Jesus. Get your group together. One of you should act as scribe or secretary, and **write down in note form an outline of the life of Jesus**, beginning with his baptism in the river Jordan and going on up to the ascension.

Put each event on a separate line.

Everyone helps in this by making suggestions, both of things to include, and about the order they ought to be in.

But be careful: quite a lot of the things in Jesus' life which you may want to include are not in the same order in all the gospels, so we do not know in what order they actually happened.

Now make two more lists.

Head the first one **Times when the disciples were happy**.

Head the second one **Times when the disciples were sad**.

Obviously some of the things you wrote on the life of Jesus do not fit in on either of these lists, so do not try to force them. Talk your decisions over in the group before you write each one down.

The Central Christian Celebration

The Last Supper, when Jesus had a special meal with his disciples on the night when he was arrested and betrayed, is of central importance for Christians. They meditate on this meal and they re–enact it in a ritual (to be explained more fully in Part Two): this is a ceremony or church service based on the account of Jesus giving out bread and wine to his disciples.

First, his closest friends were sad because they felt that Jesus would not be with them much longer. They could sense that something important was going to happen, but they did not know what.

Second, Christians now know what did happen next, and that Jesus came back to them after he was crucified, so there is hope too. The celebration is happy as well. They feel him present with them in this service.

Here it will be useful to notice three things about this Last Supper in particular:

A eucharist or communion service

Third, Christians who feel Jesus is coming to them whenever they re–enact this Supper may also be a little afraid. Christians believe that Jesus will return to judge the world at the end of time. This can be worrying for most of them. The theme of judgement links into Advent (see next section).

ACTIVITY: as a group

Preparation

Plan a party to celebrate passing your examinations, or if you prefer, some other event. Make a list of what you will need, and what preparations you will have to make.

Note ideas for the celebration itself.

Try to divide your lists into things you will need, people you will have to contact and what you will do at the party.

Some people start getting ready for Christmas months in advance. For instance shops get in stock for Christmas around the end of the summer, and some people begin buying presents and Christmas cards in August and September. Small wonder that they are tired out when Christmas actually comes.

In primary schools they begin working on Christmas decorations, parties, and perhaps a nativity play just as soon as Guy Fawkes is out of the way, and often the planning has started long before.

ACTIVITY: as a group

For a preliminary exercise on planning ahead, collect your small group of five or six and choose one of the following:
EITHER imagine one of you is the Headteacher and the others the staff of a small primary school, meeting early in the autumn term to plan your school's activities for Christmas. You will need to give roles to each group member.

- Make use of any special interests or experience which members of your group may have — for instance in art, music or acting.
- As you plan, make lists of things to be done, and when they have to be done by.
- Start your staff meeting by having a **brainstorming session**. You know how to do this (see page 2).
- The result should be a kind of calendar of what is to be done and when, and who are going to do particular things, either alone (imagine a primary school class teacher working with one class), or as a joint effort.
- Then you will need to make the programme itself, with details of the school's activities for Christmas.
- Decide whether you are inviting parents to any part of it (if so, to what) and what publicity is needed.

OR ALTERNATIVELY, do the same exercise from the point of view of someone at home. This time imagine that you are members of a large family who have invited quite a lot of relatives to stay.
For this you will need to assign roles again and also to make a list of the 'relatives' you expect.

Advent means coming or arrival. The Christian season of Advent means more than this because there is a definite idea of getting ready for the coming, and this is at more than one level. Obviously there are preparations for Christmas: almost everyone is doing that in some way or other. But there is also the idea of thinking about how we get on with other people and how to put right things that seem to have gone wrong. This could be especially important at Christmas time, when many families get together again and quarrels could flare up. At Advent Christians are not only thinking about the birth of Jesus in Bethlehem, but also of the promised return of Jesus Christ at the end of the world to judge the living and the dead. Being up before the judge may not be very nice, and most Christians are a little bit anxious (see opposite).

In the Christian calender, Advent begins with a Sunday, in fact the fourth Sunday before Christmas, and ends with Christmas. As Christmas Day is always the 25th December, it can be any day of the week. But Advent always starts on a Sunday. This means that the season of Advent lasts between four weeks plus a day (if Christmas Day is a Monday), and five weeks (if Christmas falls on a Sunday), because Advent must include four Sundays.

Advent Fellowship

In some European countries, Advent is a very special time for Christian families, and others, such as small groups of Christians living near each other.

In Germany a Christian family usually has an Advent wreath, and an Advent calendar as well if there are children. The Advent wreath always has four candles, which are lit in turn (see below). Sitting by candlelight, the family enjoy cakes, fruit and nuts, and a warm drink too, and sing songs for Advent about looking forward to the coming of Jesus. It is a very warm and friendly time, and people obviously enjoy it so much that German students may have their own little Advent parties when they are away from home, and sing the same Christian songs.

You may have made an Advent wreath or an Advent calendar when you were at junior school, but if you did not, you might like to do so now. This is what to do.

ACTIVITY: as a group

The Advent wreath is made out of evergreen twigs and leaves, and is usually about one to two foot in diameter. To get the leaves to form a circle you may decide to make a framework of wood or wire. It is not hung up like a Christmas wreath, but lies flat on a table because it has four candles standing up in it, equally spaced. The first candle is lit on Advent Sunday, that and a second candle the next Sunday, and so on until on the Sunday before Christmas all four are alight. So you have a chance to sit round with your drinks and nuts and to sing songs every time a candle is lit, four parties before Christmas.

An Advent calendar

A painting of Jesus in his Mother's arms

The Coming of Jesus Christ as Judge

ACTIVITY: as a group

The Advent calendar is also fun to make. You can buy them too, but for some reason the shops never seem to get the number of days right.

The basic idea is that there is a big chart, or a picture, to hang on the wall, and it has little doors in it. The children come and open one little door each day until Christmas. **The doors are labelled with the date when they should be opened**. The first door is opened on Advent Sunday, and the last door, a big one, at Christmas. This means that each year the number of doors is different (see above about the number of days in Advent), and if you are making a calendar you have got to think ahead and work it out. It is easy to do this if you work from an ordinary calendar or diary, and mark the Sundays and Christmas. There is a lot of scope for skill and imagination, artwork and colour.

You will need two big sheets of thick paper or card, one for the front which is the main picture with the doors cut in it, and the other for the back on which are drawn or painted the little pictures to be discovered each day when the door is opened.

You could have separate bits of card stuck on the back behind each door, instead of the second big sheet of card if that seems easier when there are several people working on different things at the same time. Remember that each door has the day or date on it when it is to be opened.

On some calendars the doors are in rows, but on others they are dotted about all over the place so you have got to search to find the next one. Peeking ahead by opening the wrong one too early is definitely not allowed! Some people have bigger doors (and bigger pictures behind them) for the four Sundays, and naturally a big one for Christmas. The pictures can be anything you like and think would be suitable.

If you are short of ideas for the pictures, you could look ahead in this section to find symbols of Advent which Christians have used — an alarm clock for waking up and so on — but anything to do with Christmas is suitable, even though it may not be at all Christian in its origin — for instance a Christmas tree or reindeer. The last picture is always either a scene of the birth of Jesus (or Jesus in the arms of his Mother), or of Jesus Christ wearing a crown as king and judge.

Making an Advent calendar helps us to think about preparing for Christmas not just on your own, but also as a group or a family. Christianity depends not on individuals so much as on the Christians who have become the Church and who hand on the tradition, the Bible and the faith to future generations.

This means that as part of their preparation for Christmas, Christians are supposed to think about their personal relationships with other people, both Christians and non–Christians.

At the first level, Christians think about their relations with other members of the family. This may include thinking of nice presents to give them, but it also means deciding to make up for times and things that seem to have gone wrong in some way. There is more about this in Part Two, Chapter 5.

Christians believe that Jesus will come back to judge the living and the dead. See in Part Four the section on Judgement (pages 199-204). Therefore Advent is also a time for thinking about being judged, and the hopes and joyful expectations of Christians who are looking forward to Christmas are also tinged with some fear and anxiety which centres on stories and pictures of the end of the world. If you have ever seen a picture of this you will know why!

Themes and Symbols for Advent

In all religions people like to show their feelings and their faith. They use pictures, words and actions to bring to mind things from their religious history, or their hopes for the future. These are called **religious symbols** and Christianity has plenty of them. Some are very obvious, like a picture or carving of Jesus on the cross to help Christians think about the crucifixion. Some of these symbols seem to have several layers of meaning: for instance, a man carrying a lamb or a calf across his shoulders symbolises the Good Shepherd, and the Good Shepherd not only recalls Jesus saying *I am the good shepherd and the good shepherd gives his life for the sheep* (John 10.11), but reminds people of symbols in the Old Testament too. God is often called the shepherd of Israel, and David, who was a shepherd boy when he killed Goliath (I Samuel 17), has himself become for later generations the symbol of the ideal king. The shepherd idea continues in the Christian tradition with the shepherd's crook which is carried by Western bishops.

Jesus on the cross

A shepherd with his crook

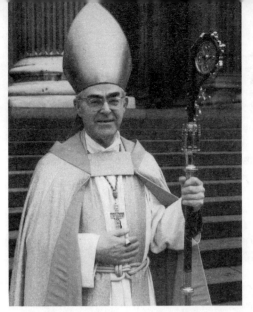

The Bishop of London holding his crook

Not all symbols are exclusively religious. That is part of the mystery and the attraction of a lot of religious symbolism. For instance, a lamb, a light, a fish, a pelican and a rose all belong in some way to Christian tradition. Sometimes people invent new symbols, but much more often they use symbols which they already know or have learnt about: that means that symbols are mostly traditional.

A symbol is in some ways like a badge or even a secret sign. As we have seen already, most religious symbols have several layers of meaning. A loaf or loaves of bread for instance is a symbol for Christians of the Last Supper, and of Jesus feeding five thousand people, and then again of Jesus himself through his saying *I am the bread of life* (John 6.35).

ACTIVITY: on your own

Symbols to do with Advent

These are some of the basic ideas:

waking up, getting up, a message about an important visitor, getting ready for the visitor's arrival, a feast (especially a wedding feast), getting on good terms with the family and neighbours, looking forward to the birth of Jesus Christ, the return of Christ as judge at the end of time.

Working on your own, take one of these ideas, for instance that of waking up, and either draw pictures or write words and phrases which you think might symbolise this idea.

Now, still on your own, choose another idea connected with Advent, perhaps a message about an important visitor, and again draw a picture.

Now that you have got the idea, work through the following list and write not more than one or two lines on each, saying what it has to do with Advent:

Christ as Judge
an alarm clock
preparing for a feast
healing the sick
putting on armour
writing a book
taking stock of your life
drawing pictures
Jesus walking on the water
the good shepherd
a cock crowing in the morning
feeding 5,000 people
a wedding party
turning water into wine
going fishing
keeping alert and awake
putting things right that have gone wrong
paying your taxes
buying Christmas presents
a watchman on a lookout tower

- Did you find that some of them had nothing at all to do with Advent? If so, you are quite right.
- Take out these misleading suggestions.
- If you can, think up some of your own which you think have something to do with Advent and add them on instead.

ACTIVITY

To be done alone or in a group if you think you need each other's help.

**Find a church hymn book, one which has headings for different festivals and seasons, and find the section on Advent.
Select two of these hymns.**

- Read carefully the first one you have chosen
- Note down words and phrases in it which seem to you to refer to ideas connected with Advent, as suggested in the paragraphs above.
- Write out clearly the words from the hymn which you think refer to one of these ideas.
- Then alongside or underneath, state briefly what the Christian idea is which is being mentioned.
- When you have done this with one hymn, do the same with the second you have chosen.
  Two or three carefully chosen hymns should cover all the ideas above more than once.
- Maybe you will find some other things which you think appropriate to Advent, but have not been mentioned in this book: if so, note them down too.

Further development

This activity can be improved on by finding Bible references for each of the ideas noted. As this requires quite a good knowledge of the Bible, you may need help before attempting it.

ACTIVITY: on your own

Draw a picture of the return of Christ at the end of the world.
You could choose a city scene, a village, farms, or another part of the world which you know something about (maybe Africa, or Australia). When the art work is finished, get together and explain your pictures to the other members of your group.

Chapter Three

CHRISTMAS AND EPIPHANY

Almost everyone knows what Christmas is. It comes round every year, and has long ceased to be just a religious festival. In fact most peoples in Europe had a midwinter festival long before they heard of Christianity. Memories of this survive, and so do some of the ancient customs.

In these days when warmth comes from electricity or central heating, and food can be bought in shops, the natural seasons mean much less to us. But try to think what it was like for our remote ancestors in northern Europe. In winter the nights are long and the days short. It is cold, and even if it becomes colder later, at least after midwinter the days start to get a little longer. Midwinter marks the shortest day. By this time, our ancestors would be getting short of food. It was not just ready for picking as at harvest time in the fields and woods and orchards. People had to rely on whatever was in store, and when snow came and the grass was deadened by frost, stored food also had to be given to farm animals. Really most people preferred spring, summer and autumn.

ACTIVITY: as a group

Write down some ideas on what you might do with friends and family to mark the shortest day, or rather to mark getting past it, because everyone is also looking forward to spring.

Together plan a celebration that will help you to forget cold and darkness and the possible threat of food shortage later on. If you think one day is not enough for your celebration, spread it out over several days. Go over your ideas and try to organise them.

People still decorate their houses with evergreens (fir tree, holly, ivy, mistletoe), light candles or special Christmas tree lights, and make the lights twinkle with silvery balls and other coloured decorations.

You have probably ended up with everyone's idea of an old–fashioned Christmas. Did you think of a party with plenty of lights to beat the darkest, shortest day? A roaring log fire for warmth? A big feast from things in the store, or perhaps a goose or pig or other farm animal which you could eat, instead of you having to feed it all winter? Did you think the family and friends could play games, sing songs and tell stories round the fire? Sometimes you could go out in the snow for fun, and our ancestors in Britain would also have gone hunting for deer which had come down from the hills in the cold weather. This would provide more meat for the feast.

The Birth of Jesus Christ

Two of the gospels in the New Testament give a certain amount of detail about the birth of Jesus. When these two are put together, we get the traditional story which is acted out in Nativity plays in countless churches and schools in many parts of the world. This composite story is also represented by a little model of the birth scene, which lots of families set up in their houses at Christmas time.

Many churches have them too, but larger, and often with carved figures. Sometimes the whole scene is set up for Christmas Day, but in other churches the Christmas night scene is set first with shepherds round the Holy Family. The wise men are added later for Epiphany (6th January).

ACTIVITY

A piece of research which you can do either on your own or with a partner.

1 **Open a copy of the New Testament at Matthew chapter 1**, and have a pen and paper ready. Leave out the bit about the ancestors for now, and **start reading at Matthew 1.18. Read carefully to the end of chapter 2, making notes as you go.**
   Divide your notes under the following headings:

   (a) before the birth
   (b) the birth
   (c) political considerations — King Herod
   (d) visitors — the wise men
   (e) after the wise men left
   (f) where they lived as Jesus grew up

Notice that at (b) you have got very little information, only the fact that a baby is born, the place (town) and the approximate date. To make it easier to look back later, write the chapter and verse reference alongside each of your notes.

2 **Now do the same exercise using Luke's gospel.** Leave out the bit about John the Baptist's parents, and **read Luke 1.26–38, then 2.1–25. Make notes now from this account, using these headings**:

   (a) before the birth
   (b) political considerations — Caesar Augustus
   (c) the birth
   (d) visitors — the shepherds
   (e) after the shepherds left and where they went next
   (f) where they lived as Jesus grew up (see Luke 2.39–40)

3 **Now look again at your two sets of notes.** They have got the same pattern, and some of the details are the same (e.g. Bethlehem), but other things are quite different.
   Now take a third sheet of paper, and write down all the things which are roughly the same in the two accounts, then write down the things which strike you as different. You can be as critical as you like, for instance in Luke Jesus is born in a stable for animals, while Matthew speaks of a house.

To follow this up, **write two or three pages about the birth of Jesus as described in the gospels**. Say why you think Christian tradition has always put the material in Matthew and Luke together, and say which things in the combined story you think are likely to be true.

ACTIVITY: on your own

Look at this picture, which shows a representation of the traditional story. Write the Bible reference or references which refer to each feature in the story.

For instance, against the manger write Luke 2.7, and against the star write Matthew 2.2,9,10.

Either make a list of these items and put the references next to each, or photocopy the picture and write the references at suitable places round the edge with a line connecting each to the relevant item.

This scene is often called simply **The Crib**. Crib is an old word for a type of manger with vertical bars, but when people began to make babies' cots with vertical bars they were called 'cribs' instead. If you are interested in language changes, you could look at the Christmas carol that begins *Away in manger*: the second line used to be *a crib for a bed* but is now changed to *no crib for a bed*.

● Can you think why this happened?

17

Jesus is both God and Man

Christians think of God as eternal and almighty and the creator of all that exists. This means that God is understood to be on a different plane or in a different dimension from mankind. But in the birth of Jesus Christians have felt that God has come as a member of the human race, becoming a particular individual at a particular time and living a human life. This is known for shorthand as the incarnation, which is discussed again in Part Four, Chapter 3.

Because this is such a difficult idea for people to understand, Christians use picture language. You have already come across the use of symbols in religion. Picture language is an attempt to explain a mystery, whereas symbolism is a way of representing it.

So in the birth of Jesus, God comes to relate to people at their own level, that is horizontally. But at the same time, the vertical dimension is there too. That is why the holy child is also called Immanuel (also spelt Emanuel) which means *God with us*.

At the human level, Jesus puts himself at the mercy of men who eventually reject his love and put him to death. Becoming a human being led eventually to the crucifixion. In most Christian thinking about Christmas the Cross is never very far away.

> The old–fashioned idea of man-kind on earth and God up above may give us the idea that people relate to each other *horizontally*, but God relates to them *vertically*.

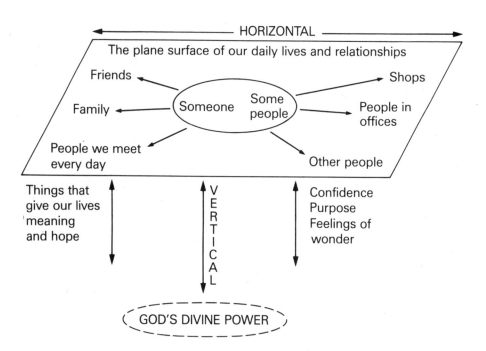

The horizontal dimension includes some of the details of the traditional account. Jesus is born in an animal shed like a refugee. He is a tiny baby, helpless and entirely dependent on his mother and other people. He only escapes being killed by King Herod's men because his parents take him away to safety. At every stage in the story the family are at the mercy of the authorities. This is exactly like the poor in every age and society.

Traditional Christian teaching develops the horizontal relationships further. The first people to meet and welcome Jesus are the poor, the shepherds who were out in the fields. The wise men who come next, turn out to be foreigners and not Jews. They are the first to recognise who Jesus is, and that he has come to the gentiles too (non–Jews), and for the whole world. The visit of the wise men is the story of Epiphany.

- Can you spot any signs of the crucifixion in this picture?

The Madonna and Child, painted by Botticelli

ACTIVITY: as a group

Design a modern version of the birth of Jesus Christ. Make notes first to plan your scene or story.

The finished product, in this case a joint product, can be a picture, or a written description — a poem if you like — or it can be acted out as a scene for someone to photograph. If you are acting this scene, a nativity in a modern setting, you may need to join up with another group.

Epiphany

Epiphany means showing something or making it obvious. The Christian festival of Epiphany, which is held on the 6th January, celebrates the visit of the wise men to Bethlehem. Thanks to the guidance of the star, Jesus is shown to them, and they recognise him as their God and King by giving him the three symbolic presents (you have read what these were in Matthew 2.11). The gospel does not mention a particular number of men, but because there were three gifts people thought there must be three wise men. They were called Kings later, and later still names were given to each of them. Because they represent all the non–Jews of the world, it has become conventional to make one of them an African and one an East Asian, the third being more or less European in appearance.

In Orthodox churches the Epiphany is the main festival of the Christmas season. Jesus was born almost in secret, in a stable or shed down a backstreet of the town, but at the Epiphany he is recognised as Saviour and King, first by the wise men and then by people of every race and language, Jews and non–Jews alike.

ACTIVITY: on your own

Find a hymn book which has a section on Epiphany and choose a hymn. Write this hymn out one verse at a time and say briefly:
(a) what it refers to in the Bible account you read earlier (Matthew 2.1–12 — you would be wise to read this again),
(b) what else it refers to in the life of Jesus and in Christian tradition.

If you cannot get hold of a suitable hymn book easily, you could use this traditional hymn by Prudentius, translated from the Latin:

1.   Earth has many a noble city;
          Bethlem, thou dost all excel:
        Out of thee the Lord from heaven
          Came to rule his Israel.

2.   Fairer than the sun at morning
          Was the star that told his birth,
        To the world its God announcing
          Seen in fleshly form on earth.

3.   Eastern sages at his cradle
          Make oblations rich and rare;
        See them give in deep devotion
          Gold and frankincense and myrrh.

4.   Sacred gifts of mystic meaning:
          Incense doth their God disclose,
        Gold the King of Kings proclaimeth,
          Myrrh his sepulchre foreshows.

5.   Jesu, whom the Gentiles worshipped
          At thy glad Epiphany,
        Unto thee with God the Father
          And the Spirit glory be.

Notes on this: *oblations* (verse 3) are offerings, gifts
               sepulchre (verse 4) is a tomb
               the last two lines of verse 5 (at the end) refer to the Trinity, which is discussed in Part Four.

Celebrating Epiphany

In Spain and Italy, and some other parts of southern Europe, the Epiphany is called **the Feast of Kings**. Given the story and the tradition which makes the wise men into kings, the reason will be obvious. It is especially a festival for the children. Just as the kings brought presents to the child Jesus, so parents and other adults give children presents.

At Epiphany Christians also celebrate the Baptism of Jesus. This marked the beginning of his ministry. See Part Three, Chapter 1.

Naturally this is instead of having presents on Christmas Day. Children and adults put on their best clothes and go to a service in church. The children have a special part in this, and the sermon could take the form of a dialogue between the preacher and half a dozen children.

The church service is followed by parties in people's houses, and the fine clothes, some of them like fancy dress, make the whole occasion like a carnival. The food includes a special cake in which a tiny figure of a king has been hidden. Whichever child gets this king in his or her piece becomes the 'king' or the 'queen' of the party. This child may simply get applause, or it may mean some special part to play in some of the games.

The Greeks have a similar custom called **Vasilopitta** (St Basil's Bread) which is popular with children. If you live near a Greek Orthodox community you may like to hear the story of St Basil which goes with this custom.

New Year

January 1st falls in the Christmas season between Christmas Day and Epiphany. It is the traditional date for the naming of Jesus, because Jewish boy babies were always circumcised and given their names on the eighth day after being born. This is still Jewish practice. But the Naming of Jesus is not a big festival for Christians.

Instead, Methodists use the start of a new year as a time of renewal and dedication to the covenant with God (friendship), and they have a special service called the **Covenant Service**. It is usually held on the first Sunday in New Year. As this service always includes the Lord's Supper (eucharist), there must be a minister present. This can mean delays when one minister has to look after several congregations.

The **Watch Night Service** is a special time of Prayer on New Year's Eve, and is kept by Presbyterians and by Methodists in Scotland and the North of England. After it is over, people visit each others' houses for first footing and other traditional customs which are not connected with Christianity.

Chapter Four

GOING INTO TRAINING

In the weeks before the Olympic Games, you can read about the training schedules of famous athletes. Of course they have been in training for a long time before, but the papers think readers will only be interested in the run–up to a big event.

Quite a lot of people train for local events, fun runs, or team sports, or just because they want to keep fit. A few years ago there was a craze for going jogging. If you want to be generally fit and healthy, then a little exercise now and then may not be enough, and your training plan is likely to cover what you eat and drink, as well as your hours of sleep, work and other habits.

ACTIVITY: as a group

Get together in your small group of five or six, and **write a plan for a training schedule for ONE of the following**:

   (a) **A sport**, either team or individual, which some of you know something about.

   (b) **Preparing for an important examination**: the schedule must include periods of revision study as well as some recreation and rest periods, sleep, meals etc.

   (c) **A schedule of Christian discipline for Lent, or preparation for something special like confirmation.** Your training schedule will include times of prayer and meditation, as well as reading, physical recreation and habits of life.

   If you choose (c) and are short of ideas, you will find suggestions in Part Two, Chapter 8 on Rules of Life.

Lent

The idea of linking Lent to athletics training goes back to St Paul's letter to the Corinthians, so it is nothing new. But Christians make use of the weeks leading up to Holy Week and Easter to think about the temptations of Jesus in the desert, and they try, by prayer and self–discipline, to prepare themselves to grow into more loyal and unselfish people. Traditionally, the season of Lent has been linked to fasting. This means usually a little more than giving up certain types of food.

The name Lent is not Christian: it just means that the days are getting longer, '*lengthening.*' In many languages the name for Lent is one that means fasting, eating less or giving something up. During this period

Christians think of Jesus, who immediately after his baptism went into the desert or uninhabited region to prepare himself for his ministry in Judaea and Galilee. In the Christian calendar Lent does not start straight after the celebration of the Baptism of Jesus (which is remembered at Epiphany), although this would perhaps be more logical.

According to the gospels, Jesus spent forty days in the desert. In this time he faced temptations and prepared himself for his ministry. Christian tradition therefore makes Lent last forty days. Lent starts with Ash Wednesday (next section), which is actually six and a half weeks before Easter. This is more than forty days. Many Christians say the Sundays in Lent should not count, and so bring the days of Lent down to forty. Others make Lent the forty days leading up to Holy Week. But Holy Week is obviously a time for special fasting and prayer (see pages 26–32).

Following the example of Jesus in the desert, Christians use Lent to go into training. The idea is to become more alert and alive spiritually and to deepen prayer life. (There are several sections on prayer in Part Two). If you think about your life, you may well find things which are not really right. Christians use the example of Jesus in the desert to try and identify these things, because they would really like to give up bad attitudes and habits.

Fasting may also be good for health, but this depends on how you normally eat. In the West it has been usual to stop eating meat in Lent, but the tradition for Orthodox church members has been to eat no meat or fish, and also to give up milk, butter, cheese, eggs and all fats. So for the whole of Lent their standard food is mainly bread and olives, or other available fruit. By the last week of Lent people can be very tired.

Ash Wednesday, people with ash on their foreheads

Ash Wednesday

The first day of Lent is called Ash Wednesday
- Can you find out how it got this name?
- Can you find out about Shrove Tuesday, which is the day before?

Many Christians still keep up the ancient practice of making their confession on the Tuesday, then burning last year's palm cross and getting a bit of ash put on their foreheads at church on Ash Wednesday morning.

The tradition with the ash includes at least two symbols. One is the dust of the ground from which, according to ancient tradition, Adam was originally created. This is taken up again in the burial service with the words *Earth to earth, dust to dust and ashes to ashes* as the body is laid in the ground. Ash therefore symbolises man and his achievements, most of which will seem very unimportant in one or two hundred years time. Secondly, there is a tradition that at the end of the world God's servants will have a special mark on their foreheads. Finally, ash is also a general sign of penitence which is fully in keeping with the spirit of Lent.

Penitence means being sorry for doing something bad or wrong, and deciding to try and make things up and do better in future.

The Desert Tradition

The desert is very significant in Christian tradition. As already noted, Jesus spent time in the desert and the gospels relate that he used to go to a lonely place to pray. If you have ever been in a desert, you will know that the desert does things to people. There is not a lot to eat, and your possessions have to be things that you can carry with you, i.e. not too much. This all adds up to saying that in the desert the people of God are dependent on God to guide them and to provide for them. It is a time of weakness and therefore of humility.

The book of Exodus relates how Moses got the children of Israel (the Israelites) out of Egypt. God (sometimes it says *the angel of God*) led them by going in front in a pillar of cloud by day and a pillar of fire by night. The Israelites crossed the Red Sea, but when the Egyptian army came with their chariots and horses they got stuck and drowned. And the Israelites got away into the desert. This was a time of hardship and a time of testing. There was hardly any water to drink and not much food to eat.

But the tradition says clearly that God provided food and water for them. This same tradition which was treasured by the Jews became also the tradition of the Christian church. That is why this story is so important.

It is little wonder that the New Testament makes so many references to the Exodus and recalls so many important events in the life of Jesus that are linked to the uninhabited country of Judaea and Galilee, the desert near at hand.

ACTIVITY: on your own

Find a Bible and read carefully the following passages, making notes as you go along. You will also need strips of paper to use as bookmarks in order to find the place in the Bible quickly when you come to make your diagram.

1 Read the following passages: Exodus 16.1–17.7; Hosea 2.1–3; 2.6–7: 2.14–17, and Isaiah 40.1–5.

2 Now read in the gospels the story of the five thousand people who where given food in a deserted place, Matthew 14.13–21.

3 On a large sheet of paper devise a kind of 'flow diagram' based on what you have just read. Make your starting point 'the desert' and then connect to this other things you have read from the Bible, both Old and New Testaments.

You might include the crossing of the Red Sea, the Temptations of Jesus, but also think of feelings and experiences like feeling lost, hungry and thirsty, but at the same time feeling free, not much luggage to carry. Let your imagination help you.

(If you find that this looks too hard to do alone, you could find a partner and work at it in pairs)

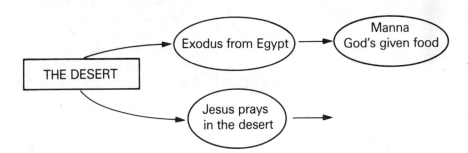

A Time of Endurance

If you are an athlete or other sportsman you will know that hard training can contribute to your success and increase your stamina. Can you think of any other example of a difficult experience or time or hardship which, looking back on it, has helped you in some way? A hard time can give you confidence in yourself, build up your stamina and powers of perseverence.

Many Christians of every generation have tried to follow the example of Jesus who went into the desert to pray and to prepare himself for what he had to do. Some Christians have gone literally into uninhabited places. Others have chosen a life of prayer even within a well–populated area, living alone for much of the time. This loneliness is their desert and their life with God.

The most famous of all the **desert fathers** is certainly the Egyptian saint, Anthony, who went out into the Egyptian desert. Other people came out to live like him. From this experimental life–style grew the ideals of Christian monasticism (this is the religious life of monks and nuns). St Anthony stayed in the same place for many years, but was much in demand for teaching and advice about prayer and other problems, and so he travelled a little. Even so, much of his life was quite solitary, and he lived to be around a hundred and five: approximate dates 251–356 A.D.

Holy Week

The gospel writers make clear that Jesus went up to Jerusalem for the Passover, knowing that he would be arrested and put to death. To this extent his death was voluntary. Christians celebrate this in Holy Week, the week which leads up to Easter.

It starts with Palm Sunday and includes Good Friday. During this week Christians follow the last week of the earthly life of Jesus. The fact that all the gospels give a lot of space to this week and to the resurrection tells us that these events were from the first felt to be extremely important. These eight days are central for the Christian tradition, and the celebration of the day of resurrection on Easter Sunday is the essence and the starting point for Christianity.

Many church groups hold special services for each day of this week. Others will mark only the Sunday, Thursday evening, Friday, and of course Easter Sunday. These will be described below.

ACTIVITY: on your own

Try to find out at the right time of year, a little before Holy Week begins, **what services local churches are planning**.

You could perhaps attend some of them and look through the books or service sheets which tell you what is happening each day. If there are to be special processions and lights and candles, you should ask permission to take photographs.

After each visit, write up an account of what you have seen. Include what you yourself felt or were thinking about it all at the time, as well as what you think you understood.

In particular, note any symbols, actions or signs which seemed to remind people of a deeper layer of meaning, or refer to something that occurred in the life of Jesus.

Palm Sunday

A Vicar giving out palm crosses on Palm Sunday

How to make a palm cross

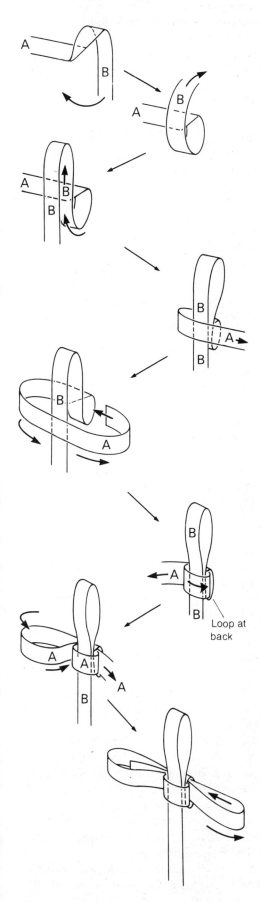

Loop at back

The Sunday before Easter is called Palm Sunday. It recalls the day Jesus rode into Jerusalem on a donkey. His disciples and the crowds welcomed him with branches, mainly from palm trees, and shouted, *Hosanna* and *Blessed is he who comes in the name of the Lord*. These same people were not to be seen on the Friday when Jesus was led out to be crucified. Christians are encouraged to rejoice on Palm Sunday and little palm fronds are given out in many churches. These pieces of palm leaf are usually made into the form of a cross. The cross shape reminds them that Good Friday is not far away.

ACTIVITY

To do either with your group or on your own

This exercise on Palm Sunday requires the use of a Bible, or at least the New Testament. You can get together in your small group and talk over the questions before writing down your answers. Or you can do this exercise on your own, if you prefer.

1 **Read John 12.12–16 and get clear what happened. Then read Mark 11.1–11 and compare the two accounts.**

2 **Now answer the following questions**, first orally, then write the answers down.

(a) Were people expecting this to happen? What evidence is there?

(b) Who was David and what has he got to do with it?

(c) Who today thinks Jesus is a king? What can this mean?

(d) *Blessings on him who comes in the name of the Lord!* is a quotation from Psalm 118.26. Look at this psalm, verses 19–end, and see if you think it suggests to you anything which might be relevant to Palm Sunday.

ACTIVITY: practical

This is an activity which might also be useful to somebody else. The palms given out in many churches at the service on Palm Sunday are usually made into the shape of a cross. They can be bought ready made, but some churches just buy the fronds and people in the congregation make them into crosses. **See if you can help in making palm crosses**.

About two to three weeks in advance, ask round local churches. You may need to be shown how to do this or you may be able to work it out for yourselves.

There are basically two ways: in one, you need two bits of palm, which fold and then fix together with glue. The other way only needs one fairly long frond which can be folded cleverly to make a firm cross without needing any glue at all. It is fun to do this as a group.

Look at the picture below and answer the questions which follow.

(a) (i) On which special day is this service taking place? (1 mark)
(ii) In which week does this day fall? (1 mark)
(iii) What is the priest giving to the people?
(iv) Why are these things given out on this day? (2 marks)

(b) Priests often wear special clothes when taking part in public worship. Why do they do so? (3 marks)

Holy Thursday — Maundy Thursday

At services held in churches on the evening before Good Friday Christians remember the Last Supper which Jesus held with his disciples. What is related about this meal gives Christians both the reason and the form for the holy communion service. Jesus took the bread and said, 'This is my body', and then over the cup of wine, 'This is my blood'. For both he added, 'Do this in remembrance of me'. These words are central for the celebration of the eucharist.

This is of central importance to all but a tiny minority of the world's Christians, and the holy communion is treated at length in Part Two, Chapter 4. The night of Maundy Thursday recalls it.

Two other important things happened at the Last Supper. Judas Iscariot went out from the meal to get ready to betray Jesus to the Temple authorities, who arrested him later that evening in the garden of Gethsemane. So this too is recalled every year on this night. The other event was the extraordinary and quite unexpected action of Jesus in washing the feet of the disciples. You can read about this in John 13.1–17. At the end we read not only why the washing of feet was important, but also that the disciples should wash feet for one another.

In the days when people travelled mostly on foot, their feet got both tired and dirty, especially if they were wearing sandals or no shoes at all.

It is quite a thought for us today to think that a legion of Roman soldiers could be posted from Jerusalem to Hadrian's Wall in the north of England, and they would have to walk on foot all the way, except for two very short boat crossings. It took a while, especially as they had to carry tools, weapons and armour, and had to make a camp every night. In those days it was a sign of welcome if you were able to take your sandals off and rest your feet. It was better still if a slave washed them in warm water.

This is just a hint at the significance of what Jesus did on that evening. Christians have meditated on it for many centuries, and it has been the custom in some churches to enact a foot washing. At one time Christian kings and rulers used to wash the feet of a number of poor and aged people on this one night in the year.

The time Jesus spent in the garden praying and waiting for his arrest is not marked by a church ceremony. It is, however, a time of prayer and meditation for Christians, and some churches organise a watch, that is a succession of people to pray in the church throughout the night up until the service on Good Friday.

Paying the Penalty

Christian teaching is that Jesus, by being put to death like a dangerous criminal, paid the penalty for the wrongdoing of the rest of the human race. This is a big claim.

Maximilien Kolbe

Jesus was arrested and led away. Everyone knew that he was innocent of any crime, but some people were jealous and the big crowds he attracted worried the officials responsible for public order. His disciples were frightened and did not know what to do. Some of them hid or pretended they did not know him.

If you are found guilty in a Magistrate's Court, the penalty is quite often a fine. But if you cannot pay the money there is usually the alternative of spending a few days in prison. If you were faced with a fine which you could not pay, and thought with horror that this would mean going to prison, then suddenly and quite unexpectedly a neighbour paid the fine for you, how would you feel? You would probably feel enormous relief, mixed with shame at not being able to cope for yourself: you would also be grateful, even if you were not at all sure of the best way to show your thanks.

If the penalty handed down was a prison sentence, there would be no choice, and magistrates in this country would not agree to let someone else go to prison on your behalf, even if someone tried to help you like this. But there have been exceptional cases.

Most people have heard about the Nazi concentration camps of 1933–1945. Some were mass extermination camps for gypsies, communists and Jews, but others were prisons. Maximilien Kolbe was a Polish franciscan friar who was arrested and put in one of these.

If anyone managed to escape, the Nazis punished the others by taking ten people for a special kind of death. They were stripped of all clothes, and put into an underground room without any food until they died. Escapes were very rare, but one day in 1941 Maximilien Kolbe saw ten men lined up for this punishment, and silently took the place of another man whom he knew had a wife and young family. The man he saved actually survived the camp and the war, and lived to see Maximilien Kolbe declared a saint some thirty years later.

It was not that Kolbe and the man he saved had been special friends. If you were saved by a friend in this way you would feel bad about losing him. On the first Good Friday the little group of Christ's disciples, men and women, lost their friend and their leader, and they felt terrible.

Detailed accounts of the trials and crucifixion of Jesus are given in each of the four gospels. There are many references to the crucifixion in the rest of the New Testament. Christians of all nations and churches have written and spoken and meditated on the death of Jesus on the cross. There can be no doubt about the central importance of this event for the faith and life of Christian people.

There must be countless ways in which people have thought and prayed about this. This book can only consider some of the things that Christians do.

PRAYING ABOUT GOOD FRIDAY — A FOCUS FOR WONDER

According to Christian legend, St Helena, who was the mother of the first Christian Roman Emperor, Constantine, went on pilgrimage to Jerusalem, and there she miraculously found wood and some nails from the cross on which Jesus died. This would be some three hundred years after the crucifixion. Her finding the wood and nails of the cross is celebrated with a major festival on September 14th, in particular by the Syrian Orthodox church, which is the major denomination in the Holy Land.

Symbols of the crucifixion include pictures of Jesus on the cross, the cross itself (found in all Christian churches, but not Quaker Meeting Houses), the wood of the cross, nails, crown of thorns. These last are also called **instruments of the Passion** and **Passion** is a special term for the suffering of Jesus on the cross. Another symbol is the blood that Jesus shed. Although it is not represented in the same way as the cross or crown of thorns, the blood of Jesus can also be a focus for devotion.

Some symbols of the crucifixion

There is also a special form of devotion called the **Stations of the Cross**.

Christians can perform these alone or in groups, usually inside a church where the fourteen relevant stopping places (this is what *Stations* mean) have been set up.

Doing the Stations is a bit like going on a pilgrimage (see later Chapter 10 pages 56–60). Each station has its own story, although not all of these are mentioned in the gospels.

- Look at this picture of the Passion Flower: can you suggest reasons why it is called this?

ACTIVITY: on your own

Find a church near you which has the fourteen places marked for Stations of the Cross — this is likely to be a Roman Catholic church.

1 Find out what each station is, and say briefly what is related to have happened there.
2 Why do so many Christians go in for this particular form of devotion and why is it so popular?
3 Write 5 to 10 lines about a Christian (woman or man) doing the stations, and how she or he might feel.

Public Witness

In a Procession of Witness in an English town on Good Friday, you would probably find Christians from at least the following churches or denominations: United Reformed, Salvation Army, Roman Catholic, Quaker, Methodist, Church of England and Baptist, maybe more.

A Good Friday procession around the streets of London

In Greece the Christians make a public procession on Good Friday, carrying a coffin. This relates obviously to the burial of Jesus after the body was taken down from the cross.

In western Europe a public procession of witness is becoming popular, especially as Christians of many denominations join in together. Different denominations may take it in turns to lead the procession, and it has become usual for a very large, full-size cross to be carried by one or more people. During the procession hymns may be sung, or the people may walk in silence. They will stop at certain places for prayers.

A procession like this is sometimes held in the streets of London at Notting Hill. Large numbers of people take part, and the procession stops at fourteen places, exactly like the Stations of the Cross. A large cross is carried in the procession. Some of the people are dressed up to act out a Passion Play. This means that someone acts the part of Jesus and is tied to the cross. At the end he is taken down as if dead (thirteenth station) to be laid in a tomb (fourteenth station).

GCSE Question — Northern Examining Association — May 1988

Look at the picture on page 32 and answer the questions below.

(**a**) (**i**) The picture shows a cross. On which day in Holy Week is this procession most likely to be taking place? (**1 mark**)

(**ii**) What event in the life of Jesus do Christians remember on this day? (**1 mark**)

(**iii**) Why is this event important to Christians today? (**3 marks**)

(**b**) A number of Christian denominations are taking part in the procession.
(**i**) Name two denominations shown here. (**2 marks**)

(**ii**) Why do many Christians think it important for different denominations to meet together at times like this?

(**c**) Giving your reasons, say whether you think that there is any value in public acts of worship such as that shown in the picture.

(3 marks)

Chapter Five

EASTER

It is night. It is quite dark. You are waiting for something, and at the same time feeling a bit chilly. You really cannot see anything, but are glad at least to feel the ground under your feet. It is hard, a stone floor or pavement. You listen. It is obvious that you are not alone. You do not know how many other people are waiting just as you are. You think briefly of some of them, and wonder whether they are thinking of you . Probably they are not. There is just about total silence, but you can almost hear the sense of expectation.

Suddenly in the distance a light shines. It is actually fairly small, but after the darkness it seems big. It is a single flame, but quickly, almost silently, more flames come from it. Now there are dozens of lights and they are coming very close to you. The person standing next to you takes hold of your candle and tilts it towards his own and lights it. You then turn to the person the other side in order to pass the light–giving flame on. But as you give it away, you do not lose it. Sharing light makes more light for everyone, and soon the whole enormous building contains a sea of lights and faces roughly level with own.

A song is started. It is familiar, but someone has given you the words on paper, and you can read them as the great procession moves off. As you walk singing, you take your eyes off the page, and something tells you to look up. Far above you, maybe hundreds of feet, the light of a thousand candles is dimly reflected on the groined vaulting of the great cathedral. It is very beautiful. As the procession turns to the East, you notice that the dawn is beginning to show through the East window.

Easter has come. The Easter candle has been lit. With the breaking of day, the Eucharist of the Resurrection is celebrated. This was the scene experienced early one Easter morning in Salisbury Cathedral in the south of England.

Darkness and Light

The Paschal candle (also called Easter candle) is placed in a prominent place in the church. It represents the triumph of light over darkness, which in turn stands for the victory of life over death at the Resurrection. Its power as a symbol will be clear from the experience just described.

Easter celebrates Jesus rising again from the grave. So Easter means new life (of which more below), and a new kind of life. People who become Christians sometimes call this experience *being born again*. This phrase is used at Baptism, so Easter is a very popular time for baptisms, as the symbolism of dying (to sin) and rising (to new life) is strong. In some churches a candle is given at baptism to the person baptised, or the parents.

An Easter Candle

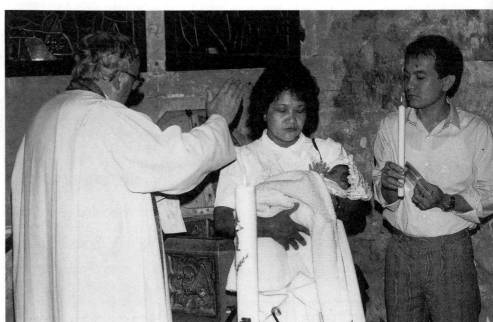

Candles at a Baptism

What the very first followers of Jesus felt, the men as well as the women, is central for the Christian understanding of Easter. Everything the disciples of Jesus had lived for seemed to have been suddenly and cruelly taken from them as Jesus was laid into the rock cut tomb in the evening of the first Good Friday. Saturday, the sabbath for Jews, was a day of quiet. Darkness seemed to them more than a metaphor, and their minds were numbed. Of course we do not really know what they felt, but their mood was suddenly changed when they first heard about and then experienced the resurrection, that Jesus had somehow risen from the dead, and then he came to them.

The gospels do not explain exactly what happened to Jesus early on that Sunday morning, just before daybreak. Some Christians today claim that they know what happened, but the traditional faith is that how God raised Jesus from the dead is a great and sacred mystery. On the other hand, how the disciples experienced this is told again and again in the gospels, and what happened to them has become the central message of Christianity. According to John's gospel Jesus was seen first of all by Mary Magdalene (also called Mary of Magdala) when she came to the tomb in the garden at dawn on the day after the Jewish sabbath.

ACTIVITY: in pairs

This activity is based on experiences of trouble and experiences of relief.

Find a partner whom you normally feel happy with, and make sure each of you has a plain piece of paper, a pencil, and some colours. This is a variation of the game called Secrets.

1 In silence for some minutes, think back in your own mind to some time in your experience when you felt terribly uncertain, or worried, or depressed about something which seemed to take away all your confidence: you simply did not know what to do.

Now take your paper and colours and try to represent in some form the doubts and difficulties you felt. You can be as symbolic and abstract as you like.

2 When you and your partner have finished your pictures, take turns to show them to each other, and talk about them. Of course it helps a lot if you feel at ease with each other, but remember, there is absolutley no need to tell the other person what your doubts or troubles were, or are. All the facts can remain quite private, unless you choose to reveal them.

3 If the trouble you used for 1 above has in fact been solved, you could now do the same exercise, but this time representing in a symbolic way the joy or relief you felt.

Traditional Ways of Celebrating

In northern countries, Easter coincides rather neatly with spring, when trees, birds and flowers are coming to life again after winter. Because of this, we find the Easter symbols of eggs, bunnies, flowers and so on. These are not in themselves Christian symbols.

To represent new life and happiness, Easter is often greeted with flowers. After the weeks of fasting through lent, there are special exciting things to eat, and people put on new clothes. In parts of Europe coloured eggs are popular. These can be simply dyed by boiling in a vegetable colour, or they can be decorated in various ways, but the most elaborate are painted. Such eggs are especially popular and traditional in the Ukraine and in Romania. Plain coloured eggs are popular in Germany and they are sometimes hidden about the house and garden for young children to go out and find on Easter morning.

ACTIVITY: on your own

If you want to try colouring eggs, it can be relatively simple: more ambitious designs take longer to do.

- Choose eggs with white shells. If you boil them with spinach leaves they will come out green. Boiled with beetroot, they go red. There are other vegetable dyes, and also artificial ones you can try.
- If you are more ambitious, fix pieces of tape or cotton round your egg before you boil it. When you take them off, the shell with be white underneath. In this way you can make simple patterns.
- Really skilful use of covering will allow you to put on several colours, one at a time, like batik.
- Otherwise you can just boil the egg in plain water and then get out your paint box. You can either make your own designs, or try to incorporate Christian symbols. If you live near a Ukrainian community, you might be able to ask for traditional designs.

ACTIVITY: as a group

An Easter Garden is fun to make too. You could do this as a group project.

- You will need a pile of small rocks, one, or perhaps three, wooden crosses, and if possible a flat round stone, to represent the door to the rock tomb.
- You build up a kind of hillside, with a cave or grotto in it as the tomb. The round stone is beside the entrance, showing that the tomb is open and empty.
- Place the cross at a little distance from the tomb. If you have three crosses, the others represent the two thieves who were crucified on either side of Jesus, but this is an optional extra.
- As it is spring, and the tomb of Jesus was in a garden, you can make any number of pockets of earth and plant flowers wherever you like, only do not obscure the point of the Easter Garden.
- Can you think of a good place to make the Easter Garden? Maybe they would like it at an old people's home. If you think it looks really good, why not take a photograph of the completed garden?

Note, that wherever you put it, you will almost certainly be expected to take it down and clear up afterwards.

Easter celebrations in a Greek village – roasting lambs on a spit

After Lent, the Easter feast is taken literally, and a meal with meat is eaten. Lamb or kid is traditional, partly because Easter occurs at the same time (not always exactly) as the Jewish feast of Passover when lamb or kid is to be eaten. This is one level of symbolism. But Good Friday recalls the self–giving of Jesus, and he is often referred to as the lamb slaughtered in sacrifice, or as the lamb of God, so this is a second level of symbol.

Easter Services in Church

This section began with an Easter service in Salisbury cathedral. In western Europe it is usual to hold the Easter services in the morning of Easter Day, but not usually as early as that one. In Greece, however, the Easter service begins at midnight on Saturday. The darkness gives extra meaning to the lighting of the candles. The key point in the service is the priest shouting, *Christos anesti* (Christ is risen), repeated three times. Each time everyone replies, *alithos anesti* (truly risen, or risen indeed — pronounce *alithos* like *alithose*, long *O*). Then the lights are passed on, and men in the square outside fire off shotguns and fireworks, bells ring, and everyone is glad not to be in bed.

ACTIVITY: in pairs

To make a study of Easter symbolism, find the Easter Anthem in a service book of the Church of England.

This could be either the Book of Common Prayer or the Alternative Services Book. It consists of extracts from the New Testament, arranged for singing or chanting.

Read it with a friend, and together decide what symbols are used, and what they suggest about the meaning of Easter. Here is the Anthem:

> *Christ our passover has been sacrificed for us:*
> *   so let us celebrate the feast,*
> *not with the old leaven of corruption and wickedness:*
> *   but with the unleavened bread of sincerity and truth.*
> *Christ once raised from the dead dies no more:*
> *   death has no more dominion over him.*
> *In dying he died to sin once for all:*
> *   in living he lives to God.*
> *See yourselves therefore as dead to sin:*
> *   and alive to God in Jesus Christ our Lord.*
> *Christ has been raised from the dead:*
> *   the firstfruits of those who sleep.*
> *For as by man came death:*
> *   by man has come also the resurrection of the dead.*
> *For as in Adam all die:*
> *   even so in Christ shall all be made alive.*

Chapter Six

ASCENSION

The word **ascension** means going up, as when someone ascends the stairs, or mountaineers begin the ascent of Everest. Aeroplanes ascend, and at the end of the flight begin their descent (coming down). So the ascension of Jesus at the end of Luke's gospel and the beginning of Acts refers to going upwards. After the resurrection, the gospel relates that Jesus spent forty days with his disciples and then was taken up into heaven while they watched. This is the event which the feast of the Ascension celebrates.

In the tradition of the Christian church, the Ascension has been one of the three most important festivals, the others being Christmas and Easter. Yet in recent generations it has somehow received less attention, as if it were now less important than it used to be. There are reasons for this change in attitude among Christians themselves, especially in Europe and North America, and these reasons need to be looked at, as well as the festival itself.

One reason is that Ascension Day is always a Thursday, so not at the week–end. The day is fixed by being forty days after Easter, that is a little short of six weeks. In some countries this is a public holiday, but in Britain it seems that people want public holidays on Mondays. There are also other reasons why the Ascension has seemed in recent years to be difficult and controversial.

ACTIVITY: on your own

Find and read passages in the Bible which relate to the Ascension. These are Luke 24.48–53; and also Acts 1.3–14.

Then write answers to these questions, putting Bible references in brackets after each answer.

The first one has been done for you, to start you off.

It will help to put markers in the places to help you find them again easily.

1 Where did the ascension take place?
   (answer: near Bethany (Luke 24.50), Mount Olivet (Acts 1.12), very near Jerusalem (Acts 1.4; Acts 1.12))
2 Where did Jesus go to when he left his disciples?
3 What promises did Jesus make to his disciples?
4 What promises or predictions did anyone else make?
5 Can you find any political references which might have affected the Jews and their governors? If so, what were they?
6 What did the disciples do straight afterwards?

A Christian minister said a few years ago: *'My church congregation includes university professors and astro-physicists* (These are scientists who study space); *so what sermon do I preach on Ascension Day?'* Look back at your answer to question 2 on page 38. Do you see the difficulty for this minister?

Another minister answered: *I shall just preach the Ascension as it is given in the Bible. I don't see any difficulty about that'.*

Discuss the problem felt by the first minister, and the anwer given by the second. Make sure first that everyone understands the problem. What is the real difference between these two ministers?

ACTIVITY: on your own

Write about a page explaining the difficulty about preaching the Ascension to professors and astro-physicists.

Say if you think the difficulty felt by the first preacher would disappear if he found that there were in fact no professors or physicists in his congregation.

Going and Coming Back

This picture from the chapel of the Ascension at Walsingham shows a pair of feet sticking through the ceiling. How can you tell whether the person is coming or going?

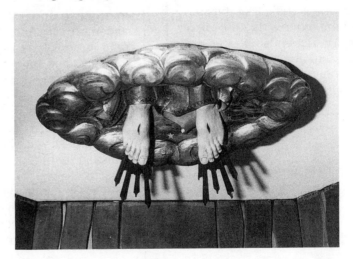

The story of the ascension of Jesus seemed at first to be very simple, simple enough for very young children to understand, but in fact it has got complications which are nothing to do with space travel. These can be seen in what follows.

Look back at your answers to question 3 in the previous section (page 38). The promises Jesus gave his disciples are about receiving strength (power) through the holy spirit and going out as missionaries. This is in fact the story of most of the book of Acts. Acts chapter 2 describes the coming of the holy spirit of God, to be discussed in Chapter 7 on Pentecost.

In the sections on the crucifixion and the resurrection, something was said about the shock the disciples felt when Jesus was suddenly taken away from them, and then their joy and excitement when they found that he was among them again. He was not with them all the time of course, but their friendship and companionship seemed to continue. At the ascension, however, Jesus goes away from them, as it seems, for ever, or at any rate until the end of the world, and no–one knows when that is. Instead they are to receive the holy spirit, provided only that they stay together, and this of course they do.

Christian teaching on the Trinity (see Part Four, pages 185–189) declares the presence of God in Father, Son and Holy Spirit, so from this point of view the disciples will still be able to feel Jesus with them and near them. But instead of the simple presence of Jesus, as it was when they were together in Galilee, now he is no longer just around. Instead of someone they can call and listen to, the presence of the spirit is within them, yet it is somehow much more problematic. It is not as simple as it seemed to be before. Two different Christians can have quite different ideas about what they think the spirit is saying to them. Often Christian leaders have to cope with this sort of problem.

At its most simple, the ascension describes Jesus going up to heaven. For many Christians the story is simply a matter of transport: Jesus came down from heaven when he was born, and then went back up again. The thought that heaven is a place above the sky is reinforced by the fact that we use the same word **heaven** actually to mean sky. But there is much more to understanding Christ's ascension than space travel.

Using the story of Elijah's ascension as a type for the ascension of Jesus, helps to stress two points: one is the gift of the spirit, and the other is that the gift of the spirit depends on the disciples actually witnessing the ascension, until he disappears from sight.

ACTIVITY: on your own

In order to understand this 'more', read again the account of the ascension in Acts 1.3–11. Put a marker in the place before you read the next passage.

Christians have always thought that the Old Testament, which was and is the Jewish Bible, spoke to them about Christ, and they looked for texts and stories to match events in the gospels.

These stories in the Old Testament are called **types**. The type for the ascension of Jesus is the story of the ascension of the prophet Elijah which you will find in 2 Kings 2.1–18. This is quite a long passage, but the key verse is 2 Kings 2.10.

- Read the whole passage carefully, and note the dialogue between Elijah and Elisha in verse 10.
- Does this connect with anything in Acts 1.3–13? Read this again, and note down anything that looks similar.

What the Ascension Means for Christians

What Christians think about the ascension can be listed briefly:

1 Jesus leaves them, and is not seen on earth again (except in visions and dreams)
2 The disciples receive power through the holy spirit at Pentecost.

Christ giving a blessing with his wounded hand

3 The disciples are witnesses, not just to the ascension, but to the life and work of Christ.

4 Christ has finished the work he had to do and goes to the Father to a great celebration, a kind of coronation or triumph.

5 But something has changed, because Jesus carries the wounds of the crucifixion in his body as a sign of his love for mankind and creation.

ACTIVITY

This is optional for follow-up work:

Look back at the exercise you did when you considered the two Christian ministers and what kind of sermon they might preach on Ascension Day (on page 39).

Using these materials, **note down on a sheet of paper three or four points which you think the first minister might make in his sermon about the Ascension**. This is the minister who had professors and physicists in the congregation.

Chapter Seven

PENTECOST, WHITSUNDAY, THE GIFT OF THE HOLY SPIRIT

Some symbols used to represent Pentecost

Power
Support
Strength
Courage

The Christian festival of Pentecost comes ten days after Ascension Day. Pentecost celebrates the gift of the Spirit which Jesus promised at the Ascension. The disciples did not know what this would be like until they received the spirit. Pentecost means that spiritual experience is an essential part of Christian religion. People of other religions have spiritual experiences too, but someone who has no religion might think of the spirit as either imaginary or an emotion aroused by crowd excitement. But the Book of Acts, for instance, makes little sense unless the power of the spirit is recognised. That is why Acts has sometimes been called the Gospel of the Holy Spirit.

The Spirit brings gifts to the community of Christians and is himself a gift. If we distribute gifts of food or money, the more people we give them out to the less each one has. This is a fact of life and a fact of economics. But spiritual sharing is not like this. A better comparison is the sharing of fire or lighting candles. As we light new fires from the one we started with, the total quantity of heat and light becomes much greater, and everyone has more. Fire and life–giving breath are the pictures often used for spiritual blessing, and not the finite goods of economics and industry.

Pentecost comes from a Greek word meaning fiftieth. Pentecost is exactly seven weeks after Easter, and is therefore always a Sunday. In New Testament times most Jews outside Palestine spoke Greek, or at least understood Greek. **Pentecost** is also the Greek name for the Jewish feast, **Shavuoth**. Shavuoth means weeks, that is a week of weeks which is forty–nine days, and is thus the fiftieth day after Passover. Greek–speaking Jews called it Pentecost.

Today Pentecost is important for Christians in three ways. Christians speak of Pentecost as the birthday of the Church because the disciples were suddenly empowered together and collectively to carry on Christ's mission in the world. Secondly, Pentecost bears witness to the power of the Spirit in the lives of Christians today and in every age, and this means that many Christians experience this spiritual power in their lives. If they did not the festival would lose most of its meaning. Thirdly, many Christians today also experience a spiritual power in their lives which they connect with the original happening at Pentecost. This experience is called **Baptism in the Spirit**.

What Happened when the Spirit was Poured Out

ACTIVITY: on your own

First read Acts 2.1–13, then write answers to these questions on 'What happened when the Spirit was poured out'.

1 How many disciples were together in one place?
2 Where were they?
3 What two things did the outpouring of the Spirit feel like?
4 What did the disciples do first?
5 How did the other Jews near them react?

ACTIVITY: as a group

Discuss your answers to the questions above. They might not all be the same within the group.
   Then discuss the following:

(a) What specific powers did the disciples receive?
(b) Why are they now called apostles? (You need to know what the Greek word '*apostle*' means)

ACTIVITY: on your own

The gifts of the Holy Spirit are mentioned in many other places in the New Testament.
Read I Corinthians 12 and also Galatians 5.22–26.
List the gifts of the spirit mentioned.

- Is there any difference between '*gifts*' and '*fruits*' *of the Spirit*?
- How do the gifts or fruits differ from those you noted after reading Acts 2.1–13?

PEOPLES AND TONGUES

ACTIVITY: as a group

Read Acts 2.1–13 again. Then:

1 List the peoples or languages mentioned.
2 Mark on an outline map of the Mediterranean and Middle East (Tunis to Iraq) the places where they came from. Note that *Asia* in Acts 2.9 does not mean the whole continent, but the Roman province they called Asia, which was part of what we call Asia Minor (modern Turkey).
3 Discuss your results to 1 and 2 above, and decide on headings to help you group these peoples and languages, e.g. they might be *Europe*, *Africa*, *Asia* — or you might decide to split Asia up into smaller groups of languages.
4 Why were all these people in Jerusalem in the first place?
5 Do members of the group think that **tongues** is a good word to use about Pentecost?

ACTIVITY: on your own

Write about a page on wind and/or fire, describing circumstances in which wind or fire is really strong — draw out both creative (helpful) and destructive forces.

Finally say why you think wind or fire is (or is not) a good analogy for what the first Christians felt about the coming of the Holy Spirit.

ACTIVITY: as a group

- Can you think of any other way of describing the Spirit's power and freedom?
- Try and imagine the experience, try and put into words what the spirit feels like, looks like, sounds like. Sometimes the coming down of the spirit has been described as a dove.
- Is this a good description, or can you think of others? If so, why do you feel they are appropriate?

Pentecostal Churches

Many Christians would like to relive the power of the spirit being poured out by experiencing it in their own lives, either when alone, or together with other people in church. There is often great excitement in Pentecostal churches. The services almost always include ecstatic speech, in particular speaking in tongues, stirring sermons or testimonies, and sessions for healing, the healing usually through prayer and touch, especially a ritual known as the laying on of hands.

ACTIVITY: as a group

1 Find out what Pentecostal Christians do
   in church, during the service
   in the community
   and make notes about the main things
2 If possible, record with a tape recorder or photographs, the high points at a Pentecostal church service. You will need to ask in advance if this is allowed.
3 Ask the minister or other members about how their activities relate to Scripture.
4 Compare what they tell you with the notes you made on the first Pentecost headed: '*What happened when the Spirit was poured out*'.
5 Could anyone have the gifts of the Spirit and it not show?

A service in a Pentecostal church

Speaking in Tongues

We sometimes talk about people being speechless with surprise or with joy. People who are very happy might break into song, or shout out for joy and happiness. Christians who practice speaking in tongues describe it as a feeling of being taken over, as if a power not their own is using their voices. Other people present do not understand what is being said, and there is a need for someone to interpret the tongues. Being able to translate or interpret tongues is also counted as a spiritual gift. This is spoken of in the Bible, but it is well known too among some groups who are not Christians.

Two things about Pentecost are often forgotten but they are important. The first is that the Spirit is felt as God working in the world. This was not a new idea and there are many passages about this in the Old Testament. At Pentecost, however, the first Christians were taken by surprise. What happened felt absolutely new and exciting. Little by little they came to see it as a new turn in the experience of their people. For them, the experience came first, and the links with the past were only understood later. But for us as students, it can only be the other way round.

The second thing about Pentecost is that the disciples were all together at the same time and in the same place. This means that the Spirit is a spirit of unity and of unanimity. He comes as a joint gift, like a fire who is given out in tongues of flame to individuals, but the light of inspiration and the heat are shared by all. That is why church services often speak of the fellowship of the Holy Spirit or the communion of the Holy Spirit.

> Speaking in tongues in a Pentecostal (or other) church is in some ways like the experience of the apostles describes in Acts 2. The words spoken may be a foreign language, but one unknown to the speaker. If this happened at Pentecost, then Christians can see this gift as a means of effective communication in their mission.

What the First Christians Might Have Known About the Spirit

The pouring out of the spirit at Pentecost obviously came on the disciples very suddenly. Yet it ought not to have been a complete surprise as the Old Testament has a lot to say about the spirit.

ACTIVITY: on your own

Read the following passages, from the Old Testament.
   Write a few lines on the working of the spirit mentioned in each.
1 Genesis 1.1–3; **2** I Samuel 10.1–12; **3** I Samuel 11.1–10; **4** Isaiah 11.1–5; **5** Isaiah 61.1–3; **6** Ezekiel 37.1–14; **7** Joel 2.28–32 (in some Bibles this is called Joel chapter 3)

ACTIVITY: as a group

Using the results of the previous work, talk over what these powers mean, and collect together those which seem to be alike.

ACTIVITY: on your own

Follow-up work
Now write a page or two about the spirit of God in the Old Testament as the disciples might have expected him. Use any notes you have made from the group's discussion.

- How far do you think the Pentecost experience seems to fulfil these expectations?

The Spirit in Christian Ritual

The fleur de lys

Other rituals which try to summon the Spirit include Confirmation and Ordination. These happen much more frequently and are described in Part Three of this book. But neither of these rites is specially tied to the season of Pentecost.

Pentecost is a major Christian festival. But because no human being can control the Spirit or predict his coming, it is not easy to fix the Holy Spirit in any ritual. No–one expected the Holy Spirit to come down on Jesus in the form of a dove when he was baptised (Mark 1.9–13).

The coronation ritual for kings in Old Testament times included anointing with holy oil. This was held to symbolise the descent of the spirit, and the spirit was believed to give the king power and blessing from God. This ritual was taken over for the sovereigns of France and England. When Queen Elizabeth was crowned in 1953, anointing with holy oil formed part of the ceremony. The *fleur de lys* was originally a stylised sketch of the holy spirit coming down as a dove. It became a badge for French and English royalty. If you look at a scout badge, you can still see the dove's outline, with a wing each side and the head at the bottom.

In the last analysis, Pentecost is to be seen as the gift of the Spirit, and this makes ritual in the sense of special time and special place, special person and special actions, unnecessary. This is perhaps why today Christians regard Pentecost as a major festival, but do not have a notably distinct ritual for the day or the season. But Christians do need to have rituals for the good order of the congregations and of the church as a whole, as St Paul found out and explains in some of his letters.

Being Able to Do Something New

But what does it really feel like to be able to do something new?

When Christians celebrate Pentecost, they are celebrating the gift of God's spirit which makes them able to do something new. This applies whether we think of this new power as coming to individual Christians or to the Church as a community, and so to the individuals who belong to it. According to the New Testament, it seems to be the group that counts, and Pentecost is often called *The Birthday of the Christian Church*.

If you were brought up in this country you probably learnt to ride a bicycle before you were eight. In fact you have been learning new skills and new techniques all your life. There is no reason why this should not go on, if you want it to. But there must have been times when you were surprised and also very pleased with yourself about what you could do.

The thing about riding a bicycle is that at first you cannot do it, and then suddenly you can! You just get it, you cannot really explain how. Think about other skills you have learnt.

ACTIVITY: as a group

Discuss and make a list of different sports and hobbies which you take part in. Sort out those which you learn once then can always do — like riding a bicycle — from skills which need practice to keep them up. Skill at football would be one of these, or cookery, because there is a real risk of losing the ability if you do not keep in practice. Learning a new skill can give you tremendous scope and opportunities for doing things you could not do before, for enjoyment, and for making friends.

How about learning a foreign language, or a computer language? Ability like this is often called a gift, or a talent, but you have got to keep it up.

ACTIVITY: on your own

Make a list of the clubs or teams you belong to, or the teams you support.
   Then write not more than two lines to answer each of these questions.

- How do you feel when the team wins an important match?
- How do you express your feelings?
- What are the signs of membership or of support? e.g. badges, shirts, scarves, etc.
- Do you need these things to feel you belong, to feel team spirit?
- Do you find you do things in special ways, even on your own, because you belong to the club or team?

ACTIVITY: on your own

To follow this up:
   Write about a page on the feelings of a big crowd.
   Choose an example that is fairly topical, and try to say how being in the crowd together felt different from being just an individual who happened to be there. Remember that crowd feelings can be good or bad, creative or destructive, heartening or terrifying.

GCSE Question — Southern Examining Group — 1988

(a) Give an account of the first Christian Pentecost (Whitsun).

(7 marks)

(b) Choose four other Christian Festivals or Fasts and explain why each is celebrated. (8 marks)

(c) Which do you think is the most important festival in the Christian year? Give reasons for your choice. (5 marks)

Everyone knows what Sunday is. There's one every weekend. But in fact Sunday can mean different things to different people, or even to the same people at different times.

BRAINSTORMING: on 'Sunday'

You will need a large sheet of paper, and someone to write down all the ideas and suggestions from anyone in the group. There must be no comments. **Ideas about Sunday can include not only what it means, but what you do on Sundays and any other ideas.**

- When you have filled the paper, or when the ideas seem to have stopped flowing, look at what has been written and try as a group to collect together those ideas and suggestions which seem to be linked.
- Cross out ones which seem to be already included somewhere else.
- At this stage too, you may decide to expand one or two things, but do not do too much of this.
- Equally, you may decide that one or two of the suggestions do not really fit after all and should be left out.

Enjoying a sunny Sunday

People who live in an industrialised society with a five day working week tend to class Saturday and Sunday together as the weekend. This makes five days for work and study and two days for leisure activities. Of course some people have to work at the weekend, and this may mean overtime pay, which also makes Saturday and Sunday different. Yet a hundred years ago in Britain it was normal to work for six days in the week, and then Sunday was the only day of rest, and it was much needed. Then Saturday became a half day, giving people time to wash and change, play football or whatever, and then start fresh on Sunday for a day with the family, a whole day of leisure.

The modern world has got the pattern of seven days in a week from ancient traditions described in the Bible. But in fact quite a lot of other societies had a week of seven days simply because of the phases of the moon. Seven days marks the time from new moon to half moon, from half to full, from full moon to half, and then from half back to new moon again. Modern Jews still observe the new moon in their religious calendar, but the moon's only significance for Christians is in working out the date of Easter.

In Old Testament times, people worked for six days and the seventh day was the day of rest. This is true for Jews still, and the day of rest is called Sabbath, and it is the seventh day of the week, that is Saturday. The main difference is that the day begins at sunset the night before, and ends with sunset again, instead of midnight. So for the Jews of Jesus' time, just as today, what we call Sunday is the first day of the new week. And it was not a holiday.

What Sunday Means for Christians

Easter Day is always a Sunday. In the gospel of John we read how Mary Magdalene came to Jesus' tomb *the first day of the week early, when it was yet dark*. Later on the same day, we can read in Luke's gospel how two disciples on their way to Emmaus met Jesus and had a long discussion with him, not knowing who he was. But when they stopped for an evening meal, Jesus took bread and blessed it, broke it and began to distribute it as he had done before, and they instantly recognised him. They knew who he was as a result of this: they recognised him at the breaking of the bread.

At other times when we read that Jesus appeared among his disciples after the resurrection, the gospels sometimes make the point that the disciples were eating together, or breaking bread. Christians believe that on many, though not all, the times that the disciples saw Jesus after his resurrection, it was a Sunday and that they were praying together and eating together, in fact celebrating the eucharist (see Part Two, Chapter 4).

That is why Sunday became the holy day for Christians. It is the first day in the week, and it is also called the eighth day (first day of next week). So for some Christians the number eight symbolises the resurrection. On Sundays the Christians wanted (and still want) to meet together to worship God, to pray and to break bread. But for the first three centuries Sunday was a normal working day, and this meant that the Christians had to arrange to meet either very early in the morning, or else after work in the evening. Mostly they preferred to meet in the morning and the following symbols of morning are found associated with early Christianity: the sun and sunrise; the cock crowing; light. The beginning of a new day also helped to remind them of the resurrection to new life, which was in any case the reason for worshipping together on Sundays.

Only after Christians became influential in government was Sunday made into a public holiday. The idea of a day of rest, of time to spend together with friends and family, appealed to the ancient world and much of what the Jews did on the Sabbath (Saturday) was adapted by Christians and applied to Sunday. For this reason some Christians still call Sunday '*the sabbath day*'.

Lord's Day Observance

In western Europe in the Middle Ages, the clergy tried to enforce Sunday as a day of worship, rest and thinking about God. Thus people were not allowed to do any work, and any games or parties held on Saturday night had to be ended before midnight. The Dancers of Stanton Drew (in Somerset) are a prehistoric stone circle (nothing to do with Christianity) but the legend arose in the Middle Ages that a party of dancers had danced into the '*sabbath*' (i.e. Sunday) and been turned to stone.

After the reformation, both Catholics and Protestants kept this rule, but it became gradually more relaxed in the twentieth century because of the increase in leisure activities, travel, sports and so on, even though these involve work for some people. This process had begun with the industrial revolution, and The Lord's Day Observance Society was founded in 1831 with two aims: to make people more aware of the blessings of Sunday, and to make Sunday a day of rest, worship and serious reading. This led members to try and stop not only work, but any kind of sport, travel and leisure activities as well. The majority of Christians in Britain do not support this Society, and people who are not Christians object to what they see as an attempt by a religious group to impose their will on the rest of society.

ACTIVITY: on your own

Write two or three lines on each of these questions:

1 Why is Sunday special for Christians?
2 What do Christians specially like to meet for on Sundays?
3 What did early Christians do, when Sunday was an ordinary working day?
4 What can today's Christians do about worship if they have to work or to go out on a Sunday?
5 Do you think it is a good idea for everyone to have the same day of rest every week, even if they are not Christian?

Chapter Nine

OTHER SPECIAL DAYS

We have got so used to some things that we do not think of them as special any more. Yet most parts of the country have some kind of local festival which happens every year, or in some cases every few years. It may concern only a particular group of people, like the annual Scout or Guide camp, or Women's Institute Garden Meeting, or the choir outing from the local church. Other events are very prominent locally, such as a local agricultural show. This does not have to be very ancient or long established, but popular and featured in news items in the local papers.

ACTIVITY: as a group

Make up a list of the local events or outings or celebrations which you know about in your district.

When you have got suggestions, organise the list into public events (open to anyone, like a music festival), club events (usually open only to members and their guests like a Guide camp), and others (if any).

With the help of the whole group, write a few lines on each event, saying who takes part, what time of year it is held, and what usually happens on this day or few days.

Example of local celebrations would include the Durham Miners Gala (not religious), village well dressings in the Peak District (each one is linked to a Christian festival, although rather loosely). May or Whitsun processions and fairs. Some of these include the election of a May or Carnival Queen.

Well dressing at Tissington in Derbyshire

Rogation and Harvest

Most churches in this country and quite a lot of schools hold a special service or ceremony to mark the gathering in of the harvest. This obviously has its roots in an agricultural way of life, but it is possible to include products of all kinds, including coal and manufactures, which are not related to seasons of the year. This festival is held sometime in October usually, but the exact date is fixed locally.

Rogation days are times of prayer set aside to pray for good weather and success in planting the crops. Many Christians in Britain nowadays pray for success in food production especially in countries of drought and food shortage. Rogation days (rogation just means '*asking*') now are prayers for food to grow in any part of the world. There are no great ceremonies attached to them.

Harvest festival decorations in a church

Saints Days and Name Days

Many parish congregations celebrate the anniversary of the dedication of their parish church. This arose because every church building was at one time sacred to the memory of a particular saint, as many churches and chapels still are.

Ascension Day is a public holiday in several countries, and also some other religious festivals are celebrated in particular places by most of the population. Cities in northern Italy were once independent states, and the festival of each one's patron saint is a public holiday and great civic occasion. Another example is the public festival of St Lazarus in Cuba (December), although the state is officially Marxist.

A very big celebration in the Near East is Holy Cross Day on September 14th. This commemorates St Helena's pilgrimage to Jerusalem where she found wood and nails from the true cross, according to tradition, and also the bones of the wise men. There are Christian processions in Israel–Palestine, Lebanon, Syria and the southern part of Turkey. (See also pages 30–31 on Good Friday).

Patron saints can also be honoured by a society: obviously a religious order wants to remember its founder and other patrons, and an obvious example is the celebration of St Benedict by members of the Benedictine order. But individuals can have patron saints too, and this is widespread among Roman Catholics. Members of the Orthodox churches usually keep their '*name day*' instead of their birthday. This works quite simply. Most Christian names (though not all) are also the names of saints, and Orthodox Christians, especially children, have a party on the saint's day whose name they have. In naming the child, parents probably had a particular saint in mind, if there are several saints with the same name.

Some saints are mainly of local importance. This place may be where they were born, or where they worked, or where they died. They are probably celebrated locally too. Examples would include Cuthbert and Bede in the north-east of England. There are dozens of local Welsh and Cornish saints, about some of whom facts may be hard to come by.

ACTIVITY: as a group

Find out about local religious celebrations (Christian) in your area. There are several ways to do this. **Read the suggestions below, talk them over and then choose one of them to follow up:**

1 A local church, e.g. Church of England parish church, will be dedicated. Find out its dedication. This need not be to a saint, but could be St Saviour (Jesus Christ), Holy Trinity, or The Ascension. But in any case there is certain to be a special feast day which the congregation keeps every year, or could keep if they wanted.

2 If there is an immigrant Christian population near you, find out if they have any religious celebrations which they have brought from the old country. For instance, Holy Cross Day (September 14th) is important for Christians from Syria, Lebanon, and Israel–Palestine, and is a big festival in the Syrian Orthodox Church.

3 Members of your small group will have Christian names. Choose one or two for the whole group to research. Or alternatively you could each choose one name (not necessarily your own) and bring the results of your individual research to the group for comment.

The way to proceed is as follows: first the group must decide what you are going to do out of 1, 2 and 3 above.

Then begin the research.

(a) Find out something about the saint (or event) in question.
(b) Ask on what day of the year this is celebrated.
(c) How is it celebrated locally (if it is)?
(d) What does it mean to the people who celebrate it?

As a result of your group research project, write one or two pages on local saints days.

MARY THE MOTHER OF JESUS

Of all Christian saints Mary the Mother of Jesus is far the most popular. Several events in the life of Jesus are also about her and a church dedicated to her can have a choice of days to celebrate. She is commonly referred to among Christians as Our Lady, or the Blessed Virgin. A project on a church dedicated to St Mary is likely to be much bigger than one of the others.

In the exercise you did above, if you chose **1**, you maybe found that a local church which was dedicated to St Mary celebrated February 2nd, the Presentation of Christ in the Temple, or March 25th, the Annunciation, or some other occasion as their special day. And if you chose **3**, your research into the name Mary could have been quite lengthy, unless you chose one of the other Saint Marys.

Christian doctrine is discussed at greater length in Part Four, and the person of Jesus Christ especially in Chapter 3, pages 196 – 199 . In order to emphasise that Jesus is God (as well as man) it was decided to call his mother **the bearer of God** or **the Mother of God**. Thus the title Mother of God refers specifically to the birth of Jesus. An explanation of what this means is given in Part Four, Chapter 3 on the Incarnation, pages 192 – 196

National Occasions

The country of San Salvador is dedicated, as its very name shows, to Jesus Christ (San Salvador means St Saviour in Spanish). Other countries have religious patrons, like St Andrew of Scotland, though he did not go there. The English adopted St George (who never set foot in England) at the time of the Crusades, in place of their previous patron saint, Edward the Confessor, who at least was an English king. Many national days of course are linked to events which are not religious, like American Independence or the French revolution.

An important national occasion in the United Kingdom is Remembrance Sunday in November. This commemorates those who died in two world wars in this century, as well as other fighting. Although this is not obviously a Christian commemoration, it is kept in churches when special prayers are said and Christian clergy also take part in outdoor services at the Cenotaph in London and at local war memorials. Its links with Christianity are sufficiently strongly felt for the Jewish ex–servicemen to hold a quite separate commemoration on the Sunday after Remembrance Sunday.

Chapter Ten

PILGRIMAGE

By using analogy or a kind of picture language you could call the Stations of the Cross a kind of **pilgrimage**, even in the home area, because Christians go to Jerusalem *in their hearts*. But this is not a literal description.

In the section on Good Friday we looked at the idea of Christians reliving the last few hours of Jesus' life by following him in meditation, and by a special ritual called the Stations of the Cross. If instead of doing this at their local church, a group of Christians travel to Jerusalem, they can follow the route that Jesus Christ took that morning. They can meditate at each Station (stopping place) on the actual spot where tradition says each event happened.

Special Places

Pilgrims go to places which are special for them, places which bring back memories or stories, and which therefore mean a lot to individuals or to a group of people.

The Eiffel Tower, Paris

ACTIVITY: as a group

Choose a country or part of a country which means a lot to one or several of you.

It may be where you live, or it may be somewhere you have been on a holiday, or somewhere you have heard about.

Perhaps your parents or ancestors came from overseas, and have told you about a country you have never seen, but you feel you would love sometime to go there.

If, for example, Australia is the land your group has chosen, make a list of five things which you all feel are special about Australia. Ask yourselves whether Australians are proud of these things, and if so, how they would remind people of them.

Of course Australia was only an example. You may have chosen Ghana, Poland, Jamaica or East Anglia or anywhere else you like. But wherever you have chosen, make your list of five special things.

These could be buildings or natural features, special customs or foods, or anything you as a group think are characteristic of the place.

Tourists going to Paris for the first time might buy a postcard or a model of the Eiffel Tower. What might a more experienced tourist take away from the place which you have chosen and discussed above? The people who live there do not have such postcards and models in their rooms, but if you have to go away, on business or study, you might take with you a souvenir to remind you of home.

If you are a refugee, someone who cannot go back to your home country for any reason, then the things which are special about your home country have even greater meaning and you may dream of it as a kind of ideal place. You long to return, even though you probably know that you cannot, or not just yet.

ACTIVITY: as a group

For a practical exercise on a fine day, take a camera and walk about your neighbourhood. Take photographs of anything that seems special to any of you, for instance an ancient building, or a place where something special happens, like a clubhouse or a football stadium.

Mount the photographs on a piece of paper or card, and underneath write a brief description of what is in the picture and what it is about it which makes it special to one (or more) of your group.

- Have any of the places in your group's collection got religious significance? This is not always an easy question to answer.

A Modern Pilgrimage

Here is a description of a pilgrimage to Lindisfarne (also called Holy Island) on the east coast of Northumberland, in May 1986.

About forty Christians from the counties of Durham and Northumberland planned this pilgrimage as a day trip. A coach was booked from Newcastle. Those from further south were picked up by a minibus, after waiting at the side of the road in accordance with a timetable which had been planned in advance. Everyone brought food to share together for lunch, and whatever clothes, etc. they thought appropriate.

Someone had designed a badge for them all to pin on, marking the pilgrimage, and there was also a song sheet, religious songs naturally, for them to sing together for the bit on foot.

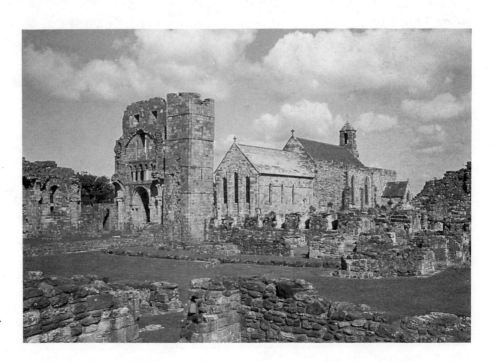

Lindisfarne, the Parish Church and ruins of the Priory

The plan was to walk across to the island at low tide along the route called the Pilgrim's Way. This was still under a few inches of water, but a line of posts in the sand mark it out quite clearly. Consequently the pilgrims had to decide whether to walk barefoot in traditional style or wear wellington boots. Most took their shoes and socks off. In modern times a road has been built along a causeway which coaches and cars can use at low tide, and pilgrims who were old or unsteady on their feet were taken over by the coach. The Pilgrim's Way is shorter, but still getting on for a mile and through shallow water across the sands.

When they had all arrived they were welcomed at a Christian hostel on the island (also arranged in advance), and then went to the ruins of the medieval abbey for an open–air eucharist. This was the climax of their pilgrimage. Then they had lunch together, sharing out their food, and hot drinks were supplied by the hostel. In the afternoon people either went for walks or played on the sand — there were some children in the party — or talked together.

The time to return also depended on the tides, of course, so had to be planned, but there was time for some tea and an evening service in the parish church (which is not a ruin) before going back by coach.

It will be seen from this description that the people who went to Lindisfarne enjoyed each other's friendship, got some exercise and recreation together with a little excitement because of the sea tides, got a badge to take home, as well as the obviously religious part.

Pilgrims sometimes have a very particular purpose when they start on a pilgrimage. One of the most usual reasons is to pray for something special, or for help over fertility or healing. From Lourdes in France there are many reports of healing miracles, and some of the pilgrims have given up all hope of a cure from medical science. Others go as a way of saying a special 'Thank–you' after being cured in their own home or in a hospital.

Pilgrims at Lourdes

Pilgrimages can be a holiday, time for a change and for meeting friends, as well as being religious journeys. Christians may make a pilgrimage to dedicate themselves to God afresh. Many Christians still go on pilgrimage as a kind of holiday. They also enjoy meeting new people, who in some way at least share their interests.

ACTIVITY: as a group

Together draw up a list of places in Great Britain where modern Christians go on pilgrimage. You will be surprised how many there are, and will not be able to list more than a few of them.

- When you have got a list, choose one to study in more detail.
- Find out where it is, and a little of the history. Be careful over this, and concentrate on the history which is connected with the pilgrimage.
- Find out if there is a special day for the pilgrimage, or whether people come at all times of year. For many places it is both, but if there is a special day, find out what people do on it.
- Find out whether pilgrims take away with them a special badge or souvenir from the pilgrimage, and if so, what this is like.

ACTIVITY: on your own

Write up the project in two or more pages.

If you cannot think of places in Britain for pilgrimage, here are some suggestions: Iona, Lindisfarne (also called Holy Island), Durham, York, Walsingham, Bradwell–on–sea, Canterbury.

Canterbury Cathedral

Pilgrimage Overseas

Almost every country has places to which Christians may make pilgrimage at some time. Jerusalem is probably the most popular place of pilgrimage for Christians of all denominations, churches and nationalities. At the same time of course it is a place of pilgrimage for Muslims and Jews. Christians may make the pilgrimage to Jerusalem at any time of the year. You can go to Jerusalem on package holiday, and spend most of the time sightseeing, but it can be a pilgrimage none the less for those who go, however they go.

ACTIVITY: on your own

Plan a family expedition to a place which specially interests you.
It need not have any religious significance, although obviously it would be more relevant to this course if it has.

- Think out how you will travel there, find out about fares and so on, and if you need accommodation.
- Then think of the things which will interest or occupy each member of your family.
- Write about two sides on this.

One Line Answers

(Write answers to these questions in one line or two)

1 How many Sundays are there in Advent?
2 Name two things Christians are preparing for in Advent.
3 Name three things that are used as symbols in Advent.
4 Name one town in Israel–Palestine which is associated with the childhood of Jesus.
5 Name two decorations on a modern Christmas tree which symbolise the story of the birth of Jesus.
6 Why do some Christians hold Christmas services at midnight?
7 What is meant by the *Feast of Kings* and where is it celebrated?
8 Why do many Christians think of the homeless at Christmas time?
9 Name one denomination which might hold a Watch Night Service at New Year.
10 Which day is remembered as the Naming of Jesus?
11 With what festival is the baptism of Jesus usually linked?
12 When is Shrove Tuesday?
13 How did Ash Wednesday get its name?

14 In what season do Christians specially remember the temptations of Jesus?

15 Name two important events in Holy Week.

16 Why do many Christians fast in Lent?

17 Why is the Thursday before Easter important for Christians?

18 What might Christians of many churches do together on Good Friday?

19 On what day in the year might special leaves be given out to Christians?

20 Name three symbols of the Passion.

21 What are the *Stations of the Cross*?

22 Why is Easter a popular time for baptisms?

23 What could coloured eggs symbolise for Christians?

24 What is an Easter Garden?

25 What event in the gospel is celebrated at Easter, and on what other days is it specially celebrated?

26 How many days after Easter is Ascension Day?

27 Where were the disciples at the time of Jesus' ascension?

28 Name one way in which the ascension of Jesus can be pictured.

29 Why is Ascension Day not a public holiday in Great Britain?

30 Why might Ascension Day present a difficulty for twentieth century Christians?

31 Give another name for the day of Pentecost.

32 What is meant by *'speaking in tongues'*?

33 Why is the word *'fire'* sometimes used to describe the holy spirit?

34 What is meant by the phrase *'born–again Christians'*?

35 Name one activity which makes Pentecostal worship different from that of most other denominations.

36 What does a dove in downward flight symbolise?

37 Why is Sunday a special day for Christians?

38 Why do some Christians believe Sunday should be a day of rest?

39 Give three different reasons why a Christian might decide to go on a pilgrimage.

40 Name two places outside Great Britain which are popular for Christian pilgrimages.

Part Two

WORSHIP

WORSHIP

Many people think they know what worship means. It is what goes on in churches and temples. But when you try to say more, it is not so easy. In fact the word worship and the idea of worship are used in a number of ways which are a bit confusing, even if after all it turns out that the meanings have got something in common.

Quite a lot of words have got extended meanings, like **ray** which can be either a ray of light or a ray of hope, i.e. not literally but metaphorically (metaphor means a transfer of meaning from one thing to another): or **sweeping**, as in sweeping the floor or sweeping aside objections. Call it picture language if you like. A lot of words in English have transferred and associated meanings, and it is worth finding out whether the word **Worship** is one of these.

BRAINSTORMING

In your small group do a brainstorming exercise on the word WORSHIP. When you have got a list of possibilities, try to sort out which apply to worship literally, and which are metaphors or associated meanings.

ACTIVITY: on your own

In the light of the brainstorming exercise you have just done — and the discussion you had over it — try to recall an example of an act or ceremony of worship which you have seen on TV or in a film, or read about in a book, or watched or taken part in at home or abroad. It need not be Christian, but could be drawn from any culture or religion.

Write short answers to these questions:

(a) Who or what was it that people worshipped or honoured?
(b) How did they show or express their worship or respect?
(c) What rituals were involved? — this includes ritual acts, things used ritually, ritual words or books.
(d) Were there periods of silence? Was music used, or other sounds? If so, how?
(e) How did people position themselves in relation to the centre of attention?

A medal presentation ceremony

ACTIVITY: as a group

Discuss the following in the light of what you have all just done in these activities:

- Is worship always religious?
- What could be meant by '*worshipping*' money, or football, or a filmstar? Is this just a metaphor or extended use of the word?

ACTIVITY: on your own

For follow-up work, write one or two pages describing an act of worship.

Chapter One

WHEN CHRISTIANS WORSHIP

You will have found from the exercises above some of the main things about worship.

First of all there is a relationship between the worshippers and the person or object which they worship. They may feel love or fear, but probably they feel a mixture of both. At the same time there is a feeling that you are drawn to worship. You can hardly help it. Here is a special something or someone, who is powerful — much stronger and more important than you. So you also have a feeling of littleness: maybe you even feel insignificant by comparison. You want to be in the presence of what you worship, and at the same time you feel you might easily not be noticed.

Christians associate with worship a feeling that God is supremely or completely good, beautiful, wonderful, deathless, and of course strong. How this works out it is not possible to explain. It is a mystery, and the feeling that worship is something you cannot really understand is the final ingredient.

What you worship is far beyond you, and on a different, higher level of being. For this reason, perhaps, you feel you ought to do whatever the one you worship wishes. This is one of the roots of moral obligation in religion, specifically Christian religion. We will come to the other root shortly.

Can there be human relationships like this? You probably found some in the exercises you did on the previous page. All these aspects of worship are to be found in Christian worship. But there is another special emphasis in addition.

Christians have got their name from Jesus Christ, and they are specially devoted to the person of Jesus. In this relationship love seems to be dominant, but all the other feelings we noted above, even fear, are also part of the complex attitudes of Christians at worship. Christians love to read and pray about the life of Jesus on earth, his death and resurrection. This they do alone and in groups and at religious services. There is more about prayer in Chapter 7, and about Bible reading in Chapter 6 in this Part.

Sacraments are particularly important in worship because through them a relationship of giving and receiving is built up. This means that in the sacraments Christians feel that God gives them special and particular help. This is because of his love for human kind, channelled as they see it through the sacraments and the Christian church.

In this Part we shall study especially the sacrament of holy communion in Chapter 4. In this service most Christian worshippers sense that Jesus is present among them and that they can become parts of him by eating the holy food. Mystery, love and fear are all components of this act.

Then in Chapter 5 we study the ritual or ceremony of reconciliation (forgiveness of sins), and here the feeling of unworthiness is strongest, a feeling that you are a hopeless case compared to the love and power of God: but by the words of forgiveness you can still be accepted in spite of it all.

Friendship and Thinking of One's Friends

Is the feeling Christians have for Jesus anything like friendship and the way we feel about people we like? This needs investigation, and may help us to see how sacraments are thought to work.

The two main things to bear in mind for this section are first, the special regard Christians have for Jesus Christ, and second, the fact that they cannot see or hear him in the way the disciples did in Galilee.

ACTIVITY: on your own

This activity is a multiple—choice exercise on the subject of friendship. For each suggestion you should choose only one of the five possible answers.

1 Yes, definitely   **4** Probably not, not much like it
2 Possibly, that is fairly probably   **5** No, definitely not
3 Doubtful, I really don't know

Here are the suggestions for what friendship is or involves:
    Friendship is

- People liking each other
- Sharing secrets
- Writing letters to each other
- Helping each other
- Thinking about someone
- Not seeing each other
- Helping with shopping, washing up
- Making jokes about someone
- Remembering her or his birthday
- Doing things for each other
- Knowing where your friend is, or is going
- Going on holiday together
- Taking his or her dog for a walk
- Standing up for someone
- Laughing at the same jokes
- Giving someone money
- Asking someone for money
- Seeing someone often (every day perhaps)
- Remembering things you've done together or gone through together
- Doing the same work
- Sharing the blame for something that went wrong
- Stopping hurtful gossip about someone
- Buying a present
- Preparing a pleasant surprise
- Preparing an unpleasant surprise
- Sharing good news
- Sharing bad news
- Reading the same books, papers, seeing same TV, films
- Having the same hobbies
- Taking an interest in someone else's hobbies
- Like a warm jersey
- Like a good pair of shoes
- Like a good film, game, book
- Like a cup of coffee
- A bowl of fruit
- A cup of tea
- Keeping rabbits
- Easily broken
- Indefinable

When you have finished your list, compare your answers with the others in your small group. Discuss any answers you found difficult, and try to decide, if you can, why you found them difficult.

Thinking of You

Have you ever had to wait for someone who didn't come? Although your friend is not there, his or her absence can be felt in every approaching footstep, every shadow in the doorway. If you have arranged to meet in a place where you have often met before, even the place, every detail, the clock, the curtains or whatever, seem to be full of the person who is not there, who has not yet arrived.

Have you ever been on your own, and wished your friend was with you? Or maybe you were already with a group of others, but there was one special friend who was not there. How did you feel? It could be hard not to keep thinking about someone who is not there!

There was once a businesswoman who had to travel from time to time for her firm, but her husband was a teacher who of course had to go to school every day and could not travel with her. When she was at a business convention in the South of France, by the sea and sunny beaches, she was really sorry he wasn't there too, so she scribbled a picture postcard with the words 'Lonely without you'. You can see how she felt. It was just unfortunate that her handwriting made it look like 'Lovely without you'.

When a special friend gives you a present, the present, whatever it is, becomes very special too. You take it out and look at it, and you think of your friend, and maybe wonder when you can meet again. This is a kind of longing, or it may be a yearning for the past, perhaps for a situation which you really know can never be the same again. You look at photographs, things you've bought together, remember a film you saw together, or a concert you both went to. In extreme cases, you could say, 'I don't want to go to the Lakes again without Lesley (or Leslie)'.

Of course there are always new things to do and places to go, people to meet, but memories can be special. It may be a sports team or a youth camp — 'What fun we had, in spite of the rain!' Maybe you have got a few photographs to remind you. Club nights at cricket and sailing clubs (and of course other sports) produce a number of old members who take an interest in the young but also like to get together and reminisce about old times. There could be trophies on the club walls or shelves, and pictures of successful teams. Other sections in this book use the idea of special places, and many of these are connected with longings, memories, and hopes for the future. Have you heard someone say, 'I can hardly wait till my holiday to get back to Iona' (or Jersey, or Majorca, or Weston–super–Mare).

A sports clubhouse full of trophies

Things to Collect and Things to be Proud Of

Is he a special ancestor?

A fan club collects pictures, records, tapes or whatever of the star or the group they support, and sometimes also press cuttings in scrap books. You can find people who collect things to do with Elvis Presley ten or more years after his death. A particular family may be proud of their ancestors — they have family portraits on the walls, shields, banners, the sort of thing you might see in a stately home open to the public. But anyone can have a rather special grandfather or great–great aunt, and photographs, a hat, a book or diaries which the family keep in memory.

National heroes as well as national events can be important, particularly for people who are living away from home. Scots may want to keep Burns Night, Irish people St Patrick's Day, and the ceremony may follow a regular pattern. If they are living in another country, they may have memories of their homeland which are possibly a bit rosier than reality — some of them may never actually have lived there!

ACTIVITY: on your own

Make a list of national days for various countries represented by people you know.

List the country, the name of the national day, and the date.

- How many of them are in memory of an important event in the development of the nation? (An example of this is the storming of the Bastille during the French Revolution. What does it do for Frenchmen to remember this?)

Reliving Historic Experiences

We know that some countries have a national day which they celebrate each year, like Independence Day in the USA (4th July) and Bastille Day in France (14th July), because the event which the people celebrate somehow gives meaning to the nation. Perhaps because of it also people think the way they do. It has helped to shape their national character and outlook. In Britain there is no independence day, and big national celebrations are rare, like a royal wedding or jubilee after 25 or 50 years of the Queen's reign.

There are also some smaller celebrations which most people are not involved in like St George's Day, the Trooping of the Colour, and Trafalgar Day. They are not public holidays. The only regular national occasion in Britain is Remembrance Day which is always on a Sunday, so cannot be a public holiday. Then there are parades, including church parades, and ex–servicemen and women get together to exchange news and to relive old experiences, experiences which have left an unforgettable impression.

Christians celebrate quite a lot of special events and many of these are treated in Part One of this book. The greatest of these is the Resurrection of Jesus which is celebrated annually at Easter, but also every Sunday. In fact Sunday is the special day for Christians precisely because it is the day of Jesus' resurrection.

The point is that the experience of the first Christians meant so very much to them. These were the disciples and those with them whom we know about from the gospels like Mary Magdalene (Mary of Magdala) and others. What they had lived through together meant so much that it was not enough just talking about it and remembering old times. They felt that the resurrection of Jesus gave meaning to their whole lives and shaped the character of the group who became the church, and therefore the event must be more than just a celebration — it must if possible be re–enacted, relived, re–experienced.

That is why still today we find mystery plays which reach their climax with the Resurrection, why local churches make an Easter Garden, and so on. Some of the rituals and customs at Christmas began like this too, even if a lot of other customs which were nothing to do with Christianity have been added on or incorporated. This is especially true of Christmas and one reason why the Puritans tried to stop it.

For the first Christians something special happened. New Christians, converts, children, were not themselves there when it happened, but they want to and need to share in the original experience, and this for two reasons: one is because it felt vitally important at the time, and secondly because it says something about what it is like to be a Christian. It is as if every Christian must somehow experience this event or relive it or go through it for him or herself.

A scene from the Gospels – the raising of Lazarus

ACTIVITY: as a group

Make a list of important Christian events or experiences which you think give character and meaning to the Christian religion.

You can draw on things in Part One and add your own as well, especially anything of more recent or local importance. If you have noted down more than four things, choose four of them, write them on a separate piece of paper, and answer these questions for these few only.

- How do Christians recreate or recall the experiences?
- How do they get young people and new converts to enter into these events?

ACTIVITY: on your own

You should find that the exercise you have just done is some help, although it will not provide all the answers

Copy out this list of things that Jesus did, and what Christians do as a result to recreate or carry on with what Jesus began.

Try to fill in the blank spaces. Keep this for later reference.

(a) WHAT JESUS DID	(b) WHAT CHRISTIANS DO
Healing people	Healing, hospital work, the laying on of hands
Spending time alone in prayer	
	Campaign for social justice
Teaching, telling parables	
	Baptism
Setting people free	
	Church order, setting up groups, mission to non-christians
The Last Supper	
	Counselling and giving support
Telling people to sin no more	
Self-giving death on the cross	

You can probably think of other 'things that Christians do' in addition to the ten suggested above. It will be obvious that some are a much better match than others, and this is due to the intensity of personal experience: how people react depends on the event or how it feels, and how they in fact look at it.

Chapter Two

STYLES AND PATTERNS OF PUBLIC WORSHIP

Most churches and chapels are open to the public in the sense that anyone can come in when there is a service taking place, although some have a notice asking visitors either to join in or to be quiet. In this section, we mean by **public worship** the religious services in which groups of Christians meet for worship, even if they are not always open to the public in general. We only want to exclude from this section private prayer, either alone or in a small group of special friends. Private prayer comes in later, in Chapter 7.

The church began with a group of Christians who met regularly, at least every Sunday. The very first Christians met for breaking bread and prayer. As the disciples were Jews, they prayed and sang songs together and read the Scriptures using the same pattern of worship as in the synagogue. They did not try to copy the system of sacrifices from the Jewish Temple.

For breaking bread together, that is some kind of meal, they would need a table. As Jews pray standing up (and some Christian still do) there may not have been benches or chairs. But to read the Scriptures they would have had a bookrest. These were written on scrolls, as Jewish scriptures still are, and they would need a stand, in fact something like what is now called a lectern.

What happens in a church service is often the reliving or recalling of an important event, and when this is repeated on a regular basis it becomes something of a routine. People talk about a ceremony becoming routinised or stylised, and that is why it is possible to talk about styles of public worship. If it is routine, however, this does not mean that it is dead or just a pretence. You may greet your best friend regularly and usually in the same way, but the friendship is all the stronger for this and certainly not made weaker. So the style is a kind of means of expressing feelings, hopes, love, respect and so on which are deeply and genuinely felt.

> The point of mentioning furniture is that the things you can find inside a church provide a clue for the kinds of activities that are done there. Many objects are also symbolic, but what they symbolise is in the first instance an activity, a memory or a belief.

Church with a notice board to show when the services are held

The Society of Friends (this is the full name for the Quakers) worship and express their religious feelings without any set pattern of words or actions. There is no service book. Instead of a chapel or church, the Quakers have a building they call a Meeting House. This is a plain building, without any altar or pulpit or lectern, just chairs. In fact Quakers can meet anywhere convenient, and once a congregation has been recognised it is called a Meeting. During worship any member of the meeting may speak, read from the Bible, pray aloud, sing, or read out anything which seems to be helpful and instructive. If no–one speaks, the whole hour may pass in complete silence. This can be a very moving experience.

Quakers feel God present with them as a spiritual force. They consider that the buildings of other denominations which contain candles, carvings and other symbols only distract the attention of the worshippers from the activity and presence of God among them.

ACTIVITY: on your own

1 These two lists give activities which take place in some Christian churches (left hand side), and objects or spaces which are likely to be needed to match each activity (right hand side). For the first ten of these you are given both sides, but they have been mixed up and you have got to sort them out.

Get a piece of paper with room for two lists side by side and write out the activities on the left, and the object or focus on the right. Your list should get them to match. As you can see, some of them may need more than one line, so be careful not to get in a muddle, and it is best to find each matching pair before you go on to the next one.

MAIN ACTIVITY OF SERVICE	CENTRAL OBJECT OR FOCUS
Reading the Bible aloud	Board of the Ten Commandments
Singing together	Desk for prayer leader
Holy Communion	Space for movement or dance
Religious processions	Place for the sick and sorrowful to kneel in front of healer or healers
Flower arrangements	No focus
Services of healing	Lectern with Bible on it
Prayer	Space with aisles
Ecstatic speech and dance and speaking in tongues	Holy table or altar
Definite moral teaching	Altar, ledges, space for vases
Silence	Seats for choir or band, organ or piano

2 Now, fill in the blanks from what you know about churches, or what you can find out, using the same layout as before.

Giving testimonies	
Sermon or preaching	
Exposition of the Sacrament (putting the sacrament on view)	
	Baptistry or font
	Place of penitence or confessional (more on this in Chapter 5)

A particular church or chapel may well make use of several of these at different times. For instance the focus of attention could be moved from the altar to the font by asking the congregation to turn round, or by simply moving to another part of the building. It would be possible, but unlikely, for one church group to make use of all fifteen of the things noted above in **1** and **2**, and certainly not all on the same occasion! So there is room for quite a lot of variety in different styles of public worship, and the frequent use of each aspect or style will affect the shape or layout of the building.

A note of warning, however, when you visit a church or chapel: it is much easier to change styles of worship and ceremonies than it is to change buildings, so you can easily find a church which was designed for one set of practices but is now used for another. The parish church in Woolwich (London) has rails set in the floor, and when the time for the sermon has come the pulpit can be moved into the centre of the nave, in front of the altar and chancel. This is an example of a change of focus for a change of activity. If you live anywhere near Woolwich you could go and see if they use this method any more.

ACTIVITY: as a group

As a practical activity find out about local Christian services in your area.

You may need to settle two problems at the start:

If you live in a city or town you will have to define your area and get it down to a manageable size. Of course if you think your own area is rather dull there is nothing to stop you choosing another part of town providing only that you can all get to it easily.

The second thing is that you may disagree about whether or not a certain group is to count as Christian. The best thing is to take them at their own word, and if they call themselves Christians, include them.

Find each church, chapel and Christian congregation in your chosen area and make a list of the religious services on a particular Sunday.

Not all of these take place in obvious church buildings, and some congregations hire a hall or use a local school or an old shop. The same building can be used by different denominations at different times on the same Sunday. For instance in Brixton, St Matthew's Church is used each Sunday by the Church of England, by the New Testament Assembly (originally West Indian), and by a West African Church.

While you are compiling your list, note down

(**a**) The name of the church or denomination
(**b**) The time when each service is scheduled to start
(**c**) What they call it
(**d**) How long it lasts
(**e**) Then write in two lines the main thing that happens there

Hints while you are looking at the inside of the building.

- Do all (or most of) the seats face the same way? If they do, what does this suggest about the person who stands in the front?
- If the seats face inwards in a square or circle, what does this suggest about what happens in the middle?
- Is there a special piece of furniture which seems to catch your attention? Is it an altar with an altar rail, a pulpit, place of prayer and healing, organ, open space?

Your answers will suggest different activities as the main ones in a particular church service: for instance, holy communion, preaching, singing, prayer, healing, testimony.

ACTIVITY: on your own

To follow this up

Choose one of the Christian church groups you came across while doing the last exercise, and arrange an interview with the minister, preacher, prophet, elder, priest or other leader.

Talk to him or her about the Sunday service, what sort of people they think come and what the Sunday service does for people. Be careful how you ask about this last: they may not think the service is doing things for people anyway, but you will find out about this.

Then write up your interview in two to three pages.

ACTIVITY

On your own or as a group

After you have found out so much about local Christian services it seems a pity not to go to some of them.

But this exercise is really only a suggestion for the very keen. You could go alone, or with a friend or two.

- Try to go to three quite different types of service and then talk about them together.
- Compare these different types of worship or service. Ask yourselves whether different denominations have different forms of worship.
- Try to consider the following: what you feel about each kind of worship, what you think most of the Christians who were there feel, and how they express their relationship to God.

Chapter Three

PLACES OF WORSHIP

A stained glass window

A crucifix in a church

A place of worship usually means a church or chapel which has been specially built for the purpose. You looked at a number of these if you did the exercises in the previous chapter.

One basic idea is to have a room or building which is a convenient place for the local Christians to meet together at the same time. Of course it is possible to worship God on the golf course or on top of a mountain, but it would be a bit inconvenient if the whole congregation had to go there every Sunday. In order to meet together a plain hall is all you need, whether you build it, borrow it or rent it from someone else. Many church buildings are therefore quite simple. Quaker Meeting Houses are all quite plain.

But most churches are more than this. The work that has gone into the design, the carving, painting, stained–glass windows, the whole layout of the building, show that much care has been devoted to this place, and so to the body of Christ which the church building symbolises. In many churches you can find pictures, carvings and other representations which directly symbolise something important for the Christian religion. In some cases pictures, perhaps in coloured window glass, show a scene from the life of Jesus or of later saints. Yet even in this picture you may find symbols which remind Christians of special events.

A crucifix is a powerful symbol of the self–giving and death of Jesus Christ. A crucifix which is on top of an open–work screen across the church may have a figure each side to represent the Mother of Jesus and the Beloved Disciple (John) at the cross. This pattern is called a rood and the whole screen a rood screen. But there are much less obvious ways of representing the cross, for instance in the ground plan of the building itself. The layout seems to be saying that the cross of Jesus is the foundation of the whole church.

All these things build up an atmosphere of worship and of devotion. So even a stranger coming in can feel that this is a special place. There is a feeling not just of prayer, but of some kind of presence. The word sometimes used for this feeling of presence is 'numinous' — a word which is purposely vague because it does not specify what the presence is, only an awareness of mystery and power which has an effect on all who come to it.

For many Christians God is felt to be specially present during the Eucharist or holy communion (to be studied in Chapter 4). Reverence in worship, and particularly eucharistic worship, may be expressed in the layout of the building itself. At the eucharist bread and wine are consecrated at the altar, so its position is important in relation to the worshippers. For instance, large churches in Europe have a long nave with a chancel, and the high altar right at the far end. In these churches distance is used to express reverence. A screen across the church where the nave meets the chancel (this might be a rood screen) deepens the effect of mystery, even though the screen is open–work and you can see pretty well through it.

Greek and other Orthodox churches are often square, or rather in the shape of a stubby cross with arms of equal length. The altar, which is in the eastern arm, is separated from the rest of the church by a more solid screen than in western churches. This screen is covered with **icons** (very special kind of picture of saints) and is called the **icon screen** (in Greek iconostasis or iconostasion). In it there are doors through which the priest comes at various times in the service, but most dramatically and ceremonially to proclaim the gospel and later to give communion.

Places with a Special Atmosphere

Some chapels and churches are built in places where visions were seen, saints died, or other important events occurred. Some natural geographical features have a numinous atmosphere, a sense of a kind of religious presence which cannot be described. This sort of atmosphere also is found in some churches and cathedrals, especially when there is silence.

Anywhere can be a place of worship in the sense that it is possible to worship anywhere — at sea, underground, in the air or out in space. But in this section we mean places which are kept specially for worship, places where people have worshipped and which seem to encourage worship.

Durham Cathedral

Worship in the Open Air

The Salvation Army often hold services of worship in the street, in city squares and other public places. They have got their own buildings for worship too, which they call Citadels, but part of their work is to go out to the people in the streets. Christians of other denominations too sometimes worship in the streets. Examples have been mentioned in Part One of processions of witness on Good Friday, (Part One, Chapter 4) and there are sometimes processions of other kinds too.

GCSE Question — Northern Examining Association — May 1988

Look at the picture of a Quaker Meeting and answer the questions which follow.

(Reproduced by permission of London Yearly Meeting.)

(a) Another name for Quakers is the 'Society of   (1 mark)

(b) (i) What name do Quakers give to the building in which they worship? (1 mark)
    (ii) Why are there no ornaments or symbols in the building? (2 marks)

(c) In what way are they worshipping God? Why do they worship in this way? (4 marks)

(d) In what circumstances might a person speak at a Quaker Meeting? (3 marks)

(e) Quakers, like other Christians, believe that it is important to worship together. Why do Quakers think it important to meet to worship together? (3 marks)

Chapter Four

SACRAMENTS

Sacraments can be hard to explain. They are an aspect of worship because they take place within the context of worship, and are also a particular kind of worship which gives a special emphasis to the idea that God is close to the worshippers. It is believed that in the sacraments God gives people special benefits.

Sacraments have a ritual form, but what they mean for Christians goes far beyond their form. In fact what they actually mean is the most important thing about them. To explain what sacraments are and what worshippers feel about them, it is necessary to look more closely at relationships between two or more people.

Some families go on holiday to the same place every year. They meet the same people and enjoy a special friendship, but the friendship is linked to the holidays which they all share. There is even a certain ritual to it all: the time of year, what they do together, the things they talk about and so on. But basically, of course, the friendship depends on their being nice to each other and being glad to see each other again. They are not compelled to be nice to each other but do so of their own free will.

Christians picture God as being present with people at all times, but there are also certain special occasions and some of these are felt to take place in the framework of a special ritual or ceremony. Men and women cannot compel God to be nice to them, or even to be present, but they believe that on ritual occasions which they call sacraments God is there and is favourable to them. They feel confident of this because they believe they are acting in accordance with God's will.

There are a few groups of Christians who do not celebrate sacraments of any kind at all. The Society of Friends, called Quakers, do not have holy communion or baptism or any ritual of a remotely sacramental nature and they feel that God is really present among them whenever they meet together in his name. Similarly they feel that every meal is a eucharist (holy communion), that every act of washing is a baptism. As we shall see, there may be more to communion than eating, and more to baptism than washing, but these groups of Christians make a point, because they stress that God is everywhere. So even the others who do use ritual sacraments respect them for it.

Sacraments are therefore special ceremonies which Christians perform, and they consider them to be channels of God's love, giving strength to those who take part in them. A sacrament may be performed only occasionally, or it may be something frequent and regular, but in either case the rite, i.e. what can be seen and felt and done, is thought of as more than a sign of God's activity: Christians believe that God has in some way arranged for sacraments actually to be part of God's relationship to man, in the way that a kiss between two people who love each other is more than a sign of that love: it actually expresses the love and helps to foster it.

CEREMONIES WHICH ARE CALLED SACRAMENTS

According to traditional teaching there are seven sacraments. Almost all protestants celebrate two of these sacraments which they also call Bible sacraments. These are Baptism and Holy Communion (the Eucharist). The other five rituals which are also called sacraments by Roman Catholics, all branches of the Orthodox and by some Anglicans, also appear in some form in the New Testament. These are Confirmation, Ordination (to be a priest or minister), Marriage, Unction (anointing with special oil) and Penance (forgiveness and reconciliation, also called Absolution). If we count all these, they add up to seven.

In this book, baptism, confirmation, ordination, marriage and unction are discussed in Part Three as '**Rites of Passage**'. This is because they can be thought of as part of the human life cycle, at least for some Christians, and they usually only happen once in anyone's lifetime, though unction can be an exception.

Other Rites of Passage include a Christian funeral, but this is not called a sacrament, presumably because the person it is for has died, but the sacrament of holy communion (eucharist) may be celebrated at a funeral (see Part Three, Chapter 6).

Holy Communion — the Eucharist

In the following sections, holy communion is considered first, and then the sacrament of penance, although not all Christians have this form of ritual.

The eucharist is the central service of worship for the great majority of Christians. Therefore it is the most commonly celebrated of all the sacraments. But the variety of ways in which different Christians regard this service make it impossible to explain in a few lines.

The general shape of the service follows the same pattern for almost every type of Christian. But it has had many different names. The name Holy Communion suggests the idea of sharing with God and with other worshippers present; Eucharist underlines giving thanks; other names like The Lord's Supper, God's Board (meaning table) and the Breaking of Bread point to the meal. The name Mass has no meaning, but may have been derived from something formerly said in Latin at the end. In Orthodox churches this service is mostly called the Divine Liturgy. Liturgy means service.

First an outline description will be given of what happens. Then an attempt will be made to explore some of the many types of meaning which Christians attach to the eucharist. It will become clear that what Christians think about the eucharist is very important and holds for them the deepest meaning. For the purposes of study, meanings will be grouped together as (1) ideas connected with eating, (2) ideas connected with sacrifice, and (3) ideas connected with the presence of God.

The Shape of the Eucharist

The eucharist has become the central and most important way in which Christians worship God. Most Christian churches celebrate the eucharist at least every Sunday, and often several times on a Sunday to give as many people as possible the chance to come. By no means all present at the eucharist receive holy communion by eating the special food (and drinking the wine if offered). For many it is enough to be there. The importance of making one's communion (by eating) depends on what the eucharist means for the people there, and this is discussed later.

Some protestant groups, such as Presbyterian (United Reformed Church in England) and many of the various 'free' churches, consider the eucharist such a solemn occasion that they celebrate this service much less frequently, only once a month, or even once every few months. Quakers do not have the eucharist at all.

The heart of the eucharist is a shared meal of bread and wine, although the quantities are so small as to be symbolic. Yet the idea of real food is definitely there. There is always prayer to God, praise and thanksgiving, which are described in the following section. The bread and wine are central, and many churches have somewhere a picture of Jesus with his disciples at table for the Last Supper.

The great prayer of thanksgiving, also called the eucharistic prayer or the prayer of consecration, includes the words: '*This is my body*' and '*This is my blood*'. These words are ascribed to Christ himself who is believed to have begun this ritual at the Last Supper. He told his disciples to celebrate it regularly in order to recall him (see Part One, Chapter 3 on Maundy Thursday). For the majority of Christians, regularly means that this should be the central act of worship every Sunday.

Basically there are four actions in the eucharist:

1   Bread and wine are brought in and offered to God on the holy table or altar. They represent both the produce of nature and the work of people in baking and processing them.
2   These gifts are then consecrated, that is made holy, by the saying of prayers of thanks. This is the origin of the word Eucharist, which means *Thanks* in Greek.
3   The bread must then be broken and this has more than one meaning (see for instance ideas connected with sacrifice below).
4   Lastly the bread is given out and eaten and the wine drunk. Some Christian groups emphasise the sharing of the bread by not permitting a minister to celebrate this service unless there are other people present who will share in the communion. But Roman Catholics allow a priest to celebrate alone, while other people, if there at all, only share in a symbolic way.

A painting of the Last Supper

The Service and the Symbols

The eucharistic prayer and the communion are central, but the ceremony includes several other parts, as can be seen if you look at a service book and follow the ritual in it. To do this successfully, you will probably need help from a regular member of the church congregation.

Here is a brief outline of the things which are done at this service in almost all branches of the Christian Church:

● Bread and wine are put ready before the start of the service. In many protestant and most Orthodox churches, the bread is ordinary bread of the kind most people eat, although the actual loaf used may have been baked specially and have a special pattern on top. Roman Catholic and Armenian Orthodox churches, however, (also some Anglicans and Methodists) use small round pieces of unleavened bread like wafers: in fact they are called wafers. (Bread without leaven is bread made without yeast. It has the advantage of keeping longer and also makes hardly any crumbs). There are symbolic reasons for both. When unleavened bread is used, it represents the manna which the Israelites in Moses' time found in the desert: it was described as a '*small round thing*'. On the other hand when ordinary bread is used in the eucharist it symbolises the sharing and meeting of God and man in daily work, because ordinary bread is made every day for people to eat.

● People are expected to prepare themselves for communion and there is a form of confession which is general, i.e. it is said by everyone. After this some words of reconciliation are said by the minister to assure people that they should take part in this service, however inadequate they may actually feel. This is like the confession and forgiveness which is studied in more detail in Chapter 5.

● Thanksgiving and praise and also prayers are said or sung at various parts of the service. A normal pattern would include praise and thanksgiving at the beginning and the end, and prayers of intercession (i.e. praying for people — see Chapter 7 on Prayer) both just before the eucharistic prayer and also as part of it.

● There are Bible readings, one of which is often a psalm. The Bible readings always include a passage from a gospel, and it is usual for people to stand for this. In some churches there is a special procession in which the gospel book is held high in the air, and various attendants stand with candles around the reader while the gospel is read aloud for all to hear. Not all churches have a gospel procession like this. All, however, have a passage read out from the gospels.

● On Sundays there is usually a sermon, and the preacher usually draws on one or more of the passages which have been read from the Bible.

● The eucharistic prayer does not begin until after the bread and wine have been put on the altar. In the last thirty years it has become common in the Church of England for two members of the congregation to bring up the bread and wine from the back of the church, forming a little procession. This symbolises their offering, their contribution to the eucharist. This is not done in Orthodox churches, as the bread and wine have already been prepared beside the altar. If there is a money collection, this too is taken up to the minister immediately after the bread and the wine. The presiding minister then puts the bread and wine ready on the altar or table. The wine is usually mixed with a little water, and this symbolises the blood mixed with water from the side of Jesus when the soldier pushed a spear into his side at the crucifixion.

● The eucharistic prayer follows and this always recalls the words used by Jesus at the Last Supper, as well as calling on the Holy Spirit to consecrate (make holy) the gifts. Communion may follow immediately, but more often the Lord's Prayer (more about this in Chapter 7) is said at

this point, and there are usually also prayers to Jesus as the Lamb of God who takes away the sin of the world.

● Then the communion, that is the eating and drinking in an orderly manner. Different churches have different ways of organising this.

● After communion, the vessels used (cup or chalice, paten or plate, and anything else) must be washed ritually at the altar, but none of this can usually be seen by the people.

● Then there are final prayers of thanks, and the people are sent out, often with a priest's blessing.

● In some churches there are devotions either before or after the main service, but these are not discussed here.

The People Receive Holy Communion

Different ways in which people receive holy communion suggest different kinds of meaning.

At a simple service with a small group of people who have formed a ring round the table, the consecrated bread may simply be passed from one person to the next, with the words, '*The Body of Christ*'. The cup is passed next, with the words, '*The Blood of Christ*', said by each person as he or she passes it on. This is like the little group of the first disciples breaking bread together.

The usual way in Roman Catholic and Anglican churches is that the people come up to the space in front of the altar, and then either stand or kneel at the altar rail to receive the host (consecrated bread) from the hands of the priest, minister, or other person appointed for this purpose. This way people think of worshipping God by a personal act of commitment at communion. In Anglican churches people wait at the rail after receiving the host until they drink from the chalice (cup of consecrated wine), and then go back to their places. In Roman Catholic churches, people only receive the host, and do not get the chalice at all.

In many protestant churches people stay in their seats, and stewards bring little pieces of bread to them and individual glasses of wine on trays.

There are also other different customs about taking communion, as well as the difference between receiving the host only (as Roman Catholics do) or getting both bread and wine. In Orthodox churches communion is received 'in both kinds' (i.e. bread and wine) in one go by using a spoon.

Look at these pictures: can you suggest which church or de-nomination is shown in each picture?

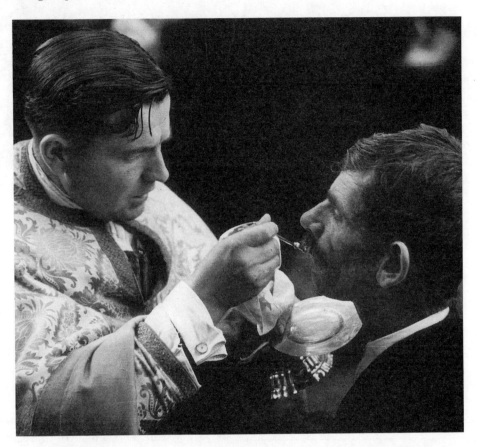

What it Means for Christians

The name Lord's Supper at once reminds us of the Last Supper of Jesus with his disciples on the night he was betrayed, just before the crucifixion. The prayer of thanksgiving, the eucharistic prayer, always includes words spoken by Jesus on that occasion: *This is my body, this is my blood*. But Christians also think of the time when Jesus distributed food to 5,000 hungry people in the desert. This story is very important for the meaning of this sacrament. And this in turn symbolises their hunger for the grace and gifts of God.

At the Last Supper Jesus used bread and wine. The five thousand people were fed on bread and fish. These two are symbolically combined in the picture from an Armenian church (Armenian Orthodox).

ACTIVITY: on your own

Look at this picture, and make a list of what is on the table.

- What do the various things mean?
- Describe briefly what is happening.
- Why did the Armenians put a picture like this in their church?

THREE KINDS OF MEANING

In order to study the meanings of the eucharist, it is proposed to consider three groups of ideas: (1) ideas connected with eating; (2) ideas connected with sacrifice and self–giving; and (3) ideas connected with the presence of God.

IDEAS CONNECTED WITH EATING

When we try to imagine a group of people being friendly, we may think of people sitting round a table eating together, or at least having a cup of tea. This is a kind of a model for being friendly and being together. In such a gathering it might seem very rude to refuse to eat or drink anything, unless there was a special reason.

The first Christians were Jews, and there were problems at first about converts to Christianity who had not been Jews before. Strict Jews do not eat together with non–Jews. This is mentioned several times in the New Testament (see Galatians 2.11–12; and Acts 11.1–4), and is still true today. It seems that eating with anyone who is not pure in a religious sense is likely to defile the faithful and make them unfit to worship God. The first Christians seemed to be very shocking because they broke this Jewish rule of purity by eating together with non–Jews. This happened both at the eucharist celebrations (the Lord's Supper) and when they ate ordinary meals together as friends. The fact that the more strict Jewish Christians made a fuss about this shows that there really is something important about eating together.

When a few friends come round to your house, do you offer them a cup of tea, or coffee, a slice of cake, or anything? Perhaps, perhaps not. But if you do, which feels friendlier, to make a pot of tea and pour it into each cup, or to give each person a cup with a teabag and just pour out the water? Is there any difference in the feel of cutting slices of cake as against giving out individual cakes in paper wrappers?

Sharing a special meal

Loaves of bread

ACTIVITY: as a group

Discuss what is said in the paragraph above. Is there in fact any difference? There is no right answer, and, as always, you are at liberty to disagree! But it is important to try and find reasons why you feel about it the way you do.

What you eat is digested and then built into your body, and actually becomes part of you. When you share an item of food with someone, you then have something organically in common. Imagine two or three people eating fruit. They feel more togetherness if they are eating the same kind of fruit, fruit out of the same bag or box, or picked from the same bush. This feeling is even stronger when one item of fruit, however large or small, is cut up and shared between them. It is like this too when you break and share a bar of chocolate.

Bread is a basic food. It used to be said that rich people had bread at the side of their main dish, but for poor people bread was itself the main dish and anything else was at the side. The very first Christians were certainly not rich people, and only very few of them were even reasonably well off. So bread and other corn products were their main food. But of course bread itself does not grow ready–made on plants, but is the result of work by several people, and several production processes.

Different climates and different farming economic systems mean that mankind's staple food is different in various countries. But in the eucharist bread stands for all of them.

The bread at the eucharist, then, is for Christians the bread of life which gives strength. Just as bread is a basic food which satisfies hunger, so this holy bread according to the gospel gives eternal life. It must, however, be received in the right way, and this means with devotion, trust, and penitence (being sorry for sin). People who come to communion in this way are accepted by God, however unworthy they actually feel themselves to be.

The Old Testament account of Moses leading the Israelites out of Egypt is often remembered in Christian tradition. God gave them miraculous food in the desert called *manna* to keep them alive. For Christians manna symbolises the communion bread, and holy communion reminds them of God's love shown in providing manna all those centuries ago. In Exodus it is described as '*a small round thing*'.

Many feelings and symbols come into play. The two elements of bread and wine become the body and blood of Christ, and this means two things in particular for all those who share in this ritual feast. First, the same food is shared out and eaten by a number of people, and, as just noted when we discussed sharing food and drink, all the Christians who eat and drink at the eucharist have something organic in common. This is stressed sometimes by the words: '*We are one body because we all partake of the one bread*'.

Secondly, if Jesus becomes the bread and the wine, it is like a new birth at Bethlehem, a new incarnation. This is symbolised in Orthodox ritual even before the service, when the bread is covered with a cloth which has a star–shaped clip and is called the Star of Bethlehem. After consecration, this food which is the body and blood of Christ also becomes each of those people present. Or rather, each of them becomes in some way a part of Christ himself.

Obviously we have jumped ahead a bit, and the idea of the presence of Christ has been combined with the idea of eating. But God is felt to be outside time and so is not tied to the normal order of events. This means that Christians can think of themselves being organically joined to Christ by eating in holy communion, just as they believe Christ has joined them to himself first, for instance when they were baptised, and is now nourishing them in the sacrament of holy communion.

Abel and Melchizadek, a mosaic in Ravenna, Italy

ACTIVITY

On your own (or with a friend)

This exercise shows how some Christians have thought of the Eucharist not just as something begun by Jesus in the gospels, but as having a kind of prehistory in the Old Testament.

Look up the passages in the Bible to which this picture refers.

(a) Read about Abel and his offering to God in Genesis chapter 4, especially verses 1–4.

- What offering did Abel bring?
- What happened to Abel soon afterwards?
- Is this significant when we compare Jesus at the Last Supper and soon after?

(b) Read Genesis 14.17–20 to find out what Melchizedek did.

- What did Melchizedek bring as his offering?
- Whom he did he share it with?
- Who was Melchizedek, and what did he say?

IDEAS CONNECTED WITH SACRIFICE AND SELF—GIVING:

Have you ever saved up something very special, then suddenly given it away to someone who seemed to need it more than you? You could have been saving money, but decided to give it to someone you know who needed it urgently. Or you might have given it to a disaster fund to help people you will never meet: think of famine relief, or earthquake and flood appeals.

The special something you have been saving need not have any cash value: it could be something that means a lot to you, but even so you decide to give it away. It might even be a secret, a piece of news or knowledge which you have been keeping to yourself, but then you decide to share it with someone.

Probably the supreme example of this is to risk or give your life for someone else. It might not end in death, but you maybe decide to devote your life and energy to someone or something — a cause, a political party, revolution, the Queen and your country, or for humanity. Everyone can think of examples of these from recent events and from history, but most obvious are men who risk their lives in bomb disposal or who undertake dangerous missions to try and free hostages held by terrorists.

ACTIVITY: as a group

Discuss whether you would risk your life for anyone, or your savings.

- If so, for whom or for what, and in what sort of circumstances?
  Now imagine you are walking along a river bank and a child falls in.
- Would you dive in to rescue a child, if you knew who it was?
- Would you jump in for a total stranger?
- Would you jump in for a dog?
- What if you could not swim very well?
- If you did not jump in, what else would you do?

Giving life and taking life

Quite a lot of people in this country are vegetarians and do not eat meat. There can be various reasons for this, but one of them is certainly that they feel it is wrong that an animal should be killed for food, because meat is a luxury for many people which they do not need. In a country where food is scarce naturally people eat whatever they can get.

In parts of Africa and South America, animals like sheep and goats are valuable, and people only kill an animal if they are going to celebrate and feast with family and friends. It is customary to eat a lamb or a kid for Easter, both because people have sheep and goats, and of course because a lamb is the traditional food at the Jewish Passover, the festival which Jesus wanted to keep with his disciples at the time of his betrayal and crucifixion. Naturally, Christians were very quick to see the symbolism by which Jesus is the lamb which is killed for Passover, saves his people from death, and then is eaten by them in holy communion.

A further idea which is also found in the Old Testament of the Bible is making a sacrifice for sin. This is called atonement (see Glossary). In the ˙r

Jewish Temple an animal was chosen which was thought after appropriate ritual to have received the guilt the whole people had deserved (i.e. in symbolic way it took the blame), and was then put to death, killing off the guilt and the threat of punishment in the process. This practice is found in a number of religions, and is not exclusively Jewish. But it was an ancient Jewish ritual, and the idea comes again in the New Testament, this time with Jesus Christ as the victim who willingly gives himself up to death in order to take away the guilt and sins of the world. This explains the old Latin word for the consecrated bread: Hostia (host) means sacrificial victim.

Have you ever seen a pub called *The Lamb and Flag*? Did you know this was a Christian symbol? The red cross on a white ground is the flag of resurrection. English crusaders who went to the Holy Land adopted it as their sign.

This kind of symbolism and thinking is definitely present for many Christians in the sacrament of the eucharist. It is made explicit in the words, '*Jesus, Lamb of God, you take away the sins of the world*'.

IDEAS CONNECTED WITH THE PRESENCE OF GOD

If Christians worship Jesus Christ in the host, what does it mean for them actually to eat it?

There is a saying that I only believe what I can see — seeing is believing. In a church service, some people feel the need for a focus, they want to be able to say '*God is here, and his presence is focussed in this special place, this special object*'.

Obviously the symbolism by which Jesus is thought to offer himself as a sacrifice for the sins of the world (see three paragraphs above), includes the thought that Jesus is present at the eucharist, and in particular within the sacrament of consecrated bread and wine.

In the picture on page 91 you can see the Host being lifted up for all to see. Both the host and the chalice (which is lifted up separately) form a powerful focus for devotion and worship, but especially the host because people cannot see inside the cup.

The belief that Jesus is present in the sacrament led to the doctrine of transubstantiation. According to this, the bread and wine stop being bread and wine on the altar at consecration and turn into the body and blood of Christ instead. This doctrine became official Roman Catholic teaching at the Reformation mainly because it was unacceptable to Protestants. Transubstantiation is a doctrine that people have argued about. It is still officially taught to Roman Catholics. Orthodox Christians, as well as members of several other churches, also believe that Christ is truly present in the bread and wine, and that bread and wine become his body and blood, but they are much less matter–of–fact about it. They teach that the eucharist is a mystery which the human mind cannot just explain in words.

It is perfectly possible for Christians to believe and feel the presence of God without needing a theory like transubstantiation. This is certainly true when Christians feel the presence of Christ at prayer meetings and celebrations of praise or at other times. Thinking of Jesus being present in the sacrament does not mean that he is not present in other ways and at other times as well. Feeling the presence of Jesus and of the holy spirit can be a deeply emotional matter, as can be seen most obviously in Pentecostal churches, again without any eucharist, although many pentecostals do celebrate holy communion from time to time.

ACTIVITY: in pairs

Have you ever been waiting for someone important to come?
Think of a crowd at a pop concert waiting for the performers to arrive. When it starts you think '*This is really it*!'

- Try and think of one such occasion in your own experience, and describe it to your partner.
- Then listen to her or his description. Compare notes, especially on what it felt like.

ACTIVITY: as a group

An old carpenter some fifty years ago wanted to describe the need for intense concentration when he was sharpening a saw. He said, '*If the King of England came in through that door I would not notice him*'.

Discuss whether there could be any circumstances for any of you when the arrival (or the expected arrival) of a hero, star or other important person would not make you stop what you were doing.

Christians who stress the real presence of Jesus Christ in the host, the sacrament of bread in the form of a round wafer (see picture on page 91), sometimes have the sacrament kept in a special place in the church, usually with a white light burning in front of it. The sacrament is said to be **reserved** and the place it is kept is called the **Tabernacle**. The **Reserved Sacrament** has two uses: the first is to be a focus for prayer and meditation, so you could see people kneeling in front of the altar where the sacrament is reserved; the second use is that it can be taken quickly to the very ill and dying, who may want to receive holy communion. This form of communion for the dying is part of the **Last Rites.** (Compare what follows here with the sections in Part Three on unction and funeral arrangements.) The last sacrament taken to the dying is sometimes called the **Viaticum** because it is supposed to see the dying on their way (via) to the next life.

Being There

So far all the examples have assumed that the important person is coming to you. It could be the other way round. You might be going to Buckingham Palace to receive a medal. Many Christians, especially in the Orthodox tradition, feel that the eucharist lifts them up from their town or their village into the court of heaven. The icons of the saints which are on the special icon screen give support to this idea because the saints are in heaven caught up in the worship of God.

You may be interested to know why the Russians first became Orthodox Christians. According to the Russian Chronicle, Duke Vladimir (who ruled 980–1015) thought that religion would help to bind his people together. So he sent ambassadors to all the religious centres he could think of. They visited Jews and Muslims, as well as going to Jerusalem, Rome and Constantinople. In Constantinople the Russians came into the great cathedral of Santa Sophia (holy wisdom) for the divine liturgy (eucharist). They reported, *'We did not know whether we were in heaven or on earth'* — they felt themselves uplifted to the presence of God and the angels and saints in heaven. As a result, Vladimir invited missionaries to come from Constantinople, and his people became Orthodox.

Memorial

For a number of Christians, the holy communion is a special occasion without them thinking that God is any more present than at any other kind of service. For them the ritual is a memorial only, and they think of events in the gospel, particularly of the Last Supper before the betrayal and death of Jesus. The meaning of the service, then, is something like a birthday celebration, or a regimental or club dinner, to mark some event or to remember something that they have all done or been through together.

Obviously the idea of memorial comes also from the words of Jesus *'Do this in remembrance of me'*, words which are part of the ritual anyway.

If there is an Orthodox church in your area, visit it and look at the icon screen. During the divine liturgy (this is what Orthodox Christians usually call the eucharist), the pictures of the saints seem to come alive (it is said their eyes glow), and represent for the worshippers that they are being taken up into heaven.

Alexander Nevsky church, Leningrad, USSR

Chapter Five

OTHER CEREMONIES — FORGIVENESS WHICH BRINGS RECONCILIATION

Look at these pictures. What do you think is happening? Everyone has had times of feeling bad, upset, ill or just very tired and fed up, and been glad of the comfort of human company. In all these cases, the human contact is expressed by more than words. Perhaps the point of these scenes is that it doesn't matter for the present whose fault it was, or even if there was anyone who is to blame. Somebody needs help, and someone else is giving it.

Now imagine that you are the child or sick person in one of these pictures. How do you feel as a result of the comfort offered by the other person? The basic situation, the cause of all the trouble may not have changed, but do you now feel a bit different about it? Do you feel better able to face the future? Do you think you can now take the first step towards trying to put things right?

Sick people being comforted

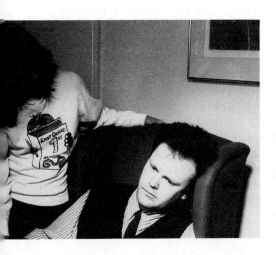

Someone to Talk To

Many better–off Americans have a psychiatrist whom they consult regularly, say every month. He (or she) is supposed to help the client become a balanced and well–rounded personality, capable of doing well at his or her job, making and keeping friends, and generally feeling fulfilled. Quite a lot of people in all modern countries, businessmen, teachers, politicians, feel that they are leading exceptionally busy and stressful lives, and they can get a lot of support from the regular visit to the psychiatrist (rudely called *the shrink*). The psychiatrist in turn is not likely to tell them that he is not needed, as he makes a living from just this kind of work.

There are several different theories of psychiatry, but they all look back into the patient's past, usually into childhood, to try and identify deep disturbances (traumas) which may account for their attitudes and character as adults. The point is that something has gone wrong in the past and this affects the way they are now. Mostly the psychiatrist does not try to put the past right — this is in any case likely to be impossible. But it is enough to find out what went wrong and to bring the patient to recognise and admit it, and eventually to be reconciled to it and so to get over it. In fact just about everyone has had something which has gone wrong in the past, a relationship with parents or such (this is the most frequent case if you go back to early childhood).

Psychiatry is a new science, which has arisen in the last hundred years. Before that people went to a doctor, to a priest or minister of religion, or talked things out with a friend. The point to notice is that something can have gone wrong in the past which affects the way you are now. You may be shy or show–off, secretive or sentimental, and this could be due to something in your childhood relationships.

An example might be a baby boy, whose parents were deeply disappointed because they really wanted a baby girl, and although they may have tried to hide this, the boy has grown up with problems in relating to women because he feels at a quite unconscious level that he ought to have been one. The method the psychiatrist is likely to use will be a series of sessions with the client (patient) talking about his childhood, his relationship with parents and so on, until the matter which, in the psychiatrist's opinion, has been the cause of the inhibition (shyness–difficulty), is brought to light, put into words, talked through and faced by the client himself. Once understood, the problem can be handled and usually clears up.

This process may take a long time, but in essence it is quite simple. Something has gone wrong in the client's past; this must be found, identified and put into words, that is confessed; and then the future can be faced with understanding and confidence.

Of course it is obvious that there is no need to go back to childhood to find things that have gone wrong in life. For many people yesterday or last week is far enough.

Psychiatric treatment helps you to feel right with yourself by getting you to recognise something that has gone wrong. In some cases, you may have to sort out a relationship with another person, possibly under guidance from the psychiatrist. Your relationship to other people is obviously important. So there are two things here: the need to be reconciled with yourself and also with other people.

For Christians there is a third relationship. Each person needs to be reconciled to God. This is not instead of the other two (self and neighbour) but is supposed to be more basic and therefore to make the other two possible, or at any rate more complete. To someone who is not a Christian this may look like pure mythology.

A psychiatrist treating her patient

Alternatively a believer might say: If Jesus has reconciled the world to God, what more can possibly be needed? But everyone knows that things do go wrong, that in fact we do things that are bad and upset ourselves and others. These are the things that forgiveness and reconciliation are for. What Jesus is believed to have done is much more basic, which Christians say ought to make reconciliation between people easier.

A recent moral education project for schools turned all its attention on a person's relationships with other people. The general line was that it is wrong to upset people, to cheat them, disappoint them or let them down, but the other side of this seems to be that if people are generally happy about what has happened, then it is all right and no harm has been done. This may be useful as a rule–of–thumb for everyday morality, but it is very easy to think of cases where it just does not work. For instance, if an individual is generally a nuisance then everyone will be pleased if she or he is put out of the way, and if this involves murder, then the victim will not even be around to complain, so of course relationships will seem to be fine. You can think of other less extreme examples. Perhaps the murderers will feel bad about it deep down in their subconscious (work for the psychiatrist here), but on the other hand they may get used to doing this kind of thing and just cease to worry.

God is important for Christians in this kind of situation because God is always around and is not fooled about what you cannot see. Most Christians in all churches and denominations stress that relationships to other people and to oneself matter and are in themselves part of the Christian's relationship to God. A Christian would say, that believing in God keeps one anchored to reality.

Finding What's Wrong to Put It Right

As with the psychiatrist, the basis of Christian confession and forgiveness is to recognise that something has gone wrong, and to say as clearly as possible what it is. If somebody else has been upset or injured by what has happened, something has got to be done about it. If it is possible to restore the damage, that may be the best thing, but in some cases something quite different is needed, a show of friendship with an apology, a present which may be symbolic rather than of any money value. In some cases it may not be possible to do anything for the right person or group, so instead it may help to be generous or friendly to somebody else.

ACTIVITY: as a group

Here are three short exercises for discussion in your small group:

1 You have broken some of the glass on your neighbour's greenhouse, and he says some of the plants have been killed in the night by the frost. What do you do?
2 You have upset your mother by staying out late without saying anything in advance, and the nice meal she got ready for you has been spoilt and had to be thrown away. What do you do?
3 Make up your own exercise and discuss it. The problem should be one which could have several possible answers for you to discuss and talk through.

And a fourth one:

4 No—one can say in advance what your group thought of for (3), but it possibly concerned the family, as (2) obviously does. Supposing that there is a family difficulty like that, decide together whether either of the following would help:
(**a**) If when you were thinking what to do, your father, or grandmother, or other respected relative, gave you some advice?
(**b**) If after you had done whatever you decided was best to try and make things right, your father or grandmother or other respected relative said, '*That was good: it'll be all right now, if you're sensible*'.

Advice and Reassurance

Christians use the words sin and sins (compare the section on the Forgiveness of Sins in Part Four pages 214–215). **Sin** means more than just something that has gone wrong, because it includes upsetting the Christian's relationship to God. One way of picturing this is to think of two children who annoy or hurt each other, and their mother is naturally upset. When they do make things up, their mother will be relieved and pleased too. There is more to it than just two children deciding to be friends again.

The first stage of **reconciliation** is thinking out what has gone wrong and putting it into words. Because this means admitting your own part in it, where you have gone wrong, it is called **confession** — more about this a little later. The next stage may be to get advice, but on the other hand, what to do may be so obvious that you do not need any advice, except perhaps how not to get into this mess again. The third stage means doing something to put things right, and restoring the broken relationship if possible.

There could be cases where the best thing to do was to be nice to somebody else, and occasionally you meet the kind of case where even an apology would open an old wound and it is best not to touch on the hurt for a bit. The final stage is a word of **forgiveness**. Obviously it is good if you accept an apology and make things up, or if two people apologise to each other and agree to treat each other normally again. But as well as this a word of reassurance from the respected friend or relative (which was suggested above) may be important too.

Confession

A Christian (or a group of Christians) may do something which seems all right at the time, but later he or they feel it was a mistake. If they (or she or he) now feel that it was a sin (wrong), and not just an embarrassment, then they will feel also that it ought to be confessed.

Sin and embarrassment are not the same. It is easy to be worried stiff about an embarrassing mistake, which is not any kind of sin or wrong in that sense at all.

Early Christians, in the first few centuries, practised public confession. People admitted their faults in front of the whole congregation, because what they had done wrong may have affected the whole congregation. This came about because at that time Christians were a tiny minority of the population, and were from time to time fiercely persecuted by the authorities. Any kind of wrongdoing or crime reflected badly on the church, and made non–Christians say, '*Well of course, that's what they're really like*'. Secondly, in days when Bibles and other sacred writings had to be copied out by hand, they were scarce and valuable, so one of the things the authorities tried to do was to get hold of Christian books and destroy them. In time of persecution Christians had to be strong to resist pressure from the authorities to hand over their scriptures, and the weaker ones gave in. In this way the whole church was harmed. In fact the English word '*traitor*' comes from the Latin *traditor*, which means someone who hands something over.

Such people needed to be forgiven in public and so they had to confess in public, if they were to be reconciled and restored to the congregation. The bishop or the elders had to pronounce the words of forgiveness (**absolution**) on behalf of the congregation and of God, and lay a penalty on the sinners which might mean wearing special clothes (penitential dress) and being banned from holy communion for a fixed length of time, or something else. This penalty was called a **penance**.

Some Pentecostal groups today and many churches who are limited to one congregation practice public confession in church, although the circumstances are often quite different. In some groups people stand up and give testimonies: these are special little speeches which start by giving thanks to God because he has, according to the speaker, brought both forgiveness and salvation, in spite of the fact that I (the person giving the testimony) was a terrible sinner — then follows a list of sins. This is certainly a kind of public confession, but the speaker is not asking the congregation for forgiveness, as he (or she) claims to have been forgiven by God already.

Some Pentecostal churches have given up public confession because some of the sins confessed were rather shocking and not a good thing for the younger members of the church to hear. They were unedifying. Instead, people who want to confess are encouraged to go to one of the church elders to confess privately, and to seek advice at the same time.

Confession and Absolution as a Sacrament

Absolution means that God's minister speaks the words of forgiveness in God's name. More than three quarters of the world's Christians believe that every Christian should make a regular practice of self–examination in the light of God's love ('*What Jesus has done for me*', etc.), and then go to a respected person, in fact a priest, and make a full confession. Of course many of the sins confessed in this way are quite undramatic and perhaps rather boring, but they are important for the people concerned.

The priest is there for at least three things: to listen patiently and attentively, to ask about what steps if any the penitent (this means the person confessing) has taken or is taking to put things right, and finally to speak words of God's forgiveness which is technically called absolution. This is a set formula, the idea being that the words are not made up by the priest, but represent the words of God. In addition to these three things, it is usual for the priest to give some advice, and to suggest a very small task which is called the penance.

A priest hearing confession

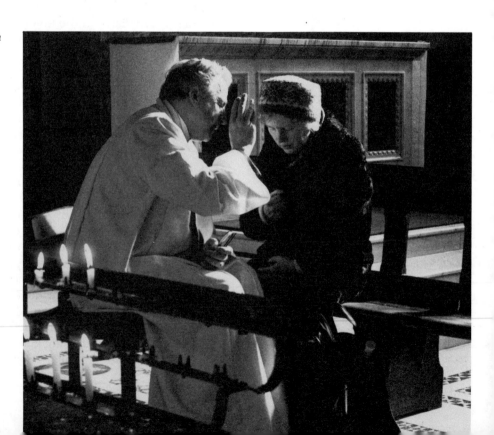

According to this usage, the penitent, after making confession, asks for *'penance, advice and absolution'*. The penance is nowadays something very small, a token. It might be to say a set prayer, or read a passage from the Bible, or occasionally to do something for someone. Nowadays the penance is never anything difficult because the teaching is that God's forgiveness is free, and the sinner who is forgiven shows his or her thanks in some cheerful and symbolic way. There should be no risk of thinking that he or she must do something difficult in order to buy or earn forgiveness.

In the section on the Lord's Prayer (see Chapter 7 below) being forgiven is linked to the Christian forgiving other people. It should be obvious that anyone who has been reconciled will want to spread this, and that is why forgiveness is meant to be passed on. If you refuse to forgive in a sensible manner, this would suggest for Christians that you have not really accepted the forgiveness that has been offered to you.

Some of the things people say to a priest or indeed to anyone they trust in confidence ought to be kept private. For this reason every priest who hears confessions and gives absolution is supposed to respect this confidence and not to pass on anything he has heard in this way, not even to the police. This is sometimes called *'the seal of the confessional'*.

In many churches the priest hears confessions either at the altar rail or in another part of the church. Many Roman Catholic churches, however, have special closed in places, called confessionals, or confession boxes. This is to ensure privacy, because Roman Catholics are taught to make confessions frequently (some once a week or fortnight) so there can be a crowd of other people waiting.

ACTIVITY: on your own

Try to visit a Roman Catholic church and look out for a kind of box big enough for one person which is called a confessional. Ask the priest how this is used, where the priest is and so on, and ask to see the form of words which the penitent is given to start him or her off.

- Now write a page or two about sacramental confession.
- Do you think it is a good idea?
- Compare it with other ways of getting help when you have done something wrong. If you like use ideas from earlier in this section.

Chapter Six

THE BIBLE AND OTHER CHRISTIAN WRITINGS

If we want to think about some of the things the Bible means for Christians, it will be useful to consider how ordinary people, many of them not specially Christian, talk about the Bible. Have you heard of people swearing an oath on the Bible in a law court? What does it mean when people say something is '*gospel*' or '*gospel true*'? Have you heard a technical handbook described as '*the mechanic's Bible*' — or accountant's or shop steward's Bible? What do you think this is supposed to mean?

The expressions just noted seem to suggest that the Bible is useful as a standard or a guarantee of truth, even if people do not read it very much, and that it can give guidance on how to work things if you do read it.

If you go to services in chapels or churches you will notice that a passage from the Bible is read aloud. When there is a sermon the preacher almost always refers to texts or short extracts from the Bible. Often the whole sermon is based on sacred scripture (Bible) and parts are quoted from it.

In addition, many people have a Bible at home, and a lot of Christians read and study the Bible alone or in small groups. Sometimes special study notes on the Bible are used as well. In this way Bible reading often leads them into prayer.

All this means that both in public and in private, in church and at home, the Bible is a special book for Christians. The way they study and read it shows their love and reverence for the Bible. The way it is used in worship, in preaching and in writing also shows that it has authority — it gives Christians guidance. By direct teaching and by examples the Bible seems to help them to think and act as Christians.

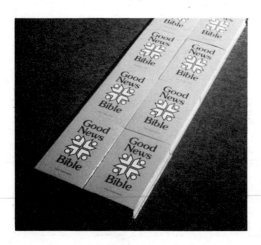

ACTIVITY: as a group

Look at these pictures. Try and decide which of these Bibles is used every day, once a week, only on special occasions.

- Can you give reasons for thinking as you do?

Almost every family in England used to have a Bible somewhere in the house, and the family would have felt ashamed if it were known that they had not got one. You could try asking your grandparents about this, and if you are very lucky, you may come across a treasured Family Bible, a big Bible, beautifully bound, with special pages at the front for keeping a record of births and baptisms in the family, and sometimes much more besides (e.g. spaces for photographs).

This chapter is really about how Christians use and value the Bible, and is not a study guide to what is in it. You presumably know that there are the Old and the New Testaments, roughly what these are, and also something about some of the main characters and events in the Bible.

ACTIVITY: on your own

Visit a church and look round to see what Bibles you can see there.

- Is there one very big one? If so, where is it kept?
- Are there also other Bibles, and if so where are these?
- Ask the minister how the Bible is used in church, how people decide which parts to read, and whether there is a plan for reading extracts in series on successive days or successive Sundays (this is called a lectionary).
- Try and find out if the Bible is used in other ways.
- Write up your findings.

ACTIVITY: as a group

If you know the Bible fairly well, you might like the following game:
You need enough space to walk about and meet each other. **Each person in your group of five or six thinks carefully about something in the Bible, and then chooses a person out of that passage.**

- Try to imagine what that person was really like, both in the Bible context and in quite new contexts and meetings you are going to make up.
- Now imagine you are that person: it does not in the least matter whether it is a man or a woman and which you are.
- Now go round and meet each other, talking and reacting as if you really were Job or David or Mary Magdalene (or whoever you have chosen to be). Some Christian groups use this as a way of studying the Bible.

The first Christians took the Old Testament over from the Jews because they thought that the life of Jesus brought the old scriptures to fulfilment. They considered that the Old Testament only made sense if it was understood as preparing for Jesus Christ and pointing to him. This means quite bluntly that they thought the Jews were missing a lot, and that the Law and the Prophets and the Writings (this is what the Jews still call their Bible) was now a Christian book or collection of books, and no longer Jewish. How the Christians read parts of the Old Testament is described in other parts of this book, for instance at the beginning, and under Baptism in Part Three, Chapter 1.

The New Testament is obviously about Jesus Christ and the first Christians, and includes letters sent by church leaders to church congregations, or to individuals. It is important to note that Jesus did not write anything down, or rather he only wrote in sand and we do not know what that was (John 8.6). Even his actual words are lost to us because he spoke Aramaic, and the gospels like the whole New Testament were all written originally in Greek.

This all means that Christians have got to make efforts to try and understand the Bible by reading, thinking, discussing together, praying and meditating on the Bible, hearing sermons, and trying to see the Bible from a variety of points of view. This is not easy. In contrast to this, Muslims consider that their holy scripture, the *Quran*, contains the actual words spoken by God and in the language he actually spoke them.

Many Muslims consider therefore that Christians are in a real mess when they find that some details in the gospel stories do not agree. Their whole understanding of Bible criticism suggests to Muslims that the Christian Bible cannot be inspired by God and is therefore a fake. Christian ideas of having to study the Bible, to 'search the scripture', and the need for interpretations like those offered within the Bible itself by St Paul and others, mean nothing to Muslims and those who think like them. This kind of Bible study seems to be quite outside the experience of the sort of people who prefer to think that every dot and letter is God's actual speech and therefore not a subject for discussion. Yet it is the activity of Bible study that makes the Bible so alive and exciting for Christians.

The fact that Jesus himself wrote nothing for later generations means that Christians must appreciate the personal impression Jesus made on his disciples and on those in every age who are affected by him. Like an outstanding teacher, he made his disciples come alive and gave them a sense of their own value as Christians, not only in what he said to them, but in what he did. The personal impression of Jesus is found in the Bible too, and the Bible as holy scripture bears witness to the inspiration of those who have written it and preserved it. We have already seen that Christians of all lands and denominations regard it as the sacred book which is read at services and studied at college, at home and in small groups.

It is in this, rather than being the original form of God's speech to man, that the authority of scripture lies.

Psalms

One part of the Bible which is frequently used in worship is the Book of Psalms. The Psalms were originally prayers and songs or meditations which Jewish worshippers used in the Temple services in Jerusalem for centuries before Jesus Christ. The first Christians took over the present collection of 150 psalms and they are made into a book for liturgical use (i.e. church services) called the **Psalter**. Psalms are said or sung in private devotions and in the course of many church services. Religious offices (services) said by monks and nuns always include psalms.

ACTIVITY: on your own

Read this version of Psalm 100

O shout to the Lord in triumph all the earth: serve the Lord with gladness and come before his face with songs of joy.

Know that the Lord he is God: it is he who has made us and we are his; we are his people and the sheep of his pasture.

Come into his gates with thanksgiving and into his courts with praise: give thanks to him and bless his holy name.

For the Lord is good, his loving mercy is for ever: his faithfulness throughout all generations.

Now write one or two line answers to the following questions:

- What are the feelings of the people who first used this psalm in worship?
- What do you think Christians feel about it when they use it today?
- Is it more suited for public worship, or for a person on his or her own to use in private prayer?

ACTIVITY: as a group

This exercise is on Psalm 23, which is perhaps the psalm best known to most people. Many children of Christian parents learn it by heart, in one of its many versions or translations.

You will need a Bible and one or more hymn books.

One of the group copies out Psalm 23 from the Bible or Psalter as tidily as possible, while the others find hymns which are versions of it or based on it. These are then written out on separate sheets and all can be put together for comparison. To help you find suitable hymns, here are some suggestions for using the index of first lines:

'The King of love my Shepherd is'
'The Lord my pasture shall prepare'
'The Lord's my shepherd, I'll not want'

You may find others. Talk over borderline cases and reach an agreed decision. As an example of a borderline case, you could look at the hymn which begins

'Guide me, O thou great Redeemer'

ACTIVITY: on your own

Write one or two pages about **why you think Christians use psalms in private and public worship**, giving some thought to what they probably feel when they say or sing them.

Other Christian Literature

The religious section in many public libraries, and even in many bookshops, is not always a good guide to the books and papers which Christians use and find valuable. Try to think of some other ways to find out more about what Christians read.

ACTIVITY: as a group

Discuss how you might find out what kinds of Christian books and magazines, etc. local Christians are reading.

- Make a note of your ideas and keep it for later.

One type of reading matter is books and papers written about the Bible. This would include Bible commentaries on specific books of the Bible, or even on the whole Bible, and notes for Bible reading, like those produced regularly by the Scripture Union, and many others. Most of these are written for adults, but there are some for children too.

A second type of literature would include newspapers and magazines, and also the news-sheets produced by missions and aid agencies. It will be obvious that this sort of literature can be used for prayer, and some groups produce regular prayer papers, with a topic set aside for each day.

A third kind of reading matter is made up of devotional literature. This would include classics of Christian devotion, mystical writings like the '*Cloud of Unknowing*' and other famous books like '*Pilgrim's Progress*'. We could also include here books, papers and pamphlets about how to pray, preparing for confirmation or some other step in deepening commitment.

A fourth kind would include books about specific people, both past and present. These might be about St Francis or Martin Luther King, and it can be hard to decide whether a book is really a biography or devotional reading. Some appear to be both.

A fifth class can include papers and books intended to encourage people to live in a certain way, in some ways like a good sermon. They may tell you that you ought to spend less on yourself, or suggest things you could do for others.

Perhaps the sixth group can be simply called 'other'. This would include books about Christian marriage, about how the church is managed, what happens in a convent, and church statistics.

A display of religious books in a book shop

- Can you find that note you made about discovering what local Christians do actually read?
- Did you think of any of the following: asking local Christians? Looking at church bookstalls inside churches? going to a specifically church or Christian bookshop?

Preaching and Sermon

We have probably all been in places where one person stands up and says a lot of things to a crowd. The audience do not always listen very carefully, and it only makes matters worse for the speaker if the crowd cover a wide range of ages and a wide variety of formal education, as well as all having different needs, problems and interests. The speaker really needs some special techniques for persuading them they want to listen.

Preaching in a church or chapel can be rather like this. The only advantage is perhaps that most people have come because they want to and are not forced to be there. Of course the sermon may not be the only or the real reason for their coming. Their ages can range from infants in arms to old age pensioners, and some may not be too good at hearing.

Yet all Christian congregations use the sermon, most of them every Sunday. Of course there are techniques for livening it up: a sermon may include a bit of music or drama, and dialogue sermons between two or more people have been tried. In Pentecostal churches the sermon often turns into prayer and praise and then back again, so it is not always easy to tell where it begins and ends.

A sermon usually is based on a text or passage from the Bible. The preacher wants to explain this text to the people and help them to apply it in some way to their own lives. She or he may want to challenge them or give them encouragement — in fact all the kinds of thing which St Paul did in different parts of his letters which are kept in the New Testament. These letters were originally sent to particular church meetings. Using a Bible text helps to produce a variety of topics in the weekly sermons, and this is specially so when the Bible readings in church follow a set guide or Lectionary. In churches where a lectionary is not used, preachers sometimes just preach on their favourite Bible texts, and some members of the congregation complain that they hear the same thing every Sunday.

While studying Christianity you have probably been to some church services, and this means you have probably heard some sermons. If not, then make a point of going to hear someone preach and notice not just what is said, but the styles and techniques used, given the difficulties we have noted above.

ACTIVITY: on your own

Which of the following do you think should or should not be in a good sermon?

Make two lists, one for should be in, and one for should not be in. Do not just copy sermons you have heard. Try to be critical and evaluate the preaching for style and effectiveness. Here are the suggestions:

- jokes or funny stories
- topical allusions to things going on in the world
- telling people to do something
- telling people not to do something
- teaching about missions in the UK or overseas
- preacher should be good–looking
- giving background information about Bible or church services
- a story with a moral
- something we hadn't heard before
- make the congregation feel good
- must say things we can all agree with
- should have something for everyone, whatever age and education
- must not hurt anybody's feelings
- sermon should have a clear shape and be easy to understand
- preacher should get worked up
- preacher should not get worked up
- must be a nice person
- preacher should have done interesting things
- asking for money
- give us local news and gossip

Do you find any things which did not fit into either column? If so, write in two lines why you think this was.

Chapter Seven

CHRISTIAN PRAYER

ACTIVITY: as a class

• Have you ever played a game called 'Gripes Market'?
You could try it out now, best with a fairly big group like the whole class because people need to write down their feelings anonymously. **Each person has a piece of paper and writes on it something that is making him or her fed up at the moment.**

It doesn't matter whether the gripe is big or little, long–lasting or very temporary. You just write it down briefly without your name. Then all the papers are collected together, mixed, then read out.

While the gripes are being read out, you should listen in silence. It doesn't matter whether you recognise anyone involved or not — you could be wrong anyway. Most important of all, you must not butt in if you think someone is making a complaint or criticism of yourself — you could be right or you could be wrong.

After doing this exercise, think a bit how you feel about each other. It is often very helpful to realise that other people have got troubles too, how they feel inside about things which upset them, no matter whether the troubles look big or small to outsiders. Secondly, think of one or two cases where you really feel sorry for someone, or you feel real sympathy perhaps because you went through something like that yourself once.

This game or exercise can be used as an introduction to Christian prayer for two reasons. One is that it makes you feel warm affection or even love for a few fellow human beings, and secondly, you get just a glimpse of people in the way that Christians think God sees them, and this viewpoint can be a basis for Christian prayer.

ACTIVITY

Either as a class or as a smaller group

Here is a second game or exercise which can be played with the whole class, or in a group of five or six. **One person tries to guess who the others are thinking about.**

One person goes out of the room, and the others all decide on a character (real person) who is well known to all of them. The person who has been out comes in again, and must guess who they've thought of by their descriptions.

Each member of the group says one descriptive thing about the person they've thinking of, but it must be both reasonably true and recognisable and at the same time not damaging or hurtful in any way. This last is most important, in fact the point of the whole thing.

If you cannot guess after one round, you could all try a second. Remember, one line of description from each player and again nothing hurtful or rude. Then you can take another character, while someone else is out of the room and so on as long as there is time for this activity, or till you've all had a turn.

The idea of this game, especially when played after the first one, is to present an individual to God, if you like, how you would like God to see someone, again obviously in a Christian context as this whole course is about Christianity. Can you think of a good name for this game?

The basis for Christian prayer is standing in the presence of God, and realising the truth about God and man. There are different styles of prayer, and many techniques for praying or for preparation for prayer. This chapter will focus on some of the styles, but there are also references to prayer in other parts of the book. There is a little more about private prayer in Chapter 8 of this Part.

Asking for things is just one part of prayer, and for many people only a very small part, but it does mean making contact, like someone having a talk with someone else. Hence putting yourself consciously in the presence of God is fundamental, and it makes no difference whether you are standing, sitting, kneeling or whatever. You may be very desperate for something you feel you need. It could even be a matter of life and death like fear of drowning or being lost on a mountainside. Christians certainly know the value of earnest and heart–felt prayer, like the parable of the widow and the magistrate (see Luke 18.1–8).

Sometimes people ask their friends to pray for them when they are in special need, so there is a lot of prayer focussing together like rays of light. Some of the friends asked to join in prayer may be departed (dead) ones whom you feel are especially close to God — this is what is behind the practice of prayers to the saints and through the saints — see also Part Four pages 212–214.

Christians often think about the prayer of Jesus in the Garden of Gethsemane just before his arrest and crucifixion (see Mark 14.32–6). What he asked for was not granted, but he was strengthened. He did not try to compel God to do what he wanted, like imposing his own will, for trying to do this, however sincere, is not Christian prayer, but either bargaining or a form of magic. A magician wants to make things happen by spells, and to force whatever powers and spirits there may be to do what he wheedles, begs or commands. There are times when Christians feel like this too, but this is not Christian prayer and should be clearly distinguished from it. In prayer Christians feel the power of God and the weakness of mankind, and a Christian ought not to think he or she is giving God advice or instructions. We shall come back to this again later.

Three Schools of Prayer

If we give names to three ways of praying, or approaches to the art of prayer, the names are just to help us to discuss them, and to do some exercises connected with them. Christians who are serious about commitment to prayer may use any or all three of these methods, and others too, in the course of their journey into God, their growth in the love and awareness of God, or whatever way they may like to describe the adventure of committed prayer. But in all three, growth or progress is an important feature, even though some of the time it is not felt.

An Orthodox (Eastern) way of prayer begins with focussing your attention or mind within your own essential being or heart. This is a kind of concentration which will be described later in more detail. The aim is a kind of constant prayer in the presence of God, and of course listening to God much more than speaking.

A Catholic (Western) way makes use of the imagination: with this method, the Christian first makes the self quiet, then pictures as vividly as possible certain scenes or situations, of which scenes from the life of Jesus in the gospels are the most obvious, and works from there.

A modern way (although it is no more modern than any other, but we use the name because this approach is widely used by modern Christians) is to concentrate in turn on thanksgiving, being sorry for failures and so on, and then trying to place people and situations in the presence of God, often by thinking of Jesus already out there at work in the mess or distress.

It may look as if only the third way is concerned about other people's lives and the needs of the world today, but in fact they all are. It is only the approaches that are different, and these must now be discussed in more detail.

A MODERN APPROACH TO PRAYER

This is a method of prayer which is often taught to young people when they are preparing for Confirmation, but of course it can be taught at any time. The basic idea is to think of prayer as four different parts or acts. In fact **ACTS** is the catchword to help people remember.

A The **A** stands for **Adoration**, that is praising God with joy, acceptance and love. You may have noticed that in religious services there are a lot of prayers which praise God, both in services which follow a more or less set form, like a prayer book, and in services where the minister or other prayer leaders make up their own words as they go along. Praise is different from thanks according to this way of prayer, although they do shade into each other. Beginners are usually taught to start from a written prayer of praise, or one of the Psalms suitably chosen, before making up their own prayers of adoration.

C The **C** stands for **Contrition** which means being sorry for your failures (feeling contrite). As the ACTS method is mostly used with words this part is often called **Confession**, which also starts with **C**. Something is said about confession, sin and penitence in Chapter 5, but it is useful to remember that contrition includes being sorry about things that are wrong in the world, even though they are not directly your own fault. One can feel kind of tainted by society: some people try to opt out, but for Christians being sorry is felt to be a much more helpful approach.

T Thanksgiving sounds altogether much easier and normal, and little children are taught to say Thank–you to parents and to each other from an early age. Saying Thank–you to God is also a fairly usual infant and junior school activity, especially in Assembly. You can imagine a Christian being thankful to God when sitting in the sunshine, but there are a lot of less obvious things for which most Christians are thankful. As with Contrition (above) you can also thank God for the sake of other people's success, luck or relief, or things that seem right with the world in general.

S The **S** is for **Supplication**, and that means asking for things, either for yourself or for other people who need help in any way. It is also called **Intercession** (which unfortunately doesn't begin with S) and is what some people think of first whenever praying is mentioned. So it is quite a useful reminder to have it last in the system we are studying.

ACTIVITY: on your own

This is based on the ACTS method of prayer.
If you have attended a church service recently where a prayer or service book was used, **find the service you attended in the book. Check through the service from the beginning, allocating each piece to one of A,C,T,S or 'other'.** Try not to let 'other' get too big, but there will be some.

If there is no service book, then the task is both easier and more difficult. It is more difficult because you cannot do it unless you have got a very good memory or you made a tape recording, but easier in that a good deal of what happens in extempore prayer, that is prayer made on the moment, falls into the **ACTS** categories.

ACTIVITY: as a group

If you have not been to a church or chapel service recently, you should do the exercise above as a group. **Get some paper and put down relevant parts of the service in note form**, but legibly, **under the headings of the ACTS system.**

If some things seem to come into both of two classes, discuss these. It may well be right, because praise and thanks, for instance, often go together.

ACTIVITY: as a group

Try and collect over one or two weeks, examples of prayer from books, papers, films, radio, TV or anything you come across. You can bring in books and papers, but for film and TV you will have to make careful notes.

It could be that some of the things people have said were not really meant as prayers, for instance lots of people say '*Thank God you've come*' without thinking of God very much, but you should include this kind of thing in this exercise, and then discuss what they meant.

- Write up your notes as a joint project.

ACTIVITY: on your own

This exercise is about prayers that weren't meant to be prayers. You need a newspaper, which could be a local or a national paper, but not a specialist journal. **Go through the paper and pick out things in it, news items as well as what people actually said, which you think might be expressions of gratitude, regret, hopes, apologies, relief, sorrow or rejoicing and so on.**

For instance a wedding announcement counts as an occasion for rejoicing, and a funeral for sorrow.

- Try to fit these into the ACTS scheme. Of course it is only fair to say that ACTS is a method designed for people to make their own prayers, especially beginners, and there is no promise that it is going to fit all other people's prayers or situations in life.

ACTIVITY: on your own

Write about two pages on the ACTS method. Describe what it is and how it is used.

- To do this make use of the other activities you have just done alone or with the group.
- Evaluate this method of prayer and say what you think of it.
- How well do you think the method would work for a Christian who wanted to pray about her or his life and the world around?

A CATHOLIC APPROACH, USING THE IMAGINATION

One way of remaining human is to spend time with a friend and talking things over if you want to. But just being together in silence is good too. All types of prayer can of course draw on this need, the need to share your feelings (whether happy, sad, cross, ashamed, over–the–moon or whatever), and perhaps to get some advice, but as often as not you would just like someone to listen, to let you feel that after all you are a human being. And it can be totally, or almost totally without words.

The first requirement perhaps for all types of prayer is the ability to be still. Have you ever found yourself sitting quietly, doing nothing? Of course you might just go to sleep, but what we mean here by sitting quietly is being at the same time fully awake and aware of your surroundings and what you are doing. If you are doing nothing, you need to know that you are doing nothing. Of course you are breathing, and your muscles are holding you in a certain position, without strain, but still in tension.

Here are some exercises for you to try before beginning with using your imagination of gospel scenes.

ACTIVITY: on your own

Find a quiet spot and sit there comfortably, or stand, if that too is comfortable and easy for you.
    Sitting comfortably does not mean sloppy, but straight and alert. This might be in sunshine, but not hot sun which will distract you and tire you. You might be alone or a group of friends, but quietness is important. Now, just enjoy the silence and the warmth.

ACTIVITY: on your own

This exercise is intended to follow your experience in the last activity. You may find that the same place and the same way of sitting or standing will work again for you, if it worked the first time — if it didn't, try another.

People who use meditative prayer a lot usually find that it helps them to have a special place for it, and also one particular way of sitting, standing or squatting which seems to suit. Whatever your best position, get into it again, then:

First, go through the last exercise again in order to empty your mind of worries and distractions.

Then, think of something in the past which has made you specially happy; try to put together the scene and the circumstances in your mind in as much detail as possible. Stay with this for just a few minutes, then let it go.

For a Christian who has begun with exercises like the two above, the life of Jesus can also be used by the imagination. The idea is to go through the preliminaries again, that is the two exercises above. Then pick a gospel scene and imagine it as vividly as possible. There are books on contemplative prayer which will give you a lot of help on techniques, much more than can be done here.

The next two exercises are suggested for those who would like to try this method of prayer, but you should not do them unless you are serious about trying, and there is no reason why you should be serious about learning actually how to pray, instead of just learning about prayer.

This book is a guide for anyone who wants to study Christianity and not a book about how to become a Christian. But it is not easy to separate exercises about prayer from exercises in actually praying, so you need to be aware of this and make your own mind up. You could meet a similar problem in one or two other places in this book.

ACTIVITY: on your own

Repeat carefully the preliminaries of the two exercises above, but this time imagine a scene in the life of Jesus.

As this becomes vivid in your mind, go into the scene yourself, feel the heat or wind, hear the sounds, then go up to someone in this gospel scene and talk to him or her. Ask the blind man (for instance) what he feels like.

ACTIVITY

Another step to take on your own, if you would really like to try praying.

Once more go carefully through the steps outlined above — if you have got this far you should be getting good at this, but it does need care and attention every time. **This time, as you walk into the gospel scene, picture Jesus turning to you and asking you how you feel.**

You begin to tell him about what you have just witnessed, but soon the conversation turns to your own life, your hopes, your problems, the troubles of the world, your friends, anything that's on your mind.

Listen carefully to his replies and to his silences, and try to picture the expression on his face.

This technique is partly used in praying with a rosary.

You may not have felt you wanted to try the last two exerc[ises] least you have read them and seen what they are about. Th[is] technique which can be used obviously for all the things not[ed] ACTS system above, and more besides. This imaginative medit[ation] sometimes called **Ignatian prayer** because St Ignatius Loyola (1[480 or] 1495–1556) developed it very much, but as a basic technique it is [of] course much older. This method of praying can be found in other religions too.

A monk in his prayer cell

A RUSSIAN ORTHODOX METHOD

The third system to look at we have called Orthodox because it is widely practised by Christians of the Orthodox churches, perhaps especially in Russia. According to this teaching, there are three degrees of prayer: (1) **verbal or bodily prayer**; (2) **praying with the mind**; (3) **spiritual prayer**, usually described as praying with the mind in the heart. While there is nothing wrong with (1) and (2), it is clear that (3) is what Christians should aim at. Spiritual prayer may often include verbal prayer and mental prayer, but again, as we shall see, often it does not. This needs a closer look.

In this system, instead of taking gospel scenes, we can begin with some of the things said in the New Testament about prayer and praying. Jesus said, '*When you pray, go to your private room and, when you have shut the door, pray to your Father who is in that secret place*'. (Part of Matthew 6.6). Your private room may indeed be a room or any other special place, like what you may have found with your exercises on imaginative prayer above. But it is also inside you, in your heart, and St Makarios of Egypt (c.300–390, also spelt Macarius) takes in this way the saying of Jesus (Luke 17.21), '*The kingdom of God is within you*' — and the fact that '*within*' can also be translated '*among*', as in some new translations ought not to spoil the main point for us. Your heart is always with you, and you can enter into it in this prayerful sense anywhere and at any time. To quote from St Makarios: '*The heart is a small vessel, but all things are contained in it; God is there, the angels are there, and there also is life and the Kingdom, the heavenly cities and the treasures of grace*'.

117

The first step then for the Christian who wants to learn this system of prayer is to try and reach the heart, i.e. concentrate with the inmost self by thinking quietly about her or his feelings, whatever makes her or him essentially what she or he is. One should not try in any way to be clever or intellectual about this. Then the second step is to place the thinking part of oneself carefully inside the heart, so that any definite thoughts and words which occur are to be seen only in the basic and human context of what or who I essentially am. This is going into my room and shutting the door. The third step is to let go of the emotions, things I feel strongly about, deliberately and one by one, until I can just experience the stillness. The fourth step is to place myself in the loving presence of God with a simple prayer, usually in words, but very short, and one that can be repeated again and again.

Orthodox Christians are very devoted to the Jesus prayer which is quite simple and simply runs: '*Lord Jesus, son of the living God, have mercy on me.*' There are other versions equally popular. When this prayer is repeated frequently, it doesn't matter whether it is aloud (verbal prayer), thought in the mind (mental prayer), or going on subconsciously in the heart, it begins to come close to St Paul's advice to the church in Thessalonica, '*Pray without ceasing*' (I Thessalonians 5.17). You may think that subconscious prayer sounds like a bit of a fiddle, but it seems to be real for those who sincerely practise this system of praying with the right preliminaries.

It is not possible to do any exercises on this form of prayer if you are simply studying Christianity for GCSE. In any case, people who want to learn about praying as Christians really need the guidance of someone more experienced. This is a spiritual director about whom a little is said later on, in chapter 8. Muslims and followers of other religions also find the same, so the need for spiritual guidance is not peculiar to Christians.

PRAYING WITH A ROSARY

A rosary is a string or chain with a number of beads on it which is used to help people pray. The person praying repeats a set of words while letting each bead pass between the fingers. You can either use one hand, or more commonly both hands. Using beads acts as a counter or time check, allowing a particular prayer to be repeated a fixed number of times. There are many uses for a rosary, but the two commonest will be briefly described.

The modern Catholic rosary is used by many Roman Catholics, some Anglicans and Methodists, and a few other individual Christians. Beads are arranged in five sets of ten, and the idea is to picture a gospel scene for each set, rather like the Ignatian method of prayer described above. At the same time the meditation is intended as prayer for someone or something as an intercession, and also as a thanksgiving. These usually follow a prearranged pattern.

There are four larger beads in the spaces between sets of ten, and four more and a crucifix are attached to the link which joins the two ends. The words repeated may vary, but most people who use this rosary say the prayer that begins '*Hail Mary*' for the small beads, and '*Our Father*' for the big ones before each set of ten. There are set prayers for starting up and others when you get to the end.

Another way of praying with a rosary is simply to repeat a prayer like the Jesus prayer quoted above and go on using the beads for as long as you want. This is like the method of '*praying with the heart*' which is popular with Orthodox Christians. Their rosary has fewer beads than the Catholic one and no crucifix.

Catholics praying with a rosary

TO SUM UP   When you have worked through this section on Christian prayer as best
you can — and it cannot be an easy section — here are some exercises to
do as a kind of revision or summing up. They can also help you to come
to an evaluation of forms of prayer which are practised by Christians.

ACTIVITY

On your own or with a friend

As a small child you may have sometimes looked at the sky. Can you
recall looking up at a sky which was blue and thinking how deep and
infinite it is? Maybe there were a few clouds about which only helped
to make the blue bits more mysterious. This exercise goes a little
further, and **you need a mirror, as large a one as you can con-
veniently carry. On a sunny day, put your mirror on the ground
outside, and look into it, so you can see the sky, but not yourself
or your friend** (you may like to do this in company).

- Just gaze down at the sky.
- Then imagine you are falling into it, away into eternity.

It can be quite frightening, and you need not feel ashamed if you and your friend prefer to hold onto each other when you try this one.

ACTIVITY: on your own

Write two pages, more if you like, **on some of the exercises you did in this whole big section on prayer.**

- Describe how you felt while doing them, and how you feel about them now.
- Did you get anything out of them?

The Lord's Prayer

The **Lord's Prayer**, also called the **Our Father** from its first two words, appears in two of the gospels. Most Christians know it very well, and in order to study it you will need to read it several times.

ACTIVITY: as a group

1 Two of you should **look up Matthew 6.9–13, and write the prayer out**, with each clause on a new line. Two of you should **do the same with Luke 11.2–4**. Then whoever is left should **get a church prayer book and find the Lord's Prayer** in one of the services, and write this out in the same way. Now put the papers side by side and compare.

- How many different versions have you got?
- Are the differences important or not important?
- List any differences you all agree are important on another piece of paper
- How do you think they arose?

2 For this the group needs a newspaper that can be divided up, so one person has the sports section, one the advertisements, one overseas news and so on, or you can just divide it out by sheets. **Find items in the paper which a Christian might bring to the Lord's prayer,** for instance news about food, people who have hurt each other, people being tempted or tried, and anything else you think you can persuade the rest of the group could be a subject for prayer using the Lord's prayer as a pattern.

After reading the two passages in the gospels mentioned in (1) above, it will be obvious why it is called the *'Lord's Prayer'*. If you also read the verse before in Luke (Luke 11.1) you will find that the disciples are shown asking to be taught how to pray. Because of this the prayer is also called the **Pattern Prayer**. Christians value this prayer very much. Some think it is so precious that they say it several times a day, as in the church offices (the offices are forms of service said at certain times each day), or in using the Rosary in the Western tradition. Other Christians, however, think that the Lord's Prayer should not be used unless they really mean it and make it a special occasion. For instance there was a group of Baptists in Wales who asked their Minister if they could say the Lord's Prayer every Sunday, but the Minister replied that once a month was more fitting. In some German Protestant churches the bells are rung when this prayer is being said so everyone outside can know that something important is happening.

ACTIVITY: on your own

Arrange the following thirteen phrases of the Lord's Prayer in the right order, without having it in front of you.

These phrases do not need a separate line each, but you can make the lines any length you think makes the best sense. Put capitals letters where you want.

give us today
lead us not into temptation
as we forgive
your kingdom come
those who sin against us
our father
our daily bread
on earth as in heaven
forgive us our sins
in heaven
hallowed be your name
but deliver us from evil
your will be done

ACTIVITY

For the whole class

How many of you know any foreign languages? The whole class might like to get together in **making a display with the first two words of the Our Father in as many languages as people can manage.** Of course, if you are really ambitious, you could write out the whole prayer!

ACTIVITY: on your own

If you have ever used the Lord's Prayer yourself, try this exercise for follow-up work.

Write about half a page on whether and why you find it easier or harder to say the Lord's Prayer in church or in Assembly after doing the exercises in this section.

The Lord's Prayer in Arabic

أبانا الذي في السموات، ليتقدس اسمك، ليأت ملكوتك، لتكن مشيئتك كما في السماء كذلك على الأرض. خبزنا الجوهري أعطنا اليوم واترك لنا ما علينا كما نترك نحن لمن لنا عليه، ولا تدخلنا في تجربة لكن نجنا من الشرير.

Other Kinds of Prayer

There is a little more about prayer in the next chapter which is about private meditation, reading, and rules of life.

All Christians believe that they can approach God in prayer because Jesus has taught them to do so and has reconciled them. But they cannot compel God to do things for them. For this reason Christians like to remind themselves that Jesus asks them to pray, and they add to their prayers the words, 'through Jesus Christ our Lord'. The word Amen was taken over from Judaism and means 'truly'.

Very many Christians belong to small, semi–private prayer groups and prayer circles. It is often not easy for outsiders to find out about these. In some congregations a special day or part of a day may be set aside for prayer, and people are asked to pray for a special purpose at some time during that day. Such a group may be attached to a particular church in a particular place, or it may be wider, or it may be open to all Christians of any church denomination at all.

The Women's World Day of Prayer is one example you may have heard of. The Christian Union starts and encourages prayer groups and meetings in schools and colleges, and gives some help about running them. These can be linked to Bible study. Some parish churches have Prayer Guilds which parish members can join, and then they meet perhaps once a week for prayer. These are very popular in some West African churches, and members of each prayer guild may wear a special sash for Sunday services, and all sit together in church.

A few Christians feel that God is calling them to dedicate the major part of their lives to praying, and this in a more obvious way than the prayer without ceasing which is mentioned above in the section on a Russian Orthodox way of prayer. Such people may be members of religious communities (monks or nuns) which are enclosed, that is they never go out of the convent. A great deal of time is spent in prayer, both contemplative prayer and praying for people and the world. There are also a number of hermits in Britain who live quite alone and spend a lot of time in prayer. Some very aged Christians, who cannot do a lot physically, give much time to praying, but they also like to keep in touch with younger Christians who often ask them to pray for special things and then visit them to keep them up–to–date.

Chapter Eight

PRIVATE WORSHIP, MEDITATION AND READING

If there is a monastery or convent near you, see what you can find out about their daily routine. This could be used for a version of the 3–D diary exercise which is described on page 126.

Everyone has had the experience of thinking about a friend, and sometimes we just spend time together without saying very much. This was the idea with which Part Two of this book began, and it has been used again and again in the sections on prayer. Something like this, but at a deeper level of intensity, is what Christians mean by worshipping God, adoring and enjoying him for ever. This is called 'the chief end of man' in some of the old catechisms — these were books used for Sunday School teaching in former years. Here 'end' means 'purpose', what mankind is for.

So it can be no surprise that private worship is just as important as public worship. Many Christians have a daily pattern of prayer, reading the Bible, and what some call a quiet time alone. Or there may be family prayers (in addition to grace at meals), or little groups which meet for the purpose. The best examples of these would be religious orders of monks or nuns. They live and work together and also worship and pray together, as well of course individually in their own rooms or cells. Lots of information is available on the daily routine of monks in different orders, and some of the orders have very different patterns. Such religious orders are to be found all through Christianity, east and west, and in Protestantism. By no means all of them wear a special outfit.

Contemplative Prayer

A very important strand of Christian prayer consists in contemplation. Christian **contemplative prayer** is in its beginning stages not unlike the early stages of Buddhist and Hindu meditation and contemplation. Not everyone agrees about the difference between meditation and contemplation. In this book it is suggested that meditation makes use of a picture, text or the imagination (like the Ignatian system described in the section on Prayer), while contemplation rather more concerns setting yourself free from conscious thoughts, feelings and emotions. A number of Westerners have tried Buddhist and Hindu methods for this, not knowing that there already is a strong Christian contemplative and mystical tradition. But what they learn in Indian religions can in most cases be very helpfully applied in Christianity too.

ACTIVITY: on your own

You could try a preparation for contemplative prayer which will help you to empty the mind and emotions.

You can do this in your own room quite alone, or in a small group as long as every member is serious about doing it.

It need not be totally quiet outside, and in fact a little bit of noise which does not concern you, for instance traffic or people in the street, can have the effect of stressing the distance between you and the activity of the world. This could be helpful.

Make yourself comfortable but alert as already described for the exercises on prayer.

Then systematically do two things: try and think in turn of every muscle in your body, from head to foot quite slowly, till each is either at rest or steady.

Then after that, think of anything that is worrying you and consciously put it aside, knowing that you will pick it up again when this exercise is over.

Now you can begin. Focus your eyes on something that is detached from you — some people use a candle flame or a single flower in a vase for this — or alternatively you could put your eyes out of focus altogether. Most people say it is better to have the eyes open than shut.

If any thoughts or feelings come into your mind, just look at them curiously, like a little dog sniffing a lamppost, until they go away.

After five or ten minutes you slowly return to normal life.

Rules of Life

A **rule of life** may be quite special to an individual or it may be based on a society or group who all try to keep a common rule. It is usually in the form of a timetable, but one which has special provision for prayer, worship and other more obviously religious activities. A rule of life can work like an athlete's training schedule. But most Christians prefer to make a simple rule which gives them a feeling of support and security. It just keeps them spiritually fit, and they can do extra things when they want to.

The sorts of things which are included in a rule of life for a Christian include obviously public worship and private prayer; for instance the rule is likely to say that you go to church every Sunday and how often you will receive communion. Other things to be included would be daily prayer, Bible reading and reading or study of other literature, and also work, perhaps both voluntary work say at the church or a prison or hospital, and aspects of daily work, that is the work the Christian does for a living. Obviously the rule cannot prescribe the work itself, but can require certain attitudes or emphases. There may be other parts which include relationships with other people, including family if applicable, use of money and life–style generally.

Two important things should be noted. One is that the rule of life is either drawn up by the individual Christian in conjunction with some advice, or at least the individual takes it on voluntarily. It is not a target to aim at, but is meant to give support as well as a kind of vision for daily living, and if it does not do this it ought to be changed. The other thing about a rule of life concerns the need for someone or possibly a group who gives advice or direction to the individual. They (or he or she) need to be alert and flexible enough to accept or suggest changes as the individual's life circumstances and needs and attitudes change. Obviously someone at work five days a week may need a rule which reflects this.

A rule may be very specialised, for instance if you join a Christian Temperance group. This rule might not be much more than abstaining from drugs and alcohol, but it probably would also include coming to meetings, some of which would be religious services — maybe a Temperance service once a year. As a member you might wear a special badge. Monks and nuns live by the rule of their order and some wear a whole outfit. It is possible to recognise what Order they are from if you know, but then again quite a lot do not wear a distinctive uniform, and you would not know they were in a religious order at all.

The **spiritual adviser** is very important for many Christians. This can be a man or a woman (often but not always an ordained minister), or it can be a small group who all relate well to each other. Those who practise sacramental confession (see chapter 5) often have a priest as spiritual director, but even for these Christians there is absolutely no need to have the same person as spiritual director and as confessor. Experience in spiritual direction is important before anyone takes on this role.

ACTIVITY: as a group

This exercise is called the 3—D diary, and is best done as a small group only because it takes a lot longer if you do it alone.

Read this all through first as you will need to plan carefully in advance.

1 Get twelve boxes, one for each hour of the day, more if it's a longer day, and the boxes should be about the same size if the activities you are going to record are equal in length.

2 Label each box either with the time, both start and finish, or with the name of the activity it is for.

3 Then you make each box represent an activity in one of the following ways:
  either Draw, paint pictures, or make models or collage to indicate the activity that is taking place
  or Collect small objects to do with that activity and put them in the box
  or Collect tapes, music, slides and so on of each activity and store them in the box. **Remember** this will take longer than you think!

4 Arrange the boxes and put them on display with suitable titles, labels and so on. This is your 3—D diary of a day in your own life, or someone else's life, such as a clergyman or a monk, or whoever you have chosen.

5 If the activities take different lengths of time, work this out in advance and you can show this by having a bigger box for a longer time and a smaller one for a short time, if you like. But maybe you will just have to use whatever boxes are available.

If successful, the 3—D diary can be used for other purposes. It could illustrate a rule of life in an attractive way.

Ideas for a 3-D diary

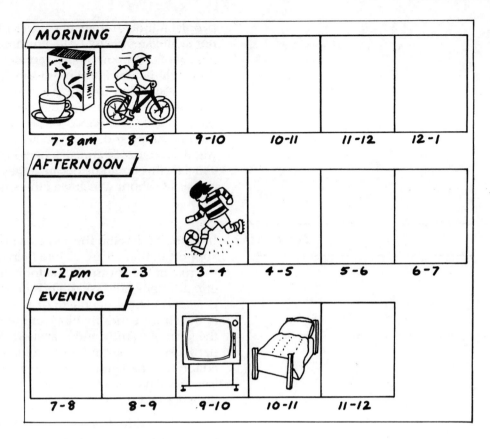

Chapter Nine

CHRISTIAN SPIRITUALITY

Christianity is not a religion of rituals and rules. It is easy to see that there are rituals and rules, but these are not the essence of Christianity and anyway they are not the same for all Christians.

Every Christian is supposed to have a life of spiritual growth and development. This is the personal relationship of the individual to God, even if it is sometimes only spoken of in groups. Many Christians of all traditions, Orthodox, Catholic, main–line Protestant, Quakers, and charismatic Pentecostals long for a closer relationship and try to make themselves ready, as they see it, for God's grace to reach out to them. They know that they cannot possess God and that their grasp of God is insecure. They do not lose heart at the thought that they cannot know God as he knows them. Yet these people seem confident in their lives, and this comes from their trust in God's mercy. They picture the initiative coming entirely from God and not from themselves, and this also means that they can rejoice to see God's grace and mercy poured out on people who have not been making any efforts to attract his attention.

They want to develop their spiritual life, and can work at this because they love God and not in order to gain anything special for themselves. That is why, unlike the labourers in the parable of the vineyard (Matthew 20.1–15), they do not want to complain about the good fortune of other people! Although there are stages in the development of spiritual life, it is not at all like passing tests or examinations.

That is why sometimes very old people, who are obviously going downhill mentally and physically, can enjoy a very happy spiritual life of a kind that is beyond the understanding of most of us. Have you ever been impressed when an old person who is suffering great pain between bouts of semi–consciousness suddenly asks you about your life, your friends, family and what you are planning to do? You may be surprised when such an old and sick person takes an intelligent interest in what you say: this could be because they have drawn you into their hidden prayer life about which we others can know next to nothing.

Retreats

In trying to develop the spiritual life, a prayer group can be a help and support in that all are able to help each other. As already noted above, the role of the spiritual director can be crucial. Many Christian organisations hold week–ends or longer periods which are specially designed to help people to deepen their prayer life, their understanding of the church and the Bible and their faith. These occasions may take the form of a study and prayer week, a holiday — and this form is particularly important for Christian parents who may want to bring their children — or a guided tour to a special place, in fact a sort of pilgrimage (see Part One). All of these devote varying amounts of time of spiritual development.

Typical is the **Retreat**. At a retreat a group of people spend a few days together in a quiet place with a retreat conductor or leader. The place may be a retreat house specially provided for this purpose, with staff who cook and so on in order to give the retreatants time to devote to their religion. But some retreat houses are more or less do–it–yourself. There should, however, be someone who is leading it, arranging prayer meetings, giving special talks, and chairing discussions. Usually the day is regulated by a succession of prayer services like the daily offices in a monastery. It is usual for those on retreat not to talk but to observe silence apart from the services, but some retreats involve discussions and study groups at which all can take part.

The Ascent of Mount Carmel

Yet to develop the spiritual life efforts are needed. Christian mystical writers describe stages in spiritual growth in different ways. It is obvious that any description must be metaphorical and rather sketchy. There are no words for a literal description. The metaphor of climbing a mountain, the ascent of Mount Carmel, has associations obviously with the Carmelite religious order. The steep climb is said to get harder as you advance and to demand a total commitment.

The basic attitude of the Christian who is trying to develop in this way is total commitment to God in adoration. This is a basic category of prayer as was seen in the ACTS method above. To dedicate the whole self to adoration must include the cares and mess of the world as well as one's own failures. It is necessary to be realistic. This means that prayer for people and situations (supplication in the ACTS method) is part of this, but the Christian does not go to God with a kind of shopping list of requests.

Writers on spiritual development speak of dangers and discouragements (think of the discouragements in John Bunyan's book 'Pilgrim's Progress'), rather as if one were caught in a snowstorm on the side of a bleak mountain. At one of the stages even prayer life seems dead:

this is called the *Night of the Soul*, but there are other landmarks on this journey. These difficulties and discouragements make the Christian pilgrim throw away any securities, including religious securities, because he or she can have no claim on God. In fact the whole world is very small and very unimportant. It is only the life and presence of Jesus which helps the Christian to see that the world matters at all. For Christians Jesus shows what God is like, but apart from that, God is beyond all human thought and understanding.

This must sound very specialised and cut off from the ordinary world in which we all have to live. But it is not so. Many Christians who have advanced far in prayer life, who maybe spend hours a day in contemplation and other religious devotions, also do a great deal for other people. St Teresa of Avila (1515–1582) is one who was very active in helping people, and another is St Catherine of Siena (1347 or perhaps 1333–1380) who worked long hours in the hospital which still stands near to Siena cathedral.

Christian spirituality and work for others seem to go together. This is a special mark of the Quaker tradition, and it seems as if for them prayer life and the service of those in need only make sense when they are parts of each other.

Chapter Ten

LEARNING FROM CHRISTIAN WORSHIP

Christian worship covers a wide range of activities, but it is also something very deep. Many people say that the depth is the most important part, but it is also true that the fellowship of Christians worshipping together is an essential part of their relationship to God as they understand it.

You will find it helpful to keep in mind much of what you have learnt in this Part when you are studying other aspects of Christianity. Worship obviously affects what Christians feel about life and death and the world around them. This means that Christian worship is also basic to the understanding of Christianity in a non–Christian world (Part Five), and for Christian belief (Part Four).

One Line Answers

(Write answers to these questions in one line or two)

1 Why do Orthodox churches have a screen? What is it called?
2 Why do Quakers (Society of Friends) call their place of worship a Meeting House?
3 Name one piece of furniture usually found in a church (but not elsewhere) and say what it is used for.
4 What form of worship would you expect to find in a building where organ and choir are the focus of attention?
5 Which part of a Western church is called the chancel?
6 What do Salvationists call their church building?
7 Name three denominations in which only an ordained minister is allowed to preside at the eucharist.
8 Name one sacrament which is recognised by nearly all Christians.
9 Name one Christian denomination which celebrates no sacraments.
10 Give two other names for the eucharist.
11 Give one reason why a church might have a reserved sacrament.
12 Name two things which are consecrated at holy communion.
13 Give another name for the sacrament of reconciliation.
14 What is the Host at holy communion?
15 What is a gospel procession?
16 Why is Jesus sometimes called the Lamb of God?
17 Give two meanings for the words 'Body of Christ'.
18 Who or what is a penitent?
19 Why is confession important for some Christians?
20 What is meant by the phrase 'the seal of the confessional'?
21 What is meant by giving testimony in church?
22 Name two different types of Christian prayer.
23 Give an example of a prayer without words.
24 What is the Jesus prayer?
25 Describe one form of prayer often used with a rosary.
26 What are the first two words of the Lord's Prayer?
27 Why is the Lord's Prayer so called?
28 Describe one way the Bible is normally used in a church service.
29 What is the Psalter?
30 Name one church service that is connected with agriculture.

Part Three

RITES OF PASSAGE

Chapter One

BAPTISM

Baptism is a Christian ritual by which new members are joined to the Christian community. People sometimes talk about being born a Jew or born a Christian, but strictly speaking you cannot be born a Christian. You have to become one, and baptism is the ceremony for marking this.

The word '**baptism**' just means dipping in water. In the picture you can see that the person being baptised (till this moment called the candidate for baptism) is going right under the water. He or she is being held by the person who also says the words of baptism. These words are also part of the ritual.

Do you like diving and swimming in water?

Next time you go under, try to stay down long enough to look up at the surface of the water, especially if you are out of doors, in the sea, a river or a lake. What does the surface look like from below? What if it is raining? — Or the sun is shining on the water? When you come up again, how do you feel? You may have dived dozens of times, but try to reflect on one such experience. It is linked in some way to the meaning of baptism.

Baptism in the River Jordan

Joining and Belonging

You probably think that belonging to the human race is simply a matter of being born. Of course that is the biological start, but there is more to becoming human than that. Newborn babies need someone to bring them up if they are even to go on living. They cannot fend for themselves: they must be fed; they need care and protection. As well as eating and sleeping safely, young children learn almost everything they need to know from their parents and other older people. This shows that being human means much more than the biology of conception, pregnancy and birth.

Biology today includes the study of ecology and the environment. For human kind these are essential, and more important for what it means to grow up for humans than for any other species. Human kind is a social animal.

Experiments have been done with the young of different animal species, in which they have been taken away from their mothers soon after birth and reared in a humanly controlled environment. As soon as they reach the age when they ought to be able to cope for themselves (obviously this varies with different species), a suitable natural habitat is found for each to be released. Then they are observed, to see whether they show the behaviour typical of their species. If they do, this must be instinctive as they obviously have not been taught it. Insects and fish have no problems, and even some of the smaller mammals seem able to fend for themselves after just a few moments hesitation. But this is not so for larger mammals. For example an adolescent baboon does not know how to find its food unless it has been taught. It cannot even tell the difference between good food and what would be bad for it.

Have you seen a mother cat training kittens in the skills of the hunt? The young of the human species require far more nurture and education, and for far longer, than any other species of animal, far longer even than the really big mammals like elephants whose gestation period is longer than man's and whose adult life also stretches over several decades.

All this means that to grow up recognisably human, in behaviour as well as in looks, we need to belong to at least one human group. Without this we would not grow up at all, and a small baby alone must quickly die.

In fact everyone belongs to more than one group at the same time. The most obvious groups are those based on family and relations, on where we live (neighbours) and on the school we go to and the job we do.

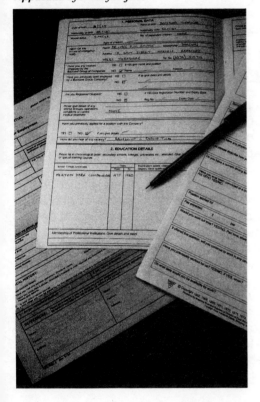

Application forms for jobs

APPLYING FOR A JOB

If you are applying for a job you will probably also be asked to write down some of the following:

- Schools Attended
- Examinations Passed
- Sports and Teams
- Religion
- Hobbies
- Medical Record
- Previous Employment (including part–time)

GROUPS WE BELONG TO

ACTIVITY: on your own

Make a list of all the various groups and communities you belong to.

ACTIVITY: as a group

Compare notes on the groups listed by each person in the last activity, and sort them out into:

    (a) groups you cannot help belonging to
    (b) groups you have chosen to join
    (c) groups which have chosen you

ACTIVITY: on your own

Now on your own again **make a new list of the groups you belong to under these headings.** You may have found some more as a result of the discussion. (Some of the groups will be included within others on your list — if this happens, arrange them in columns to show this.)

- Next, list any special sign that marks you as a member of the group (e.g. family name, local dialect or accent, badge or special clothes, typical habits and so on). These will need thinking about.
- Pick out the groups from your list which you would look on as life–long commitments, i.e. you would never try to leave them.
- Now look back at the lists you have made of the groups you belong to.
- Choose two or three of these with care, and write about two pages altogether about them.

  Describe them briefly, say how you came to belong to them, say whether there was a ceremony for joining and if so describe it, and mention anything else special about them.

FAMILIES CLUBS AND FRIENDS

Being born into a family is not a matter of choice. Yet parents and children naturally love each other without thinking too much about it. Before the child starts going to school, playmates and friends are other members of the family, or neighbours, or children of your parents' friends. Children only really begin to choose their own friends after they start school and there are a lot of other children to choose from.

Friends are fun, but they are not usually made by rational choice. Most people of all ages would find it very difficult to explain why they have the friendships they enjoy, or to give reasons for spending time with the people they see most. It is like this throughout adulthood, and shows that making friends is not exclusively a matter of rational choice.

Joining clubs and sports on the other hand is usually a matter for the individual to decide. You have got to choose between a number of ways of spending free time: everything cannot be fitted in. Your reasons for choosing particular hobbies, sports and pastimes are quite complex, and usually influenced by friendships and going along with the group.

A family group

A group of friends

ACTIVITY: on your own

Make a quick list of up to five clubs or societies you have joined in school or college.

Think of the reasons why you joined them. Try to do the same for the sports, hobbies, clubs, etc. you take part in out of school or college.

Belonging and Being Different

An ethnic minority:

We are all born to particular parents, but somewhere for nearly all of us there are special ancestors or connections. If you find out you have got Scottish ancestry somewhere, you may like the idea so much that you want to express this, bring it out, support Scottish teams, or generally enjoy Scottishness. Many people in the U.K. today are of mixed descent and so have ancestors from different groups. If they know this, they could have a choice in what they would like to be. Obviously this applies too if your ancestry is Polish, Jewish, Asian, African, French, Italian, Australian or something else and you may well be proud of it!

'Choosing' to be Scots, or African, or Polish, or something else which has the added attraction of being slightly unusual, can be fun. It can also be deeply meaningful, especially when ideals and hopes are brought into play.

Japanese ladies in their national dress

ACTIVITY: as a group

1 **Imagine that you are members of a different ethnic or cultural group (not your own) now living in Britain. Choose together who you are going to be**, as you will all need to belong to the same group!

2 Compare your group, your '*new group*', with the rest of the population living around and discuss the following questions. Make some notes of your answers and decisions.
   (a) How are your customs and tastes different?
   (b) Are your leisure activities different?
   (c) Are the same kinds of behaviour admired and disliked?
   (d) Can you make friends easily with the locals?
   (e) Where do your children go to school?
   (f) How can you make sure that your children grow up proud of their origins?

3 If you found the exercise above difficult, you might like to try things another way round.

   Imagine you are British people living abroad, perhaps in a Third World country. Now answer the questions above for this situation.

Joining the Christian Community

In Christian communities, baptism is a **rite** or **ritual of initiation**. The term initiation means joining something, making a start, and also learning how to behave and how to belong. Baptism marks the coming of new members into the fellowship of all Christian people. This means that baptism is the first of a series of rituals which happen at special times in the life of Christian men and women. Quite a lot of learning is involved, like bringing up the young in any society.

Later rituals, which are also in their way kinds of initiation, are discussed later in this Part. They include confirmation, Christian marriage, and for some people ordination to the ministry. At the end of mortal life there is a Christian funeral.

ACTIVITY: on your own

First **look at the picture of a baptism in the River Congo.** It is clear that the people to be baptised are going to be dipped under the water, while being held by the minister who says the words of baptism (see next section). This is just like the picture of baptism in the Jordan in the first section on Baptism.

Now look once more at the picture and **answer the following questions**:

(a) Which are the candidates for baptism? How many are there?

(b) Is there more than one minister? If so, how many?

(c) Why are they in a river? How deep is it?

(d) Do you think the water is flowing past them?

(e) Would you like to be baptised in a river rather than in a church? Give reasons for your answer.

You will find later if you do not know it already that there are two ways of administering baptism: one is by putting the candidate right under, which is called **total immersion**, and the other, called **effusion**, is done by pouring some water over the head or forehead with a scoop or cupped hand.

Some people think that the ritual of baptism actually makes people Christians, but it is more traditional to think of the rite as the public acceptance of the newly baptised who are making a personal commitment to the Christian way. When a baby is baptised then the personal commitment is made by the family who are going to bring the child up.

Baptism is a symbol of a new start in life and looks forward. At an everyday level we wash ourselves in preparation for going out or meeting someone special. Baptism is also a response to a call to repentance and a new kind of life. Baptism means both that a new start has been made, and at the same time it is a stimulus for making this fresh start. Some people call it new life or the beginning of life in a truer and deeper sense.

The idea of a fresh start can be illustrated from pre–Christian and non–Christian baptisms or purification rituals all of which are done with water. Such rites can be found in some Jewish rituals, and in the regular washing that Muslims and Hindus perform in order to purify themselves before worship and prayer. Christianity, however, has given a new

137

The different kinds of groups you can join and listed earlier can be seen as a picture of the different ideas Christians hold about the meaning of baptism. Do individuals choose to join the church, or is the choice made for them?

meaning to baptism and this is shown partly in that a Christian is only baptised once.

There is in fact an important difference of opinion between Christian denominations about who may join the church. The great majority of Christians, notably Roman Catholic, Orthodox, Lutheran, Anglican, Methodist and many others, encourage Christian parents to bring their children to be baptised. The baby does not make promises for her– or himself, but the family promise instead that they will bring the child up as a Christian. In most cases there are also other adults who represent the whole Christian church and make these promises together with the parents. They are called **godparents**. In particular the godparents are expected to help the parents bring the children up as loyal and faithful Christians.

Some Christians, however, do not agree with this. They believe that a person can only become a Christian after making a conscious decision and by personally taking on responsibility for the promises. If this is the case, then candidates for baptism can only be adults or near–adults who can declare their belief and make the promises for themselves. This is called **Believer's Baptism**. The Christians who first insisted on this were called Baptists. Today there are a few other denominations who agree with this.

Still other groups have gone a step further. They feel that if what really counts is the decision, then the ritual of being baptised does not matter at all. For this reason the Salvation Army and Quakers for example do not have baptism. Instead, adults join them by making a simple declaration.

Baptism in Church

The words are an essential part of baptism. The candidate is given a name, for this reason called a **Christian Name**. A candidate may have been using this name already, especially in the case of an adult baptism, but it is the ritual of baptism which makes it a Christian Name. The person who administers baptism must say:

'(name), *I baptise you in the name of the Father, and of the Son, and of the Holy Spirit*'.

So Christians are always baptised in the name of the Father, Son and Holy Spirit, who is together the holy and indivisible Trinity. New members are baptised into Jesus Christ, that means they are made members of his body which is the fellowship of all Christian people, no matter whether these are seen as a visible church group or an invisible multitude, most of whom are unknown to each other. At the same time, because the apostles took over Jewish religious history together with their scriptures (Old Testament), the new Christian is baptised into the entire scriptural tradition and fellowship (more about this on pages 141-143).

Right: an infant being baptised in a font

Below: an adult being baptised by immersion in a church

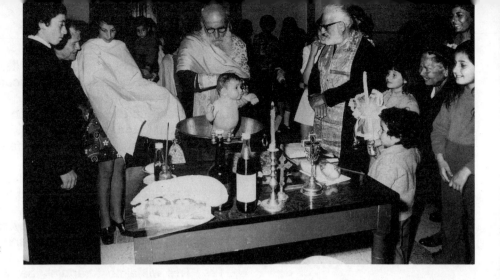

An infant being baptised by immersion in a Greek Orthodox Church

All this gives Christian baptism a significance and a symbolism which is different from all non–christian baptism rituals.

Christian baptism is frequently spoken of as rebirth or a second birth: '*born again in Christ*'. The implication of this is that physical birth is either incomplete or somehow not enough. We have already seen that this is true in the biological sense.

When a baby has been baptised, she or he needs to be brought up (nurtured) in the Christian faith. This can be expected to take a long time, just as physical growth and education take a long time. But even an adult who is baptised requires some nurture too, although generally there has been a thorough course of instruction and even examination beforehand.

Note: Do not confuse the phrase '*born again in Christ*' (which refers to Christian baptism) with the similar phrase '*born again Christians*'. This phrase refers to a pentecostal experience which is also sometimes called '*baptism in the spirit*'.

Baptism implies more than joining. Those who are baptised into Christ are baptised also into his death, and from that into his resurrection. You could say this means that they take on somehow a share in the death of Jesus Christ and therefore also in his resurrection to new life. This is not so obviously different from being born again, and yet it clearly does also have different implications. To be baptised into Christ's death can involve suffering, persecution and self–sacrifice, and therefore resurrection must at the very least involve a different level of life from before. This theme is frequently taken up in the letters of St Paul.

ACTIVITY

Either on your own or in a group

It would be a good idea to go to a baptism.

Before you go you should find out what is going to happen and what it means to the different people who take part.

Visits can be organised for the whole group, or you can go alone.

If you want to take photographs you will need to get permission in advance.

Check up whether adults, children or babies are to be baptised.

All churches baptise adults, but some denominations refuse babies and children on the grounds that they cannot make an individual commitment personally.

Make careful notes on each of the following:

1 Infant baptism
- What church (or denomination) is this?
- What happens?
- In what part of the building does it take place?
- What is the method used (dipping or pouring)?
- What preparations are made?
- Are the parents given any special teaching?
- Is baptism followed up, and if so how?

2 Adult (believer's) baptism
This will almost certainly be at a Baptist church.
Answer the same questions as above (except about parents).
- Now write a report of about two pages about your visits to two different forms of baptism,
  1 Infant baptism (Church of England, Roman Catholic, Lutheran, Orthodox)
  2 Believer's (adult) baptism in the Baptist Church
- In your report be sure to describe what happens, and what is different in the two rites.
- Compare them and say which impressed you more and why.

John the Baptist

A painting of John the Baptist

To understand about Christian baptism today it is helpful to read about John the Baptist. This should tell us at least three things. First we read that John was baptising people before Jesus appeared and this shows that baptising was a Jewish ritual. Second, Jesus came himself to be baptised. This gave baptism a new direction allowing the apostles to make it a regular Christian ritual which means something different from purification rituals in other religions. Third, Christian baptism is not an end in itself, but gets us to look forward, to expect something else.

ACTIVITY

On your own, or after discussion with the group

Read Mark 1.1–13: then write answers to the following questions:

- Where was John the Baptist?
- Where did the prophet Isaiah say the voice would be?
- Where was Jesus after his baptism?
- What did John the Baptist look like?
- What would people think of when they saw him?
- What did the people of Judea and Jerusalem do when they came out to him? (The parallel account in Luke 3.1–14 will give you some help on this if you want any.)
- How did John speak of Jesus (the one who is coming)?
- What did John say that Jesus would do?
- Why did Jesus want John to baptise him? (If you are short of ideas the account in Matthew 3.13–15 may help you.)

> **Then for follow-up work, write about a page comparing the baptism of Jesus as described in Mark 1.1–13 with baptism in a modern church.**
>
> ● Why do you think they are so different?

Jesus Christ was himself baptised at the beginning of his gospel ministry. This rite was performed for him by John the Baptist in the waters of the river Jordan. John was calling the Jews to confess their sins and then he baptised them as a sign that they were sorry for the past and wanted to make a new beginning in life. The fact that they came out to him in considerable numbers suggests not just that he was a powerful preacher, but also that they were expecting something special to happen, something that was going to make a difference to their lives, and perhaps the life of the whole Jewish community.

Some Christians look to the baptism of Jesus as a model for all new converts to follow. This is misleading. The great majority of Christians say that Jesus' baptism was unique: for example, the opening of the heavens, the coming down of the spirit, and the divine voice do not occur at modern baptisms, nor should we expect them.

Jesus did not take a new name when he was baptised. He had been called Jesus at the Jewish naming ceremony when he was eight days old. The dove coming down, however, symbolises a vocation, that is his being called to a new phase in his life.

When Jesus was baptised by John with water in the Jordan, this was the sign that his ministry had begun. When at Pentecost the holy spirit was poured out on the apostles, this was the sign that they were to take on his work. This was their baptism in the spirit (see Chapter 7 on Pentecost in Part One).

Symbols and Similarities

The four gospels were written by the first generation of Christians and were sent out to be read in the early Church. The disciples were Jews as Jesus was, and they looked for new meaning in Jewish religious practices and Jewish scripture. This scripture is what Christians call the Old Testament, and even today most Christians know some of its most important stories.

This next bit is very important in order to learn something about the meaning of baptism. To understand how Christians have traditionally thought of baptism it is necessary to look back to the great events in the Jewish religious tradition because this led up to the first experiences of Christian baptism.

People always try to understand a new experience which they feel is important by drawing on or comparing it with great events from the past. Obviously these are events which have made a deep impression. A modern example of the power of great events to shape the thinking and experience of a whole people is the terrible event when an atomic bomb was dropped on Hiroshima in 1945. The attitudes of most modern Japanese towards war are deeply affected by this, although the great majority of the population were not born at the time. Great events of the past can shape the thinking of a people for centuries to come. This is definitely how the Christian Fathers of the early church thought and taught, and many Christian theologians still do.

The Israelites crossing the Red Sea

In the Old Testament God saved the Israelites from slavery in Egypt. Moses led them out of Egypt through the dramatic Red Sea crossing. All Jews, including of course Jesus and his disciples, have always known this story. It is a fundamental part of Jewish awareness, what it means to be a Jew, and indeed it has for centuries been relived every year at Passover. Without Moses the Israelites would never have come out. As soon as they saw the Egyptians coming after them they wanted to turn back and give in. But Moses lifted his stave over the sea, and the waters parted. When the Israelites were through, the waters closed again and drowned the army of the Egyptians.

ACTIVITY: on your own

Read the account in Mark 1.1–13 again, and answer these questions:

    (a) How many quotations are there from the Old Testament?
    (b) How many times is the desert (wilderness) mentioned?
    (c) Is there any mention of a prophet and anyone who might look like a prophet?
    (d) How many times are water or a river mentioned?

ACTIVITY: as a group

Compare your answers to these four questions to see if all agree.
    Now discuss and list on the board or in a notebook

    (a) What important Old Testament events happened in the desert?
    (b) What important O T events are connected with water?

(c) Name any important O T prophets or leaders who are connected with the desert (any leader who acts as God's spokesman is sometimes spoken of as a prophet).

At least one important story from the Old Testament will be well–known to you which fits these questions. You may find you know of others.

ACTIVITY: as a group

To follow this up:
Go back to your discussion of the desert, water and a great leader in the Old Testament.
Does anything that happened in the Old Testament seem to you to forshadow in some way the experience of Christian baptism? You are guided by the clues in Mark's gospel which you have drawn out, but you may need some help through the group to make the connections with baptism — e.g. why is crossing the Red Sea (or Reed Sea) like being baptised?

The crossing of the Red Sea is so important for the Jews that it too is taken up into the symbolism of baptism. The chosen ones are saved by water, and the evil perish in the same water. Some people see this reflected also in the miracle of the Gaderene pigs and the storm on the lake in which the disciples are saved (Mark 4.35 — 5.17). The idea of salvation by water is taken up again in I Peter, using the picture of Noah's Ark in which the chosen eight persons are saved while all the rest perish. (The reference is I Peter 3.18–22)

ACTIVITY: on your own

Think very carefully about what you have just discussed. Now **write a page or two on any of the Old Testament stories you discussed in connection with baptism.**
In each case mention the clue you found in Mark 1.1–13 (this might be no more than a single word), outline briefly the relevant story from the O T.
Finally say in a couple of lines whether and why you think this is helpful for understanding what baptism means for Christians.

Salvation

Christian baptism is a sign of salvation and the experience should be one of joy. Salvation is so important for understanding religion that it needs a special exercise.

Salvation or being saved is one of the key values in any religion. If you feel that the world and your life in it are not quite as they should be, then you have an idea, however vague, that things could be better. This is a kind of ideal, and reaching it is what salvation means in a very general sense. For Christians, the chance of salvation is offered by God through Jesus Christ. That is why being joined to him is so important as the means of being saved.

Since the beginning of Christianity and even while the New Testament was still being written, baptism was widely used as the admission ritual for all who were to be saved through Christ. This salvation was pictured in a variety of ways: for instance many people experienced the new beginning in life as spiritual rebirth — death to the old life and rebirth in the new. For this reason it became the custom to take a new name, and infant baptism today is closely linked with naming. God has called the new Christian, rather as Jesus called his first disciples.

Other turning points in life are sometimes marked by a new name, for instance kings at coronation, monks and nuns at profession (when they take vows for life), and a newly elected Pope. This means that baptism is a kind of vocation, just as much as becoming a nun or a monk, or being crowned king. It is as if one were to say, '*I am called by God, and I am called Mark*'.

What salvation means for Christians is taken up again Part Five, Chapter 1.

To Sum Up

ACTIVITY: on your own

Questions to answer:

1 Which stories and events from the Old Testament have been used by Christians as models or types of Christian baptism? How appropriate do you think they are?

2 What analogies (or kinds of picture language) for salvation through baptism can be found in the Bible, both Old and New Testaments?

3 Do any of them tell us exactly what baptism does for the Christian?

This next one needs a bit more thought:

4 Can you think of other cases outside the Bible and religion where it is hard to represent something by means of another medium? As an example, how is the globe of the Earth represented as a map on a flat piece of paper? What is the best way to show that it is really a sphere?

Source: May 1987 GCE + CSE

Look at the picture below and answer the questions which follow.

    (a) Why is this baptism taking place in a pool rather than at a font?

                          (2 marks)

    (b) **(i)** Name one denomination in which people are normally
            baptised in the way shown   (1 mark)

         (ii) Why are infants not baptised in this denomination? (3 marks)

    (c) What may the woman in the picture have said to the
       congregation immediately before being baptised?   (3 marks)

    (d) **(i)** Name one denomination in which people are normally
            baptised as infants.   (1 mark)

         (ii) Why do some Christians think it important to baptise very
            young children?   (2 marks)

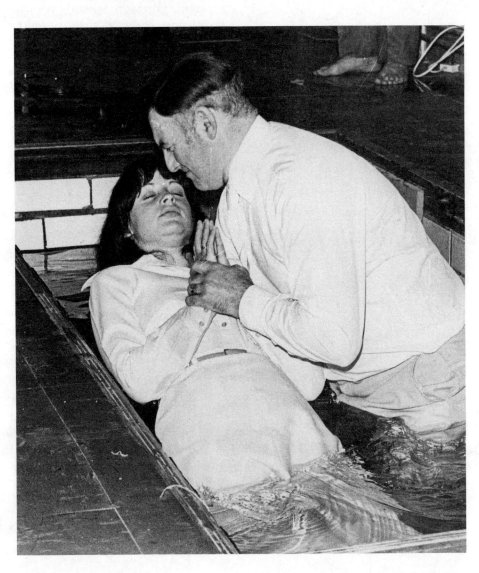

Chapter Two

CONFIRMATION

Have you ever had a dream (or day–dream) in which you score the winning goal in a football match? (It could be any sport you play). Everyone congratulates you. You are pleased, and pleased that everyone else is pleased. At one time, school stories were very popular, in which the girl or boy hero manages to do something rather special, and of course it helps the story that what she or he does is for the good of her friends, or the school, or some group of people, not just herself. Stories like this can still be read in books and teenage magazines. The readers are supposed to feel with the central character, and share in some way the admiration and congratulations. You feel strengthened. You feel that you (she, he) were right to go on, in spite of discouragements, or people saying you were wasting your time and such like. So your sense of purpose, your persistence paid off in the end.

Everyone could have an experience a bit like this in real life, by doing something marvellous — even sometimes by just being in the right place at the right time — and you get a bit of appreciation for it. You can feel good about it afterwards, although it would get boring if you were to go on about it the whole time.

A winning experience – the winners of the London Marathon

Christian confirmation is more than saying '*Well done*'. Christians think that confirmation at least makes people feel stronger, more assured and a bit more confident. Confirmation is thought of as a sacrament, but not quite on the level of baptism and holy communion. There are of course accounts in the New Testament which serve as patterns for what is expected to happen at confirmation, and these are events in which the spirit of God, the holy spirit, comes to new believers, sometimes as individuals, but more often in groups.

This can be illustrated by the story of what happened when the apostle Philip began to make converts in Samaria. You can read about it in Acts 8.14–17. Philip apparently baptised the new Christians, and they received the gift of the holy spirit when Peter and John came from Jerusalem and laid hands upon them a few days later.

This is what is done at confirmation today. Like the apostles, bishops put their hands on those who are being confirmed. This touch, called the '**laying on of hands**', is the same as they themselves received. This means that the touch has come over centuries from the first apostles, and is now being passed on. This action is considered to be very important.

This is something like the apostles' touch which is handed on at confirmation.

ACTIVITY: as a group

- **Have you ever shaken hands with the Queen?** Do you know anyone who has? Have you shaken hands with someone who has shaken hands with the Queen?
- **You could imagine a series of handshakes** which might reach back to Queen Victoria, or to Lord Nelson, or Julius Caesar.
- **Have any of you shaken hands with somebody famous**, your Member of Parliament for instance? Your MP has almost certainly shaken hands with the Prime Minister at some time, and perhaps former Prime Ministers, or heads of foreign governments.
- If you think a about it, it is not difficult to get back to someone well–known, yet long before your own lifetime.
- See how long a chain you can make, and write out all the steps.

ACTIVITY: as a group

Read the Bible passage from Acts 8 about Philip in Samaria, especially verses 14–17. This is how things are meant to happen.
Now read about the 'household' of Cornelius in Acts 10.44–48, when Peter came to him in Caesarea. This is rather a problem story for Christians, because in it the holy spirit came to Cornelius and family before baptism, whereas in all Christian churches confirmation always comes after baptism, never before, and sometimes quite a long time after.

- Discuss the two passages and compare them.
- Can anyone suggest why the order of events in Acts 8 became the normal one, instead of the order of events in Acts 10? Try to think of a number of possible reasons, but the most likely would be something to do with an orderly ritual which can be repeated in future generations.

It was explained at the beginning of the chapter on sacraments in Part Two that a sacrament is thought of as a mark of God's favour and help and friendliness, yet it is at the same time a ritual performed by members of the church, who know full well that God cannot be forced to show favour, etc. But Christians carry out the various sacraments in faith, because they believe that God wants them done, and done in their particular way.

The Confirmation Service

The Confirmation service is a special occasion which has been planned weeks, even months in advance. During this time, the candidates have been attending special classes to prepare them, not just for confirmation, but for their lives in the church as adult Christians.

Confirmation service

Methodists officially call this ceremony '**Public Reception into Full Membership**', but many Methodists in fact speak of it as Confirmation. In the Methodist church, this ceremony always ends with the Lord's Supper. Nowadays Anglican confirmation services mostly include holy communion as well. At one time this was not so.

The centre of the event is the action of the Bishop or other presiding minister placing his hands on the heads of the candidates in turn, and speaking a prayer to the holy spirit. In some ceremonies specially prepared oil is used as well, and each candidate is anointed with a very small amount of holy oil and this part of the ritual is known as **chrism** (or **chrismation**). It is also usual for each candidate to be given a text from the Bible which may be spoken aloud by the presiding minister or bishop during the ceremony, or it may be written in the front of a little book given individually to each candidate at the end of a series of preparation or instruction sessions. When the ceremony is over the local church may decide to hold a party for candidates, their families and friends.

In England, **Anglican** confirmations are usually held in parish churches, and the bishop of the diocese, or an assistant bishop, comes to administer confirmation. During the service he preaches a sermon addressed to the **confirmands** (technical name for those to be confirmed) and their families. If a parish has only a few candidates then nearby parishes arrange for all their confirmands to go to one of the churches and all be confirmed together. Confirmands can be any age from ten upwards, but the usual age is 14–19. The confirmation of adults who have not already been confirmed is quite common too.

Among **Roman Catholics**, the normal age for confirmation is ten to fourteen, but these children have already been admitted to holy communion some three to six years earlier at a different ceremony known as **First Communion**. Confirmation in Roman Catholic churches is also performed by a bishop, usually with oil (chrism) as well as laying on hands.

Orthodox Christians, Greek, Russian, Syrian and so on, have confirmation at the same time as baptism. Both are done by the priest who uses oil (chrism) which has been specially prepared by a bishop. The bishop is not actually present at the confirmation. This means that tiny babies are confirmed and may receive holy communion also in Orthodox churches.

In **Presbyterian**, **Methodist** and other churches which do not have bishops the confirmation is performed by a presiding minister who lays his or her hands on the heads of the confirmands. This is usually the parish minister. Confirmation, or Public Reception into Full Membership, may be quite a local affair, and it can happen that there are only one or very few candidates for this at one time.

Lutherans are confirmed by the parish minister too, or sometimes a visiting minister is specially invited. This makes the ceremony more of a special occasion. Even though Lutherans have bishops, they do not come to the confirmation services in the parishes. Obviously denominations which do not have baptism do not have confirmation either. For **Baptists**, believers baptism needs no extra ceremony like confirmation.

This is what is thought to happen:

- The Spirit of God confirms each candidate, who is often a young person, encourages him or her, and generally helps him or her to keep going as a Christian. The bishop's or minister's hand passes on the touch of Jesus to his disciples and friends.

• This is an occasion for public recognition that the newly confirmed are now full members of the church.

• The newly confirmed are now able to receive holy communion (only except Roman Catholics who have already been admitted to this).

• They are now thought old and mature enough to take personal responsibility for their baptism promises (this does not apply in the Orthodox churches).

Here is a description of what you might observe at the confirmation ceremony in a Lutheran church.

The confirmation is on Sunday morning, at the usual service time, and this encourages the usual parish congregation to be present as well as families and friends of the confirmands, some of whom may have come from a long way away. The candidates, boys and girls together, come in a little procession just before the start of the service and sit in rows reserved for them at the front. The service includes hymns, prayers, Bible readings and a sermon.

When the time for confirmation has come, the parish minister stands at the chancel step, that is in front of the altar, facing the congregation, and three or four confirmands come out and stand in a line facing him. The minister takes the right hand of the first in his, says his or her name aloud, and then reads (or says from memory) a text from the Bible which the candidate is expected to remember and keep as a special confirmation text. He then takes the hand of the next, announces the name and reads a new text, until all three or four who are standing there have had their hand taken and their names (Christian name and surname) announced to the church, together with a text for each. There are obviously some sentences or texts from the Bible which the minister particularly likes, and so it is possible for two or three candidates to be given the same text in the course of one confirmation service.

Now the three or four confirmands kneel. The minister says the words of confirmation, which is a prayer for strengthening (confirmation), while laying his hands on their heads. He may place one hand on one head, the other on the next, then move them to the next two heads while speaking the prayer, or he may put both his hands on the head of one confirmand, and move them on to the next while still speaking. When all have been confirmed, they stand in a line in front of the minister as before, and he gives them a blessing, making the sign of the cross over them, and tells them to go in peace. They go back to their place. The next three or four come up and the ritual is done again, until all have been confirmed. The Sunday service then goes on to its normal end. Afterwards everyone congratulates the newly confirmed. The presiding minister may be a man or a woman.

ACTIVITY: as a group

On a large piece of paper make a chart to show the ceremony of confirmation in different churches or denominations.

Along the top: Write the names of various church denominations which you already know about or which you can find out about. e.g. Anglican, Baptist, Coptic, Lutheran, Methodist, Orthodox, Presbyterian, Roman Catholic, and others.

Down the side, write these seven questions:

1 Do they have confirmation?
2 What is the usual age for this?
3 Who performs the ceremony?
4 What difference does confirmation make to those confirmed?
5 Are they given any special teaching?
6 If so, who gives the teaching?
7 What are they taught? — give a brief example of the content of what they have been taught.

ACTIVITY: on your own

A sentence from the Bible is often given to each confirmand.
A favourite text for confirmation might be:
  '*The Lord is my light and my salvation*'. Psalm 27.1
Such a text might be only part of a verse. It can be a whole verse.
More than one verse is possible but very unusual.

- **Can you think of a suitable Bible text which you would like EITHER to have yourself** — is it appropriate in some way?
  OR for a friend — think of someone particular.
- Carefully write out the text you have chosen, with the book, chapter and verse of the Bible from which it comes.
- Keep this text to use later.

ACTIVITY: as a group

Now as a follow-up get together in a group of four or five.
  Each of you in turn reads out the text you have chosen and explains to the others

(a) what helped you choose this text
(b) who it is for
(c) why you think it is likely to be suitable or helpful for yourself or your friend.

Continue round the group until all have had their say.

ACTIVITY: as a group

Go to a confirmation (or equivalent) service. You can either go alone, but it is probably better to go with one or two others because each of you will notice different things.

Make careful notes on what happens. To help you it would be a good idea to note down some headings before you go to remind you what to look for.

Afterwards write a page or two about the confirmation service you went to.

Compare this service with the Lutheran service described above.

Mention anything in the service which seems to you to stress the new status and new responsibility of those confirmed.

Chapter Three

CHRISTIAN MARRIAGE

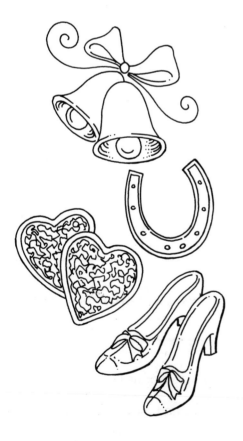

You know lots of people who are married and also many who are not. Some of them may be Christians. Before going on to study Christian marriage, try these two exercises about marriage and your own views.

ACTIVITY: on your own

Do this exercise fairly quickly: you will have time to think about your answers later. **Just put 'Yes' or 'Maybe' or 'No' against each of the following:**

When I hear the word 'love' I think of,

- a paperback romance you buy at the station
- marriage
- a really good friend
- sex
- being accepted
- one person exploiting another or others
- forgiving and being forgiven
- a long–lasting relationship
- being trusted
- a sweet little pet animal

Compare your answers with other people in your small group. **Discuss whether the word 'love' means the same in all your answers.** If it doesn't, then what different things can love mean?

ACTIVITY: on your own

Try the 'Yes', 'Maybe' and 'No' answers on these statements about marriage. 'Yes' means that you agree with the statement.

Marriage is
- a wedding reception and party
- for life
- brings lots of in–laws together who don't really like each other
- a bit of a bore
- someone to iron your shirts or mend the car
- OK for old–fashioned types
- important if you're going to have children
- socially acceptable
- old hat, not socially acceptable among people I like
- temporary
- expensive
- a convenient way of dealing with property and inheritance
- a good way of linking two influential families
- good for business
- something for other people to talk about

Then as a group, talk over your answers. There may be more to think about here than you found in the first activity.

130

Marriage and the Christian Churches

Marriage as an institution existed long before Christianity. The Christian church had some married members from the start — do you remember the gospel story about Peter's mother–in–law in Mark 1.30–31? (He was still called 'Simon' at that time and was given the name Peter later.) You do not get a mother–in–law unless you are married. In Paul's letters there are plenty of references to Christians who either are married or want to get married, and also some to the question of divorce.

At the same time there are specifically Christian ceremonies for getting married, and also most churches have teachings about marriage and the family. All societies of whatever religion recognise that there is a connection between people being married and the bringing up of children. Children are important because they are the next generation of society.

For the majority of Christians, Christian marriage is one of the seven sacraments, and derives its holiness in part from the fact that the gospel shows Jesus performing his first miracle at a wedding party in Cana in Galilee, when he turned water into wine at the wedding reception (see John 2.1–11). We say '*in part*' because all Christians derive marriage from the creation of humankind as related in Genesis 1 and 2 and the command to multiply (have children). This means that there is something universal about marriage which is not exclusively Christian, although Christian marriage is thought of as being under God and according to God's will.

In nearly all churches Christians are taught that marriage is very important. In its most extreme form, this teaching can be taken to mean that if a couple are not married in church, the marriage does not count, and there has been at least one instance of a famous film star, several times married and divorced, celebrating her latest wedding with all the

A wedding in Jamaica

splendour of the Italian church because it was the first of her weddings to take place in a church. But many Christians, including Italian Christians, found this scandalous, and such a rigid line of church teaching on marriage is not found everywhere. (see below on Divorce and on Monogamy)

For those Christians, mainly Protestants, who do not regard marriage as a sacrament in a special and necessary sense, a wedding in church is really a form of blessing and thanksgiving. For them, the church service does not make the marriage, which really happens through the civil registration. Marriage must also be legally recognised by the whole of society, and in most countries couples must have a non–religious ceremony in front of the Registrar. If they are Christian, the church ceremony is in addition. It usually follows straight away. In the Church of England, however, the legal priest or curate is also a Registrar for marriages so in a sense performs both ceremonies, that for the Church as well as that for the State. The same is true in Denmark and one or two other western European countries.

Marriage and Divorce

What Christians think about marriage goes back to how Christians understand creation. In the two stories of creation, in Genesis 1 and Genesis 2, marriage is designed for a man and a woman as a very close physical relationship. Two things are expected to follow from it: one is mutual friendship and companionship, and the other is having children. Because in some societies, including Europe until fairly recently, many babies and children died young (and some mothers died in childbirth), some church leaders have stressed the need for children above that of mutual companionship between husband and wife. The future of society, and of the church on earth, depends on there being an adequate supply of children growing up.

The two conditions of marriage have been stated as follows: one, the couple consent in public to marry, and this consent is either solemnised as a sacrament or blessed or recognised by the church; and second, there should be a physical act of sexual intercourse between the two parties to this marriage. A marriage ritual which is not consummated, that means completed by sexual intercourse, is not a valid marriage, although in cases of dispute, the truth may not be easy to establish. Some Christians have taught that sexual intercourse is exclusively for the purpose of having children. If this is accepted, then techniques of contraception are ruled out. But many other Christians, including some Roman Catholics whose official church teaching is against contraception, believe that sexual intercourse is not exclusively for having children, but is an important part of the mutual love and companionship of the couple concerned.

Many Christians who value the mutual love and companionship of marriage, must also recognise that this side of a marriage can go wrong. Christian teaching is traditionally strongly against divorce. This is shown by the words spoken by the minister as soon as the couple are joined in marriage: 'That which God has joined together let not man divide'.

At the same time many Christians recognise that when a close relationship has gone badly wrong, staying together can have the effect of destroying each other psychologically. This raises the question of divorce.

The Orthodox churches have always recognised the possibility of a marriage ending in divorce, and there is a special form of divorce which is conducted in the church. It is a very mournful affair, like a funeral, because it marks the death of a relationship. It is rarely used, however, and only after all else has failed. The Western churches have traditionally allowed marriages to be annulled, which means saying that it was never a real marriage in the first place. In effect, this has tended to be used mainly for rich or politically important people, and can sometimes give rise to arguments.

Monogamy

Monogamy means one wife with one husband. Divorce raises the question of being able to marry again. If the first marriage has been annulled (declared to be not a real marriage), then marrying afterwards counts as the first time, however odd it may all seem to outsiders. But a divorce is different because it brings to an end a marriage that has been recognised as valid and real, and therefore it may not be just assumed that both partners are free to marry other people. In civil law they can marry again, but some churches may have to treat their own members as special cases.

Christian tradition teaches monogamy. The creation passages speak of one man and one woman living together, whether we like to call them Adam and Eve or not. The New Testament also expects Christians either to be monogamous or not to marry at all. In other parts of the Old Testament, however, quite a lot of people had more than one wife (polygamy), and this has been the custom in some non–Christian societies. Christian missionaries had problems when they made converts in a society where some of the men had more than one wife, or women had more than one husband. Faced with the question often put to them by the convert who asks, '*What ought I to do?*', many missionaries told them to keep the first partner and dismiss or divorce the rest. But it is obvious that this must cause unhappiness for those who have been sent away, with no husband at all now, and perhaps with little prospect of marrying someone else, even if they want to.

A discussion of divorce in Europe and America is also relevant here. Europeans think that polygamy means having more than one wife (or husband) at the same time. But it is just as reasonable to think that having more than one marriage partner in succession is also polygamous, even if there is an interval between the different marriages. This system too can be very unkind to the individuals who have been put aside by divorce. This is a subject which Christians in the modern world have got to try to decide.

The Marriage Service

A Christian marriage service includes a lot of symbolism. The marriage between a man and a woman symbolises the love of Christ for his Church, and this means that Christian marriage is a permanent commitment of two people to each other in the same way. In most ceremonies rings are given, sometimes only one ring which the man gives to the woman, sometimes each gives a ring to the other. In Orthodox churches wreathes which are linked together are put on the heads of bride and bridegroom and exchanged and this is called the crowning. The eucharist may be celebrated immediately after the wedding and holy communion may be received by bride and bridegroom, or by the whole congregation as well, if they want.

It has been traditional in many countries for the bride to wear white, also for the bride's father to present her to the bridegroom (this is called '*giving her away*'), and for there to be lots of flowers, a photographer and an iced cake. It must be clear that all these things are matters of social custom and do not relate to Christian teaching or symbolism.

The crowning at a Greek Orthodox wedding

The best way to find out about a marriage service is to go to a few and take notes, or discuss them with Christians who were there.

The following two exercises should help you to do this:

ACTIVITY: on your own

Attend a wedding in a Christian church. It may help if you are a friend or relative of one of the people getting married, but it is not necessary as the churches are public. To understand the service better, it may be useful to ask the priest or minister in advance to let you read through the form of service which is to be used. Copy out the key passages after consultation with the minister or with the group you are studying this course with.

After the service arrange two interviews:

(a) with the priest or minister who conducted the wedding and who can help you clarify details of the service and answer your questions;

(b) with a Christian husband and wife who have had a church wedding no matter how long ago (but not the couple newly married).

Prepare yourself before each interview by discussing with your group what kind of questions and clarifications it would be useful to ask about. What has been mentioned already in this section should start you off, and you will think of other things.

Afterwards, either write up your interviews in one or two pages, or write one or two pages on a Christian marriage ceremony and what it means.

Marriage and Celibacy

It is obvious that being married requires commitment to another person and this is bound to take up time and effort. In fact, marriage usually means some commitment to a whole lot of people, including children and the families on both sides. Someone who is not married, then, might have much more time and energy to spend on working with other people and on more obviously religious activity like worship, prayer and pastoral work. This is one of the reasons why many Christians (and not only Christians of course) think it is a mark of dedication to give up of one's own free will the decision to be married and to live instead a single life, in a state of celibacy. Being celibate of course also involves self–control.

Nuns and monks of various kinds and in various churches and denominations feel that God has called them to the single, celibate life. Being celibate is a requirement for Roman Catholic priests (some few exceptions) and bishops, and also for Orthodox bishops. Orthodox priests in parishes are actually required to be married. Orthodox bishops are always chosen from the monasteries and are therefore unmarried.

From this point of view it may seem that marriage is only for people who have not got a vocation to celibacy, that is for the left–overs. But this is misleading. Most Christians say that marriage is also a vocation and is only to be taken on after thought and prayer. Christian marriage is a commitment to God and to another person, or to a number of other people (the children) through the marriage partner. This is in many ways like the commitment and vocation to being ordained priest or minister. Therefore marriage can be seen as a vocation equal to that of a nun or a monk. (See also the next chapter on Ordination)

Some of the very first Christians expected the world to end and Jesus to return in their lifetimes, and that is why in some of St Paul's letters Christians are advised not to get married. There are people in all ages who think that sexual activities are either bad in themselves or can be too easily misused (as is obvious in our own society), and therefore they have opposed marriage for Christians altogether. The American sect of Shakers provides an example for this view, and they did not have marriages or children.

In societies which are strongly male dominated, men tend to be frightened of things that women can do either better than men, or which men cannot do at all. Society in Bible times was usually run by men. Christians today usually stress the openness of Christianity and teach, following St Paul, that there are no barriers between Jew and Greek, male and female, rich and poor, etc. But the ancient and quite pre–Christian fear of certain aspects of womanhood have contributed to a strange fear of marriage or of relations between the sexes. This feeling can be found in books and in people to some extent even today and should not be forgotten.

Rites Connected with Having Children

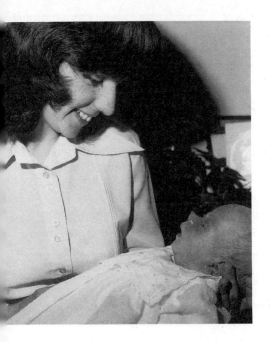

Bearing children is almost always painful for the mother, an anxiety for the father, and unless there is good medical care available, can be a time of danger, both for the mother and for the baby. This means that in any society a successful birth is a time of rejoicing, great happiness, and thanksgiving. Friends and neighbours congratulate the father and mother.

Christian parents usually express their relief and happiness in natural ways, leading up eventually to the baptism of the baby, or in churches which have adult baptism or no baptisms at all (a few), the baby can be dedicated in some way combined with thanksgiving to God.

Several churches have a form of service called **Thanksgiving after Childbirth**. An alternative name for this is sometimes **The Churching of Women**. The ancient thought behind this is a certain fear of childbirth as something that is mysterious to males, rather as outlined at the end of the last section on marriage. Very many non–Christian societies think that mysterious events, especially death and birth, require purification for the main participants. Christians recall in the gospel the Jewish Temple service when the baby Jesus was dedicated, and it is known as **the Purification of the Blessed Virgin Mary**. There are obviously pre–christian elements mixed in with the service of thanksgiving after childbirth which is still in use in many Christian churches today.

GCSE Question — Southern Examining Group — 1988

'Friends, I take this, my Friend — to be my husband promising through divine assistance to be unto him a loving and faithful wife, so long as we both on earth shall live.'

(Said during a simple Meeting for Worship on the occasion of a Quaker wedding.)

(**a**) Describe a marriage service from any other Christian denomination.

(7 marks)

(**b**) Explain how the beliefs of a Christian couple might affect their decisions in two of the following situations:
  (**i**) planning to have children;
  (**ii**) bringing up children;
  (**iii**) coping with elderly relatives;
  (**iv**) facing break-up of their marriage;
  (**v**) making choices about moves in career and changes of home.

(8 marks)

(**c**) To what extent do you think two people, who are planning to marry, should have the same belief? Explain the reasons for your opinion.

(5 marks)

Chapter Four

ORDINATION

Many people get married, but only a small number of Christians get ordained. The service of ordination is a ceremony which sets selected people apart for a special place in the organisation of the church. This usually means that they have a special job to do, and usually also an official position. Ordination makes people priests or ministers and fits them to conduct church services, as well as to teach in the church and to look after a congregation.

ACTIVITY: on your own

Look at this list of different names which Christians give to ordained men and women.
  Try to picture what each of them suggests to you:

  minister, priest, pastor, padre, chaplain, father, prophet, prayer–leader, healer, parson, vicar, curate, captain, confessor, bishop, deacon, monsignor, dean.
  • Can you add other names to this list?
  • Now add after each name, what church or denomination (maybe more than one) each seems to fit in with.

Choosing a Leader

A leader is usually appointed to head up a team. But in some cases the team elect their leader from among themselves. The team usually has an aim or purpose which defines its job and that of its leader. It may be a sports team, or a team engaged in research, or an expedition. So the leader is chosen with a particular end in view, and this means that particular qualities or qualifications will be required, and probably some special training too. When the task is done, perhaps the team disbands, and the leader is no longer needed.

But an army officer remains an army officer when the battle or special operation is over, and retains his rank. The captain of a sports team is likely to lead the team in a series of matches, and the leader of a successful research team is likely to find new projects and either get together a new team, or be invited to join another team, perhaps as its leader.

If you imagine that you are a member of a group or team planning to make an expedition to a remote part of the world, there will be various jobs to be done which must given to particular people. You would need a driver or pilot, at least one scientist who is a specialist in what you are

On an expedition

Ordination to the Ministry

Ordination of a priest in a Methodist Church

going to study (for example a geologist, anthropologist, botanist or whatever), you would need someone who knows the language of the people you are going to meet or work among (a linguist), and you can think of other useful people such as a photographer, mapmaker, mechanic, doctor, etc. These people are not called leaders, but each has a specialised function. One is not senior to others or more important. Yet there could be an emergency when suddenly the mechanic is the key person, and all the rest are keen to do whatever he or she tells them in order to rescue the whole team from big trouble. But when the emergency is over, that person's key role also disappears.

So leadership is of many kinds, and to some extent this applies also to church officials. Most Christians regard ordination as a rank or order which is permanent and can never be removed, while for others, someone is just doing a job, and when the job is over, then the official position goes too.

Leadership can be quite informal too. Someone can be a centre of attention at a party because he or she brings important news, or tells good jokes. There are individuals whom you almost without thinking choose to run a discussion, hold an auction at the village fete, lead singing or whatever is going on. Again there are people whose opinion or good advice you respect and listen to, even if in the end you decide not to follow it. In one sense such a person can be called a natural leader, and yet be useless when what you need is help on a technical problem, like the mechanic two paragraphs back.

Individuals are selected and trained for ministry in the church, and then dedicated to the work at an ordination service or ceremony. It is important that the person should have a sense of being called by God, a sense of vocation. This can be felt in a great variety of ways, and most of them are not very dramatic.

The esssential part of the ordination ritual is the laying on of hands. Someone with an official position and who is already ordained, lays hands on each of the candidates in turn. In some ways this is like the ceremony of confirmation. All the people present pray for the spiritual gifts which the holy spirit brings to be given to the candidates, now and during the course of their work. Also they are given authority from the whole Church to take services and to teach, as well as having pastoral responsibilities. The teaching aspect is symbolised in Western churches by giving each newly ordained person a Bible. This Bible is specially treasured, although the newly ordained presumably possesses one or more Bibles already.

Different groups of Christians have slightly different views on what an ordained person is entitled to do. In practice, before a minister is put in charge of a church congregation, he or she requires either a licence from the bishop (in churches that have bishops, the majority), or else a call (invitation) from the congregation. This call from the parish is seen as part of the vocation from God.

For most of the world's Christians, the essential Christian ministry consists of three grades or orders: bishops, priests and deacons. This explains what is meant by the phrase **ordination to holy orders** (orders in the plural). In all these churches, only a bishop is authorised to lay hands on people to ordain them priest or deacon, and sometimes more than one bishop and other senior clergy take part, laying their hands together on each head in turn. The orders are hierarchical, that means that one must first be a deacon before one can be ordained priest, and a priest before one can become a bishop.

In some churches, for instance the Ethiopian, there are grades below the level of deacon, and these are called minor orders. People in minor orders are typically subsistence farmers in rural areas or small tradesmen. They have some part to play in church services and sometimes also in parish life as assistants to the priest, but they earn their livings in other ways. Roman Catholics also have minor orders, but these appear to have no function and are merely unimportant steps on the way to being ordained priest.

Deacons

The order of deacon is one of the three main orders, along with priest and bishop. The Western churches have for centuries used this office simply as a staging post on the way to priesthood. In the Roman Catholic and Anglican churches a man spends one year as a deacon before going on to be ordained priest. In all Orthodox churches, however, there are permanent deacons and they have a recognisable and distinct job to do in church services and in parish life. They are not allowed to celebrate the Eucharist, but they may, and often do, take the holy communion from the church to give to sick and old people who cannot get to church.

Three New Deacons

Priests

Most of the ministers you normally see are priests. These are the vicars and parish pastors in Anglican, Catholic and Orthodox churches. Denominations which do not have bishops (see below) do not usually use the name '*priest*' for their clergy. This is reasonable because they do not have all three orders, bishops, priests and deacons.

After the ordination, friends and relatives of the newly ordained want to congratulate them and they may all have a party. Ordination is an important event in their lives. A priest is expected to celebrate the eucharist as presiding minister. He was not permitted to do this before being ordained priest. His first celebration of the eucharist, sometimes called shortly **first mass**, means a great deal and a group of his friends may be invited to be present.

Two other important occasions are preaching the first sermon and hearing the confession of a penitent for the first time (see Part Two on the sacrament of reconciliation). Yet neither of these occasions is celebrated with a group of friends. There are reasons.

Those training for the ministry often go out and preach sermons as part of their training before they are ordained. Confessions, however, can only be heard by a priest (in the Orthodox, Roman Catholic and Anglican churches) because only a priest can pronounce (speak the words of) absolution (forgiveness). Look back at what is said about this sacrament in Part Two, Chapter 5, and then imagine you are the person making his or her confession: can you now think of reasons why the priest and the penitent are alone together?

Bishops

In many churches there are bishops. Bishops are considered to be the successors of the apostles and they are responsible collectively for the good order of the church and for teaching true Christian doctrine. A bishop has pastoral responsibility for a district or a number of parishes usually called a diocese. The diocesan bishop has authority over the clergy in his diocese. There are sometimes also assistant bishops whose job is to assist the diocesan bishop, and if the church needs office departments, a bit like the civil service, then the men in charge of departments may be bishops too. This is usual in the Vatican (Rome). The diocesan bishop is also responsible for ordaining new clergy in the diocese. He is officially in charge of selection and training, but normally delegates these jobs to others.

Groups of bishops are usually under the leadership of a specially chosen bishop who is a kind of president. In most cases this person is called an **archbishop**, but in some cases the title is that of presiding bishop, metropolitan, or patriarch. In the Roman Catholic church, the **Pope** is elected to a position which is superior to all other bishops,

A bishop of the Russian Orthodox Church, London

The Roman Catholic Bishop of Liverpool

An Archbishop in Russia

A Greek priest

patriarchs and archbishops. The title Pope is also found in Coptic churches, but a Coptic pope is only another sort of patriarch or archbishop and is not superior to other archbishops. Bishops therefore form the highest rank of the three main orders of clergy. Archbishops, patriarchs, and senior clergy with other titles like cardinals, are also bishops. Churches which have these three orders consider bishops to be essential for the continuance of the church. Some Protestant denominations, however, think differently, and either do not have bishops at all, or if they have them, consider them an optional extra. Some Methodists have bishops (Methodist Episcopal Church) who are senior clergy and administrators. They are not considered vital for the existence of the church and most Methodists do not have bishops at all. Presbyterians do not have bishops either but teach that the clergy act as bishops collectively. This means that they consider the office of a bishop so important that they share it out.

A bishop can usually be recognised during church rituals by the special clothes he wears. Roman Catholic and most Anglican bishops wear a mitre on their heads and carry a stave shaped like a shepherd's crook. Orthodox bishops wear a different kind of mitre which looks more like a crown, and their stave is not crook–shaped. Lutheran bishops are bareheaded in church.

Priest and People

Ordination sets a person apart from ordinary people, no matter whether called a priest or a minister or a pastor. In the European middle ages when most of the population were illiterate and few people had any education, the clergy stood out as educated people because of their training. The village priest was also the spokesman for his community in many cases, thus he came to be known as the person or 'parson' of the village. People looked up to him, asked him for advice about matters where education was needed, and usually respected him as an educated man, quite apart from his work as a priest in the church.

Now that education is widely available, however, the minister is not necessarily the most educated person in the community. This is true even in matters of religion, as laypeople, both men and women, can go and study theology if they want to. So the parson is losing this aspect of leadership, but of course still retains the authority and respect due to a leader in the church organisation and in presiding at religious services, visiting people in the parish and preaching.

In Greece, there has been a long tradition of schools for ordinary people, so the Greek (Orthodox) clergy were not always the only educated person in the village. The priest's position among the people owed much more to his ordination and to his priestly functions than to his general education.

The Job of the Minister

It is not easy to define a minister's work — as in a normal job description — and in any case different Christian groups and denominations have rather different ideas about ordination and just what it means to be ordained to holy orders.

The best way to study the work of a minister is to spend time with one and note down what he or she does. It helps obviously if you know what to look out for. The job can include a lot of things and there are different kinds of ministry. People usually think in the first place of the priest or pastor living in a parish, who has one, or maybe more, church congregations to look after. This almost certainly means that church members live in a parish, a fairly small area — say a village, or part of a town — and that there is a special church building in which Sunday (and other) services are to be held.

In addition to the normal rituals and services, the job includes a whole range of pastoral work, visiting people in their homes or at work, especially the sick and housebound, preparing people for marriage, or baptism or confirmation, and maybe looking after the running of Christian groups such as Bible study, prayer groups, youth clubs and a lot else. Of course there are likely to be some people to help him, who may be assistant clergy, often called curates, or may be laypeople (where 'lay' means not ordained). This is typical of Western Europe, North America and countries of the Third World whose churches have been influenced by them.

There are also ministers who have other kinds of work, such as teaching in a school or college, or as a prison or hospital chaplain or a chaplain to the armed forces or to industry. All these obviously involve some pastoral responsibilities, not unlike those of a parish minister. They are likely also to get many invitations to preach and to take services, including the eucharist, in chapels and churches.

For a lot of Christians the minister's function centres on pastoral work, preaching and the sacraments. The regular celebration of the eucharist is very important. For some Christians who have inherited protestant traditions, preaching is a more important function than the eucharist. Preaching is the proclamation of the word of God, based on scripture. Some Christian groups emphasise both the eucharist and preaching, and feel that God's word is given to them in both activities.

Christians who stress the importance of the sacraments obviously also stress the importance of ordination to the priesthood. They consider the order of priesthood to be indelible, which means it can never be taken away or abandoned. Allied to this thinking is the theology noted in Part Two which sees the eucharist as a sacrifice which only the priest may perform. A different view of the ordained ministry is that the position depends entirely on the job, and that when the job ends, say the pastor leaves the parish, then he or she is no longer a pastor. Of course he or she is ready perhaps for another pastoral post and it will not be necessary to have another ordination.

ACTIVITY

Exercises and questions to do on your own, or after discussion

Write down the answers to these questions:

1 Find out about local clergy in your area
   - What churches or denominations do they lead?
   - Do they include men and women?
   - Have they had special ordination?
2 Find out about the way in which clergy are ordained
   - Is there an ordination service?
   - Who does the ordaining?
   - Is there a ceremony when a minister starts a new job? (This may be called commissioning or induction)
   - How long is the training before ordination?
   - Have they had any follow–up training after ordination?
3 Find out what ordination allows them to do
   - What are they entitled to do that ordinary church members cannot?
   - Do they need a special licence or special permission to preach? to celebrate the eucharist? to hear confessions and give absolution?
   - Are non–ordained members allowed to do any of the above?
   - What happens when he or she retires?

ACTIVITY: as a group

Design a group project on ordination
EITHER: on the life and work of a minister
OR: on the ordination ceremony
Decide on a distinct contribution by each member of the group, according to his or her interests and skills, e.g. as photographer, artist, or musician.

Chapter Five

ANOINTING THE SICK

When someone is lying ill in bed all day, it is nice to have a visitor. Even when you feel too ill to talk, it is lovely to know that people out in daily life have not forgotten all about you, and still care whether you are around, and want to ask if you are getting better. The ritual which Christians call **anointing the sick**, or **unction** (means putting a special oil on someone's forehead and often hands as well), involves three things. The first is to visit the person who is ill; the second is prayer; and the third is the anointing. At the same time the visitor touches the sick person with his hands. This is usually called **laying on of hands** and is the same kind of thing as at confirmation and ordination, but with the special intention of helping the sick, and in the context of prayer for strengthening and healing.

When you are sad or upset or feeling bad, it can be good just to sit with a friend or workmate, not saying very much, but just being together. When your friend is upset, it helps just to put an arm on his or her shoulder. The comfort of the human touch is something we all appreciate in the right circumstances, just as much as the tiny child who runs to its mother and buries its face against her side.

The practice of anointing the sick goes back to the earliest Christian times, that is the New Testament. It has brought comfort and encouragement to those who were suffering illnesses over the centuries when many diseases were not understood and medical science was much more primitive than today. Maybe doctors were anyway not available. It is important to realise, however, that even in the best modern hospital and with excellent medical care, the simple act of the visit, the praying together and then the anointing bring great comfort, and because the sick person appreciates it, he or she wants to get better and is in a more relaxed frame of mind. The connection between physical illness and mental and spiritual stress and distress is still little understood, but there can be no doubt that it exists.

Of course prayers for healing and the laying on of hands can be done without any unction (oil) and often are.

Unction is traditional and several groups of Christians think of it as one of the seven sacraments. This is nothing to do with any idea that oil may have a direct healing effect perhaps on an open wound, the kind of injury which is today treated with modern medicines.

For centuries people only received unction when they were about to die, and the practice was then called **extreme unction** as the word extreme means last. Because unction was for so long associated with being at the point of death, people in some country districts are a bit afraid of it still. In many case the sick person also receives holy communion if he or she is able to. This, sometimes called **the last sacrament**, was believed to mean that the person was about to die.

In the present century, unction is used on the request of the sick person or the family also for less serious cases, and if the family feel that it will bring encouragement and strength. In the Bible, health and healing are often thought of together with forgiveness, and anointing the sick is thought of in this way still.

The anointing is done by a priest who has brought the specially prepared oil from the church, and it is usual to invite the sick person to make a confession first, after which the priest gives absolution (forgiveness from God, as described in Part Two under other sacraments). This is not necessary, however, and the ill person may be unable to speak or say very much.

EITHER — **Recall an occasion when you have either visited someone who was ill, or been visited when you were ill yourself.**

Write a page about what it felt like when the two people, one ill, one well, were together, and what you talked about, and so on.

OR — **Get to know a hospital chaplain or any local minister who does a lot of sick visiting.**

It is helpful to talk about the ministry to the sick, and about the ritual of anointing with oil, and this will be good whether the minister in fact uses unction or not. Many use prayer and touch without oil, and it is worth writing a page on this.

Chapter Six

FUNERAL

Have you every made a sandcastle at the sea–side? Or written names on the wet sand? Part of the excitement is to watch the tide come in and gradually all your work returns to sand. For a short while you can still see the little sticks and paper flags of your fortress, but these too are soon washed away.

So it is with the body after death. People die, just as animals die, and return again to clay and dust. But the Christian belief in life after death makes the sorrows of the mourners at a Christian funeral both an expression of love for the departed friend and the hope of meeting again in happier circumstances. To study Christian belief in the resurrection, including the resurrection of the body, you should look at the section on this topic in Part Four, pages 215-217.

ACTIVITY

Do this short exercise either alone or with a friend

Read two short passages from Genesis.

The first is the creation of mankind, **in Genesis 2.7**. The first man is described as being made from the dust of the earth.

The second verse to read is **Genesis 3.19** which is part of the so–called punishment of Adam, but describes vividly the death of someone who works the land.

Write a few lines about what each of these texts suggests about the human body.

This belief in the decay of the body as we know it lies behind Christian teaching about the resurrection, and the resurrection through Christ is all the more startling and important for Christians as a result.

That is why in the funeral service, the committal part (see below) nearly always includes the words: '*Earth to earth, ashes to ashes, dust to dust*'.

In countries which have a generally Christian cultural history, like Germany, Greece and Great Britain for example, most people have some kind of Christian ritual at a funeral. Even when the dead person has had little or no church connection, the family usually ask for a priest or minister to conduct a short service, and public cemeteries and crematoria have a minister on hand for this purpose. In fact local clergy of several denominations may get together and draw up a rota in order to share out this work. Obviously when the deceased has been a church member, the family will ask the minister of their own choice to come.

The subject of death and dying has recently become a frequent topic for discussion and project work in schools, including junior schools. So it is assumed that the emotions and feelings of those who mourn will have been already explored, and will therefore be reasonably familiar, even to those who have not themselves lost friends or family who were close to them.

Until almost the present century, Christians have preferred burial of the dead, rather than cremation. Jews and Muslims do too. The idea behind this is connected with the belief in the resurrection of the body. Obviously this is only a preference, and Christians have never believed that those saints and martyrs who were burned or eaten by lions suffered any disadvantage when it came to resurrection. So there are no doctrinal problems about how a corpse is to be disposed of, provided only that it is done reverently and lovingly so far as possible.

It feels good in a Christian community if the mortal remains of departed members, and they are still members of the community only thought of now as '*in the nearer presence of God*', can lie in ground near the church building itself. For this reason an enclosed area or churchyard was consecrated. The only condition for burial there was that the deceased must have been baptised.

In Part Four, a visit to a churchyard is suggested as an exercise, with notes on what to look out for. If you want to go at this stage, two things can be suggested.

ACTIVITY: on your own

The first applies to Church of England churchyards only (the majority in England): **see if there is a special area in which priests are buried**.

This is not common, but in some places priests are buried just outside the East window, i.e. near the altar. If there are graves also in the church which have a figure in stone on top, you might note which way they are lying. In some places in England it was the custom to bury priests the other way round from laypeople, in order to suggest that in death too they were leading their people to God.

The second applies **for all burial places: see how old the oldest grave is**.

An old churchyard

Many Christians now choose cremation instead of burial, and the ashes may be buried in a churchyard — there is still room for these, and the place marked with a small memorial stone or cross — or scattered over the consecrated ground.

All this means that the full funeral service takes place in two parts. The first part is in the church. It may begin with the mourners all waiting and the coffin being carried in for the start of the service, the minister walking in front of it, speaking passages from the Scripture which have been specially chosen. Alternatively, the coffin may be already in the church or chapel before the service begins, and the minister may read the Scripture sentences (as above) or they may be left out. Then the service proceeds with prayers and a hymn (sometimes several), and almost always there is a Bible reading and an address. Sometimes a friend of the deceased is invited to read and to give the address about her or him. (As the address is usually saying nice things about the deceased, it is also called the **eulogy** by some people). In some Christian communities a eucharist is celebrated, with intention and special prayers said for the dead person, to rest in peace, '*for the repose of the soul of (name of person)*'. This eucharist is called a **Requiem**, or **requiem mass**.

The second part of the service takes place outside or away from the church and is called the **committal**. If the body is to be buried in the churchyard, the coffin is carried out to the place where the grave has been dug in readiness. Special prayers are said and the coffin is lowered in. The burial place may in fact be some distance from the church, and may need a car journey, but the form of service is exactly the same. Some people have the tradition that the principal mourner should throw the first handful or trowelful of earth on the coffin, but this is not found everywhere.

Inside the chapel at a crematorium

For a cremation, this part of the service is similar, except that the coffin slides away inside the building. Often a curtain is drawn as this happens. The mourners are not outside but still in the chapel. This is the committal. It may be that both parts of the funeral take place in the same building which is of course the chapel at the crematorium.

It used to be the practice for prominent people, landowners, noblemen and so on, to leave money in their wills to buy a black cloak or other suitable clothes for all the tenants and villagers who would come to their funeral. People, suitably dressed would line the street as the coffin passed on a hearse drawn in the old days by horses which also had black feathers and harness, before crowding into the church. It is easy to see why this kind of thing was called *'funeral pomp'*. It is not seen nowadays in Britain, but occasionally a black–edged notice can be found in a continental newspaper, stating that the funeral of some notable has taken place, *'with the full rites of the Church'*, and listing the names of principal mourners, tenants and servants.

In West Africa, funeral notices are placed in the local paper and they usually include a photograph of the deceased. The notice is then repeated at the first anniversary, together with notice of a party to be held. This is not limited to Christian funerals, and illustrates how important traditional custom can be at times of crisis. The same goes for the traditional funeral dance after a Greek funeral. This is performed by men, not women, and is very dignified. It is still to be seen in parts of the Greek world. British soldiers in the First World War who were fighting alongside Greek troops, often witnessed this special dance after a battle. But the tradition is older than Christianity and has been adopted into the ritual for the death of Christians.

One Line Answers

(Write answers to these questions in one line or two)

1 Why is the font often placed near the door of the church?
2 What is meant by *'total immersion'*?
3 Name one denomination in which baptism is by total immersion.
4 Give one promise which is normally made by the candidate or the candidate's parents at baptism.
5 What is a godparent in relation to Christian baptism?
6 What is meant by *'believer's baptism'*?
7 Name one Christian group which do not practise baptism.
8 Why in some churches is a candle given to the family of the newly baptised?
9 What is the significance of a new name at baptism?
10 Name two meanings for the use of water at baptism.
11 Why do some Christians think that the Exodus is like Christian baptism?

12 What is the common name for the ceremony Methodists call *Public Reception into Full Membership*?
13 Name one denomination in which children are admitted to holy communion before they are confirmed.
14 Name one Christian denomination in which confirmation is administered by the parish minister (i.e. not by a bishop).
15 What is the normal age for confirmation in the Orthodox churches?
16 What is First Communion, and in which denomination is this specially celebrated?
17 Why are prayers to the Holy Spirit offered at confirmation?
18 What is the significance of laying hands on the heads of candidates at confirmation?
19 What is meant by the phrase *baptism in the spirit*?
20 How do Christians justify monogamy?
21 Name one ritual which is only found in Orthodox wedding ceremonies.
22 Why do Christians want to be married in church?
23 What is celibacy?
24 Name one denomination which does not have married bishops.
25 Name two things that ordination authorises a priest to do, in the Roman Catholic and Anglican churches.
26 What is meant by minor orders?
27 A Bible is given to the new priests at an Anglican ordination: what is the significance of this act?
28 Name two things outside church services which are part of the work of a parish minister.
29 Name the three orders of Christian ministry (Anglican, Orthodox, Roman Catholic).
30 Name one Christian ritual which might be administered to the sick.
31 What is the usual name for a eucharist which is celebrated in memory of a deceased Christian?
32 What single sacrament must a person have received to permit burial of the body in a churchyard?
33 What is being done when the minister says, *Earth to earth, ashes to ashes, dust to dust*?
34 Why do some Christians prefer burial to cremation?
35 What is meant by the *committal* at a Christian funeral?

CHRISTIAN BELIEFS AND THEIR MEANING FOR CHRISTIANS

An agreed statement of beliefs is called a creed. This Part describes what Christian creeds mean and how they are used. Many Christian beliefs and doctrines also come up in Parts One, Two and Three of this book. For each section of Part Four, this part, we recommend that you also look back to the relevant sections earlier in the book.

Chapter One

BELIEFS AND BELIEVING

If you were asked to say briefly what Christianity is, quite a lot of people would begin by trying to list Christian beliefs as if beliefs were the main essentials. Many Christians, however, would say that while beliefs are important and in the form of creeds perhaps even very important, the essentials for being a Christian are how you live and what you do, together with commitment to the Christian community, that is a church.

Festivals are important for Christians, and these are studied in Part One. So is worship which is the subject of Part Two. Every religious community has rites of passage which accompany their members virtually from birth to death and celebrate turning points in their lives: these were the subject of Part Three. But the way Christians act in the world, and react to the world, both among themselves and with non–Christians, is also an essential aspect of their religion. This is the theme of Part Five. All these aspects imply beliefs, but they are not in themselves simply the result of particular beliefs.

There are many reasons why beliefs are held to be important, notably that people have died for them and in some places Christians still do. In addition to this, there are historical reasons why people often think that beliefs, rather than rituals or behaviour, are the essence of Christianity.

The philosophy of the pre–Christian Greek thinker Aristotle had been ignored by the Christian church. His writings were suddenly rediscovered in western Europe in the twelfth century. There were special reasons for this which are beyond the scope of this book. But the philosophy of Aristotle led to new developments in Christian teaching from the 13th to the 20th century, especially among Roman Catholics. Christian theologians wanted to do more than show the reasoning of Aristotle did not contradict Christianity. They wanted to prove that Christian beliefs were true, using the philosophy of the ancient Greeks to support the Bible. The result was that educated Christians in western and central Europe started thinking up intellectual reasons for what they believed, and they became much more argumentative as a result! The invention of printing in the fifteenth century and the spread of literacy allowed more people to join in.

Delegates and their families at a World Council of Churches Meeting

About the same time the Reformation grew out of protest movements against the power of the Roman church. A number of protestant churches and groups were formed. Each of these tried to state what they believed and to give reasons for their protests in a form of words. These statements were called **confessions** or sometimes just **creeds**.

The Christian Council of Nicaea in 325 had drawn up the form of words on which what is today called the Nicene Creed was later based. This creed applies to all Christians, east and west. The last section of this part tells you about the forms of creed which are most commonly used in this country. Other famous creeds and confessions include the Confession of Augsburg in 1530 (Lutheran) and the Westminster Confession of 1646 (Presbyterian).

ACTIVITY: as a group

Do a brainstorming exercise on the words belief and believe.
Collect together different kinds of believing, for instance cases where you might say, 'I believe the Browns live at number 77', as well as 'I believe in democracy'.

- See how many classes of belief you have collected.
- Do any beliefs make much difference to the way you live?
- Which ones, if any, are important enough for you or for those who hold them to risk persecution and imprisonment, and maybe even death?

Hitler giving the Nazi salute at a huge rally in Berlin

Belief and Action

Creeds are mainly about belief in God, Jesus Christ, the Holy Spirit and other doctrines which all figure in this section. But Christians also believe in certain types of behaviour in relation to other people (as well as alone). This obviously can have social and political implications. To give an example from history: Hitler's hatred of Jews was definitely racial and not religious. In 1933 the Nazis in Germany decreed that no Christian pastor who was of Jewish descent was permitted to minister to a congregation of Christians who were not of Jewish descent. A number of Christians objected to this because they believed that Jesus Christ does not favour any race or people above others. Therefore they issued a statement of their own in opposition to the Nazis which is known as the Barmen Declaration, and so the Confessing Church was born, in February 1934. This is a good example of the bond between belief and action.

ACTIVITY: as a group

Christianity from the earliest days has been against racism and sexism, although Christians do not always live up to these ideals today, any more than they all did in the time of St Paul.

1 Look at what St Paul says about '*all one in Christ Jesus*' in Galatians 3.28.
2 Discuss in the group: Could this be applied by Christians today? If so, what are the circumstances, in this country and elsewhere?
3 What has belief in Jesus got to do with political and social matters?

Stalin

Sometimes people are put in prison for their beliefs. Or people start wars, especially religious wars, for the sake of their beliefs. But can beliefs really make such a difference? In political terms, communism and the capitalism of big business are strongly opposed. In Europe of the 1930s Hitler got a lot of support from people who were not themselves fascists but gave him some support because they were so strongly opposed to the beliefs and practices of communism, at that time only to be reckoned with in its Stalinist Soviet form. Yet the kinds of government which Hitler's Germany and Stalin's Russia produced seem to have been equally harsh, authoritarian and oppressive in controlling what ordinary people could eat, do, earn, read, learn, and where they were or were not allowed to travel.

ACTIVITY: as a group

Think about the following and discuss in your small group:

Make a list of countries where people can be put in prison for their beliefs.

At the same time name the groups which governments are trying to suppress or get rid of.

Then each person in the group chooses one example from your list, and prepares a clear statement, saying what the people who are getting rough treatment believe in, and why the government think these beliefs are harmful and ought to be suppressed.

These can be read out to the group or to the whole class.

ACTIVITY: on your own

Think about one such group whom you think you agree with.

Say what you would do if a government was trying to suppress the group you belong to.

- Would you try to leave your country, and your family and friends?
- Would another country accept you?
- Which would be most likely?
- Write about a page about this.

Chapter Two

THE BEGINNINGS OF CHRISTIAN CREEDS

The first disciples were convinced that Jesus rose from the dead. This is very clear. As well as this, during the time he lived with them, they felt he was a unique revelation of the love and purposes of God. After the ascension experience they felt him with them still as a spiritual and strengthening presence. Two factors stand out. These can be called belief in the resurrection and belief in the divinity of Christ — that God was in Christ bodily.

This early preaching met with difficulties. The first Christians felt that they must spread the good news (gospel) because people only had one chance and the Lord might return in judgement at any time. But they met strong opposition wherever they spoke. St Paul writes that the gospel was a scandal to the Jews and to the Greeks foolishness. You can read about this in I Corinthians 1 and 2, but the phrase actually comes in 1.23. You can find accounts of how they spread the message if you read the Acts of Apostles. All this means that we can know something of what Christians believed (and believe) from listening to preaching.

Christians faced rejection, riots and then persecution, and yet many converts joined them. Why were the Jews scandalised? Their strong belief in one unique God, who is very distinct from man, meant that it was blasphemy for any human being to be thought of as divine. Of course people with spiritual power from God they believed in, like the kings and prophets of the Old Testament. Some of the Jews also believed in resurrection for everyone at the end of time. The Greeks on the other hand (the Jews thought of all non–Jews as 'Greeks') were quite used to the idea of gods walking about on the earth and of heroes, both men and women, becoming divine, but the thought of resurrection from the dead seemed absurd to them and therefore foolish nonsense.

Build–it–yourself Creed

ACTIVITY: on your own

Find Paul's speech at Athens as related in Acts 17.16–34. Select the main points and list them.

- Could your list form the basis for a statement of Christian belief?

Now do the same with Peter's speeches in Acts 3.12–26 and Acts 10.34–43. (Acts also has longer speeches ascribed to Peter and also to Stephen).

Write down in single sentences what appears to be **the minimum belief for Christians.**

It ought to be said that there were no tape recorders around then and no-one has found Peter's or Paul's notes for their speeches (if they ever used any). So the speeches in Acts are the writer's estimate of what they are likely to have said. Of course this means that these speeches really do represent preaching by the apostles. These speeches must have made a deep impression on converts and many were still alive when Acts was written.

ACTIVITY: on your own

For an exercise rather more demanding than the previous one, **read Philippians 2.6–11 (notice how to spell Philippians) on the subject of the divinity of Jesus Christ, and I Corinthians 15 on the resurrection** — read especially I Corinthians 15.3–7, and 15.12–15.

These are not preachings but originally the actual words written by St Paul. The passage from Philippians may be a kind of hymn which was used in liturgy (church services).

. After studying these passages, **write a few lines of Christian doctrine on each of these two subjects**
the divinity of Jesus Christ
the resurrection

Saying What You Mean and Meaning What You Say

Many people today would think it very odd to sit down and write a creed or even just a list of beliefs. Not all beliefs are religious, and even religious ones are not just in the mind, but can have social and political and economic implications. Some people just say, '*Oh that's all theology*', when they mean they don't want to listen to arguments or examples which they think are quite irrelevant to what they want to do. Theology has got a bad name and perhaps using this book will go some way to change that. But it is important to stress that beliefs can be put into words. Words are the means of public communication and putting things into words helps to get ideas and beliefs clearer in our minds. Christians have certainly found that.

ACTIVITY: on your own

Get yourself somewhere where you can have about twenty minutes without interruption. You need pen and paper. **Write a page or more on '*What I believe*'.**

Try to time this, so you spend at least fifteen minutes and not more than thirty minutes.

Keep this piece of paper for future use. Never mind at present if you find the result a bit confusing!

A candidate in an election for parliament

People go into politics for different reasons, but it is obvious that if you think something ought to be done about housing, roads or social services, you could lobby your M.P. or local councillors, especially when an election is coming up. If you feel strongly enough on a matter of principle, you could talk about it, find others who think the same, and then perhaps stand for election yourself. You would make sure that the electors knew what you were standing for. To do this you would have to use words, in your speaking and in what you wrote. Someone who is standing for Parliament usually writes an election manifesto not just to give personal details, but also to say what needs to be done. These are most likely the policies of the party — the reason why you joined in the first place. There will also be local issues.

When Something Needs to Be Done

ACTIVITY

As a group of seven or eight

For this exercise, form slightly larger groups than usual, perhaps up to eight.

Tackle a topical problem of housing, education or health, or some other topic of current interest in your locality. Form yourselves into a shadow town (or district) council and plan what you would like to do about it.

Draw up a plan, be sure to consider the costs, in money, time and resources that will be needed as far as you can estimate.

When you have done this, **jointly write an address or appeal to the voters** which you think will get them to vote for you as a group. You should include not just policies, but also matters of principle, in fact what you stand for.

If you are forming a group to run the council, or if you are joining a group which feels as you do about important issues, then it is not going to be easy to work with anyone who thinks quite differently and has principles which are opposed to yours. Thus a statement of policy can serve to exclude people who do not agree with you. The same is true of the creeds of Christianity. A statement of belief works to define the community of all those who accept the statement, and at the same time keeps out anyone who is unwilling to accept it. If anyone is not quite decided, this could be difficult, but in practice many Christians are not totally clear about all the doctrines their church expects them to agree with. The same goes for those who belong to political parties.

If people know that you belong to a church, or to a political party, they will come to expect certain attitudes and reactions. Fellow members of your group are people you can trust. At least you ought to be able to trust them within certain definite limits, because you know what they stand for. You would also expect their deepest beliefs and their principles to be consistent, that is not to contradict each other.

In the history of Christian creeds certain forms of words have been agreed in order to make clear what Christians believe and what they ought to believe. At the same time these words have excluded those who cannot agree to them. This means that creeds, like political statements,

Surrey County Council holding a meeting

have the effect of making people decide to join the group (church, party) or to leave it. Those who have refused to accept the creeds worked out at councils have been made excommunicate (i.e. refused holy communion) and eventually called **heretics**. This is a matter of history.

ACTIVITY: as a group

Take another look at the piece of paper on which you wrote 'What I believe'.

- Are you willing to show it to your small group?
- If you are, discuss what you wrote and see if there are matters of principle, or hopes, or other things which some, or maybe all of you share.

Here are some of the things written by school pupils who have done this exercise:

'My first thought was that I didn't believe in anything in particular: here are a few of the things which after a few minutes thought I discovered I believed in . . .'

'I started by writing down everything I thought I believed. On reading these through, I realised that every few lines I was contradicting myself'.

'When I sat down and thought about this it struck me that the word "believe" has much more power and strength than I had at first imagined. It is not just a case of writing down a few things that seemed to be good ideas. I think that what you "believe" is the basis of the way you run your own life'.

Why Words are Important

In our everyday life we use words to express ourselves and to share our feelings, thoughts and intentions. But as well as enabling us to express ourselves, putting things into words should help us to clarify our thinking and to be consistent. In the Christian religion also, words are used both to express or communicate and also to make things clearer and more consistent. Both these points (communication and clarification) are important in the tradition because they suggest to us how Christians understand God's dealings with them.

One of the surprising things in the Bible is the way in which Jews and Christians hear God speaking to them. Sometimes it is in actual words by means of the prophets, sometimes in answer to prayer, and sometimes by happenings which are understood as specially significant, i.e. something happens which is thought to reveal God's will.

This tradition is so strong in the Bible that individuals can claim to hear and even to 'see' God's words. Words are considered the prime means of communication and therefore the way God reveals his will, plans or warnings.

In the New Testament and Christian tradition Jesus is called 'the Word of God'. This is meant to show that he somehow expresses what God is like in his dealings with humans and that in Jesus God has communicated to mankind — and continues to do so.

Before you go any further, it would be useful to think out how the idea of words and speech from God is used in the Bible of Judaism, that is the Old Testament. This will not be easy if you are not fairly familiar with it, so here are some examples. God spoke to the prophets. This experience was so vivid that sometimes they spoke of 'seeing' God's word. God spoke to Moses and the Ten Commandments are actually called 'Ten Words'. Then the picture of God's word creating everything is found in many places in the Bible, especially some of the psalms.

ACTIVITY: on your own

Read Deuteronomy 4.10–14. This is part of a sermon about the commandments given to Moses for the Israelites at Sinai (Horeb).
Now answer these questions:

- How many times is speaking mentioned?
- What is the voice contrasted with?
- Why do you think this is important?

One of the most basic texts for Jews is found in Deuteronomy 6.4: '*Hear O Israel, the Lord our God is one Lord*'. Notice again the emphasis on direct speech as opposed to an image or written message which you could look at or not as you might please.

Have you ever tried to talk to someone who did not speak your language? Imagine a stranger comes to your door: he or she seems to need help, but cannot say anything. You say, '*What do you want?*' What do you expect in reply? After a few inarticulate noises you decide that the stranger is dumb, and you get a pen and paper. The stranger writes, '*Parlez–vous francais?*' or '*Sprechen Sie Deutsch?*' No doubt some of you can cope with this. But if he or she writes '*milate ellenika;*' how will you cope? Do you even know what language this is?

When is the voice of God found in the gospels? It might help you to refer back to the section on Baptism.

The 10 sections in this Chapter are based on Articles of the Creed.

1 The Trinity

Belief in God as Trinity is fundamental for Christians. What is to be understood as man's relationship to God in Jesus Christ and in the Spirit depends on some notion of the Trinity. Trinity means threeness and oneness combined, and St Patrick (approx. 389–461) is said to have picked a shamrock in order to explain the Trinity to his converts, the natives of Ireland. This leaf is a picture of how the threeness can easily be seen, yet all are at the same time one thing, the leaf itself. If you pulled the bits apart you would no longer have a leaf, yet every bit of it is the same stuff as the whole leaf. The shamrock may not be the perfect model to explain the Trinity today, but it meant so much to the Irish that the shamrock has become a national symbol.

The doctrine of the Trinity came about because Christians felt themselves impressed in two different ways, by reason and experience. Reason leads thinkers to believe in one God (if God is to be worth believing in) because a bevy of gods and goddesses cannot be consistently all–powerful, that is without squabbling among themselves. Monotheism (this means belief in one God only) is also, of course, a strong Jewish tradition which Christians inherited. For thousands of years Jews have repeated '*Hear O Israel, the Lord our God is one Lord*'.

But against this, the experience of the first Christians was deeply formed by Jesus Christ who appeared not simply as a superhero (crucifixion is not a good fate for superheroes) but expressed the love and humility of God so powerfully that they were convinced that God was active and living in him. The same happened when they experienced the power of God in the Spirit. This meant that reason pulled one way and experience another. All sorts of people became Christians, including some philosophers and thinkers with a formal education, and the doctrine of the Trinity emerged.

ACTIVITY

Either on your own or as a group

Read again the paragraph above.

- What made the early Christians want to believe in one God and more than one (two or three) at the same time?
- Do you think that reason is a better guide than experience?

ACTIVITY: on your own

Write down as many words as you can think of that refer to threeness, for instance tricycle, threesome and some others.

Write about half a page about these words, and say whether any of them could be applied to the Christian idea of God. If not, why not?

The picture shows a famous Russian icon by A. Rublev, and it is called the Old Testament Trinity. It refers to the '*three men*' who mysteriously met Abraham (Genesis 18) and spoke to him as God. Is there anything special about the number three in Genesis 18? Rublev has tried to tie them to the Christian idea of the Trinity by the way he has painted the icon. Can you say how he has done this?

For centuries many Christians have paid special devotion to Mary the mother of Jesus. There are many pictures and other representations of her, either with the baby Jesus or alone. One or two devotional pictures show God the Father, Jesus, and Mary (often called Our Lady), as a kind of threesome in the holy family. Why do you think this could be very misleading? Who do we really mean when we talk about the holy family?

If you want to take the doctrine of the Trinity further, two more points must be made in addition to what has already been said about trying to match reason with experience. The first is that if man is made in the image of God then there must be some kind of similarity between God and humankind, in spite of all the human faults and shortcomings we all know about. This suggests that qualities which we recognise as good in individual people and in relationships between people can reflect something which is part of what God is like. This kind of thinking about God is called **analogy**. But of course God is not really like human beings, so no analogy can be thought to fit exactly.

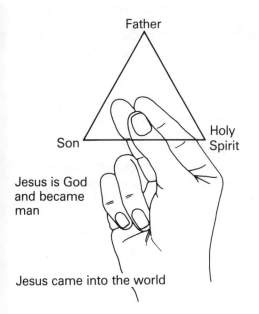

Orthodox Christians remind themselves of the Holy Trinity every time they make the sign of the cross.

Father

Son

Holy Spirit

Jesus is God and became man

Jesus came into the world

So the first point then is that if you take what seem to be good aspects of human nature and relationships, you can apply them to God. But the second point is that nothing made can be superior in understanding to its maker. The gap between man and God is so wide, that any human quality can only be reckoned as a characteristic of God in a very different sense. Just what the difference is, of course, always presents a problem.

The Christian doctrine of analogy can be put another way by saying that God is thought of as the source of all perfections. Although the nature of God is way beyond all human understanding, yet as far as it is possible for people to experience and know God, the divine qualities must include at least all the good qualities we recognise in ordinary life. This means that God is beautiful, just, loving, powerful, far–sighted and so on, all to a perfect degree. In order to help sort this out, it could be useful to consider qualities in human life which we think ought also to form aspects of what God must be like.

ACTIVITY: on your own

Make a list of all the things in life which you think make it most worth living.

If you like you can head your list '*Things to be thankful for*' but do not think about having to be grateful to anyone in particular: just aspects of life you think are the best.

ACTIVITY: as a group

Imagine that you have parachuted from a plane over the sea, or have been shipwrecked, and come safely to a lovely island where there is plenty of food and water and the weather is good, but you are all on your own.
- Discuss what you would most miss, and what you would like most if you were there for a year or more.
- Do most of the group agree?
- Did anyone think it funny to be talking in a group about what it would be like to be alone?

ACTIVITY: on your own

As a follow-up write about a page on of the things you missed most on your deserted island.

Try to describe how the good thing you did not have might tell us a bit about what God is like. This could be difficult, and need a lot of thought, but it depends a bit on what it was you came up with!

Keep this piece of paper for use a little later on.

Trinity means tri–unity: one God but three presentations. Each of these presentations is called a person. The description, '*three persons and one God*', uses the word '*person*' in its sense as a distinct representation (e.g. a particular person played by an actor in a drama). The doctrine of the Trinity is hard and in the end beyond human understanding. Many Christians have not thought too much about it and either see Jesus and the Spirit as simple manifestations of God, as if God appears in different forms or even disguises. Or they just think of three gods (or maybe two if the Spirit seems a little vague), one of whom is the chief, and Jesus a kind of superbeing who does what God says but is really on a lower level. Both these views (and many similar) have been ruled to be wrong by official Christian councils who drew up the creeds.

In talking about doctrine, it is strictly true that Christians are trinitarians, i.e. they believe in God as trinity. A number of congregations, however, who were influential particularly in the nineteenth century in Britain, North America and other countries where they did a lot of social work, call themselves Unitarians. They deny that God could be both three and one, and they regard Jesus as a good man who should be an example to us all, whether we are Christian or non–Christian. Unitarians are usually called Christians, although this would not be admissible from a strictly doctrinal point of view.

The Need for Company

> Three and one are numbers, finite numbers. All the numbers you can think of are finite, and yet God is always thought of as infinite. This means that God must essentially be beyond any number that we could possibly imagine.

When you did the exercise about the deserted island, did many of you think that what you most needed was human company? Look back at what you wrote then. Companionship is certainly seen as a very important quality of human life. At its best community is a good quality which we would expect to be in some way part of God.

It was said a little earlier that all human perfections are thought to find some counterpart in the being of God, and therefore they tell us something of what God is like. Now if society is one of these perfections then God must be plural in some respect. Perhaps the heart of the Christian gospel is the deep belief that '**God is love**', but love cannot be expressed in total isolation. So this is another reason for Christians to think that God is two or more persons or personalities within the oneness of the divine being, and is therefore important for an understanding of the Trinity. The Holy Spirit fits into this scheme as the third person of the trinity, although it is a matter of history that the main arguments about the Trinity centred on the relationship of God and Father and God the Son. More will be said about God the Son (Jesus Christ) in the sections on Incarnation, on the Person and Work of Christ, and on the Spirit.

Models or pictures or ways of thinking about the Trinity have been thought up by many Christians. At one time the so–called psychological model of the trinity was popular, and it goes back to St Augustine of Hippo (354–430). This model pictures the Holy Spirit as the mutual love expressed between Father and Son.

Ways of Saying What God is Like

Christian theology teaches that although God is by nature infinitely removed and different from anything created which includes humankind, it is still possible to know something of the character of God from two sources. One is the work of God in creation and in history, and the other which follows from this is to take the best human qualities and think that God has these qualities too, but in an infinitely better form. This is a way of saying both that God is like man and at the same time that God is not like man. The unlikeness is often represented by saying not, that is using negative words. God is not mortal, not finite and so on.

ACTIVITY: on your own

Read these two verses from a hymn popular in English–speaking churches.

> Immortal, invisible, God only wise,
> In light inaccessible hid from our eyes,
> Most blessed, most glorious, the Ancient of Days,
> Almighty, victorious, thy great name we praise.

> Unresting, unhasting, and silent as light,
> Nor wanting, nor wasting, thou rulest in might;
> Thy justice like mountains high soaring above
> Thy clouds which are fountains of goodness and love.

Make two columns on a piece of paper, and head one '*Positive Descriptions of God*' and the other '*Negative Descriptions of God*'.

Read through the two verses carefully and note each thing said about God in one column or the other.

It will be obvious that '*nor wasting*' and '*inaccessible*' are both negative descriptions, but you will have to make your own mind up about '*hid from our eyes*' and '*silent as light*'.

You should end up with quite a lot in both columns.

Now compare notes with other members of your group. Can you agree to sort out any differences?

Notice that the writer of this hymn (W. Chalmers Smith, 1824–1908) has arranged the descriptions in groups of three in each of lines 1, 2, and 3 in the first verse, and in lines 1 and 2 of the second verse. This is because it is a hymn to God the Holy Trinity. Each of the descriptions apply to each of the three persons, Father, Son and Holy Spirit, without any difference or inequality.

Representing the Trinity

Representations of God as Trinity are not very common. Tri–unity can of course be symbolised by a shamrock, or a leaf of clover (trefoil). A triangle can also be used to stand for the Trinity.

More often God is represented as Father (see page 192) or Son or (less frequently) as Holy Spirit. If the three persons of God are to be represented then God as creator has the look of a man, God as saviour is shown either by a cross or as the lamb of sacrifice, and God as life–giving spirit by something which conveys the sense of movement. This can be shown in stone or stained glass by flame or wind or water or clouds, or as a bird in rapid flight. Sometimes the Spirit is shown as the bond of love or link between Father and Son, and this might be in the form of a rainbow.

In Jewish tradition, God must not be represented by any figure or shape. God speaks, and is therefore perceived as a voice. The story of the baptism of Jesus (see Part Three, Chapter 1) illustrates this neatly. As Jesus comes up out of the water, there is the divine voice and at the same time the dove comes down quickly upon him. This is a symbolic representation of the Trinity.

189

When thinking about God as Trinity, Christians often talk about believing and trusting in '*God the Father who created me and all the world; God the Son who redeemed me and all mankind; and God the Holy Spirit who inspires and guides the people of God*'. But if God is one, then these differences are only a kind of shorthand or picture language, because God is the creator, redeemer and inspirer of all. Bible texts actually speak of the Spirit being active in creation, and Jesus too.

God is reckoned by Christians to be the creator of heaven and earth. This is just another way of saying everything that there is. Obviously the way God is thought of as creating is different from what we mean when we talk about humans creating something. But there is some similarity all the same. It is possible to think of the creator as a divine watchmaker who makes the universe like a perfect machine, winds it up (or puts in a superlonglife battery), and then leaves it to carry on working. But the Christian understanding of creation requires more than this, and God is seen as sustaining or keeping the world and all the galaxies going all the time.

ACTIVITY: on your own

Look at this picture, painted on wet plaster (fresco) on the ceiling of the Sistine Chapel (in the Vatican, Rome) by Michelangelo (Michelangiolo Buonarroti) some time between 1508 and 1512.

Based on the Biblical account from Genesis 2.7, we see God breathing life into Adam by his touch. God appears as a figure of tremendous power and wisdom, and his human form is to emphasise that Man (Adam means mankind, the human race, in Hebrew) is made in the image of God. On the other side of God we see the idea of woman, that is Eve. She has not been created yet, but exists as a kind of plan or idea in the mind of God.

With the picture in front of you, write answers to these questions

1 What separates Adam from God?
2 What is passing between them?
3 What is Eve looking at?
4 What does this picture suggest about the future relationship between Adam and Eve? — between all men and women?
5 Do you personally agree with your answer to 4?

In spite of what this picture may suggest, the Christian doctrine of creation is not really about how things began, but rather to explain that everything is dependent on God. The universe has its origin in God (even if this is somehow before or outside time), and God is active in keeping it in operation, no matter how regular and predictable this may be.

Human Responsibility

Human inventions and discoveries have given mankind the ability to control a lot of what goes on in the world. This power has become much greater in the last 150 years, yet people have felt some sense of responsibility for thousands of years. Humans are able to think about the environment and universe in a way that other animals do not seem able to. They also have a sense of right and wrong: this means that moral choices must be taken seriously and that human beings are responsible for the consequences.

ACTIVITY: on your own

Read the two stories of creation at the beginning of Genesis. The first is Genesis chapter 1, and the second chapter 2.4–25. Both stories represent creation as a sequence of events.
  Write answers to these questions:

1 At what stage in chapter 1 are human beings made? At what stage in the story in chapter 2?
2 What is the point of putting the creation of the human race in the particular place we find it in each story?
3 What did the people who put these two accounts together have in mind?
4 Did they aim for the same effect or for different ones?
5 Is there any suggestion in either story that human beings have special duties or responsibilities towards the rest of creation?
6 If your answer to 5 is 'Yes', make two lists of these, one headed 'Chapter 1' and the other 'Chapter 2'.

ACTIVITY: as a group

Compare your lists with others in your small group.
  Now make a new list that you can all agree on, combining the contents of both lists, and cutting out any duplication.
  Discuss whether you think any of these duties and responsibilities could apply in space, on other planets, in other galaxies.

God the Father

The creed speaks of '*God the Father almighty, maker of heaven and earth*'. The word Father is not only an attempt to make the force behind creation into some kind of personal being. The effect is first to stress that in the Christian view, all people, animals, plants, in fact everything in all the galaxies, are dependent on God. And second, Christians want to stress that God, like an ideal father, takes an interest in what he has made, so there is a two–sided relationship between God and all creatures. Christians say it is important to be aware of this.

When the creed speaks of God the Father creating '*all things visible and invisible*' this phrase can be understood as meaning absolutely everything. This must include subatomic particles as well as endless galaxies in space. Further, we could take '*seen and unseen*' to mean: perceptible and imperceptible; or concrete and abstract; or (for the philosophically minded) particular and universal.

Because of the emphasis that God created men and women in his image, God as father is usually represented in Christian pictures as a man. If he is an old man with a white beard, this is a reference to the vision of Daniel. More often God is shown as a man at the height of his powers. The Jews never represent God in any picture or image. Instead, the Bible speaks of God as a voice. This idea is found in Christianity also. For instance, in plays based on the Bible story, God is often a voice rather than an actor on the stage.

3 Incarnation

You may be at a college or school where they have a tie or a badge. Even if you do not wear the school badge, people who know you will probably think of you a 'one of them', that is one of the lot who go to that school, or who live on that estate. If you have ever suffered from being labelled in this way — or it may be that the label is so good that it is a great help to you — you will know what it feels like to be a representative of something.

Some school badges

Here is an introductory activity which gives a new slant on an old problem.

ACTIVITY: as a group

This is a simulation game. You need at least three characters. These are the main ones. Other members of the group can either advise, or take on minor parts (e.g. secretary, engineer's mate) which help but do not obscure the main roles.

The first person can be called Les. Les is an engineer who works for a big oil company which sells petrol, diesel, heating oil, lubricating oils and allied products. One of the company's customers, a big retail shop or department store, has called Les out because their heating system has packed up and they blame the heating oil. Les has come to fix it, and arrives wearing the company's badge and driving a van with the oil company's name on the side.

The second person is the manager of the shop. He or she is so angry that he won't let Les go down to the boilers to see what's wrong, but keeps shouting and blaming the oil company and the oil.

At last Les is able to phone back to the **manager at the oil company** (branch manager) and get him or her to come out in a company car (with the badge on its side) and try to calm down the customer enough to let Les get on with finding out what is wrong.

Act out this scene.

When you have finished, discuss it and try to analyse what happened.

Think of these specific points and get one of the group to write down answers to each when you have talked about them:

1 Do the engineer and the manager represent the oil company?
2 Does how they act, what they do and say, tell us anything about the product, in this case heating oil? Or about the firm?
3 Will the customer want to go on buying their heating oil from this company after the scene you have acted, or will they change to another supplier?
4 What might the customer tell his friends in the pub (or club) about the 'X and Y' oil company? that is, about the company, not about the engineer and branch manager as individuals.
5 Would it be fair to say that Les, the engineer, somehow is the 'X and Y' company as far as those who meet her or him are concerned?

ACTIVITY: on your own

In the light of all this,
EITHER **write one to two pages about the impressions the customer is likely to have formed once he or she has calmed down.**
OR **write a letter to the 'X and Y' oil company to apply for a job.**
To do this you must think that you would like a job with them, and have formed (from the scene you acted) some idea of what they would be like to work for. Address your letter to the Branch Manager.

God Becomes Man in Jesus Christ

If you have already worked through Part One on Festivals, you will remember the picture language about *'horizontal and vertical dimensions'* and the diagram that went with it. In any case it is a good idea to look back now to Part One, Chapter 3.

The exercise you have just done indicates one possible way in which a single individual can be taken for a large and powerful concern, in this case as representative of an oil company. The point to stress is that the personnel (reps and other employees) 'tell' the public what the firm is like, not in words only, but in what they do and in their attitudes. In this way the disciples felt that Jesus showed them what God is like, in fact that he was God.

The incarnation is central for Christianity. It is important to see that this must not be pictured as God putting on a disguise in order to spy on people, nor is it God in fancy dress, just able to pop off home again if things get difficult or embarrassing. In fact this was one of the temptations which Jesus faced straight after baptism.

Jesus became man, not man in general but a particular person with parents, family, friends and other contacts. He also had enemies, in particular political and social ones. Eventually he was arrested, sent for trial, and executed by crucifixion, the usual Roman (gentile) punishment for serious crime.

A Fact–finding Mission

This subsection has been planned to bring out another aspect of what incarnation means in practice.

ACTIVITY: as a group

You are worried about people who are homeless, both single people living on the street and homeless families. **You want to do something about it.**

Think about this together for a few minutes. It is obvious that the homeless need a home. Or is it as simple as that? Are there other important questions like, where? what kind? at what cost? and so on. If you really want to find answers to these and similar questions, what will you do?

In your group of four to six, try to explore this problem further — **You all want to find out about the needs of the homeless** (or if you like you could choose some other minority group who are in difficulties), and you really want to be able to put things right if you possibly can. But of course mistakes can be expensive, so it is no good finding homes that are too small, or too big, or too expensive, or in the wrong place, so there is going to be quite a lot of research to do.

- So, how do you go about trying to find out?
- You could try asking homeless people, or some of them.
- How do you choose who to ask?
- Are they really going to tell you about their long–term needs or what just happens to be worrying them at the moment?

Perhaps talking to some homeless people (like an investigation on the telly) is not enough, although obviously it is better than nothing.

Having nowhere to live may turn out not to be a simple problem, but for many people it is one aspect of something else, perhaps a whole list of difficulties.

Think out what these might be and make a list of them.

A homeless man with all his possessions

Your list probably includes things to do with health, unemployment, family and loss of hope. In fact despair could be the worst aspect, and the biggest obstacle to finding a solution, because an attitude of mind often affects all you do.

So the task you have now got to face is a double one: first, how can you really find out what it's like to be without a home, and second, how can you show you care? These two are connected, because it is only when people trust you and believe that you care that they are going to let you see what it is really like.

The suggestion now is that you should become homeless yourself (or yourselves, but you will be very noticeable as a group) and share the hardships, the insecurity, the homeless life, even when the weather is bad. Think, and discuss how you would do this. Could you be 'homeless' for a day? Can you be homeless when you've actually got a nice home somewhere? Can you be both homeless and not homeless, or both employed and unemployed at the same time? And what would you do when you had finished, write a report?

Do you think any of these people are homeless or unemployed?

Jesus Christ in the Everyday

What Christians believe the incarnation means today can be illustrated by the following prose–poem by the Russian writer Turgenev.

All at once some man came up and stood beside me.
I did not turn towards him: but at once felt that this man was Christ.
Emotion, curiosity, awe overmastered me suddenly.
I made the effort . . . and looked at my neighbour.
A face like everyone's, a face like all men's faces . . .
What sort of Christ is this? I thought.
I turned away. But I had hardly turned my eyes from this ordinary man when I felt again that it was really none other than Christ standing beside me.
Again I made an effort over myself . . .
And again the same face, like all men's faces, the same everyday, though unknown, features.
And suddenly my heart sank, and I came to myself.
Only then I realised that just such a face — a face like all men's faces — is the face of Christ.

4 The Person and Work of Christ

This section is centred on Christian belief about who Jesus is (i.e. the person of Christ) and what he has done and continues to do (the work of Christ). The next section on Judgement deals with the future return of Jesus Christ, from the point of view of humankind.

The creed states in outline the gospel story: the birth of Jesus Christ by the Virgin Mary, his crucifixion, his resurrection, and his ascension. For each of these see the relevant sections in Part One: on Christmas; on Good Friday; on Easter; and on Ascension. Closely connected also are parts of the sections in this Part on the Trinity and the Incarnation.

The Experience of Knowing Jesus Christ

The statements of the creed declare for Christians their sense of personal commitment. The doctrines therefore are much more a personal testimony than a list of historical facts. It is clear that for the first Christians the experience of meeting Jesus Christ is primary, in fact the most important thing in their lives.

ACTIVITY: on your own

How the disciples knew Jesus:

1 Read the opening of the First Letter of St John, I John 1.1–4. This is about the disciples' experience of Jesus.
2 Count the number of times the words '*we*' '*us*' and '*our*' come in these four verses.
   Then write short notes about their contact with Jesus: notice especially the words used for different kinds of experience, seeing, knowing, etc.
3 How did the writer intend to share this experience of Jesus with those who would read the letter?

Jesus came as a particular person to a particular family in first century Judea and Galilee. The Jews had their own history and religion. Jesus grew up within the Jewish tradition and was taught about God's creation, God's word in law and prophets, and the Jewish hope for a future king. *Messiah* (in Hebrew) means '*anointed one*' i.e. king, and the Greek for Messiah is *Christ*.

ACTIVITY: on your own

The Messiah the disciples expected:
   Now read the start of the Letter to the Hebrews, Hebrews, 1.1–4. This is religious language, but it shows something of the other side of the person and work of Christ, the tradition to which he came.
   If you compare this with the disciples' experiences, and the lists you made for the last exercise, you will get a composite picture.
   Look again at this passage, and write down what it says about Jesus the Son, in the past, the present, and the future. As the style of this letter is rather literary, you may need help.

Some people might say that the gospels tell us what it was like to be with Jesus at the time, the letters of St John try to share this experience with others, and the letter to the Hebrews looks back from some time afterwards. By this time the Christians had identified Jesus as the Christ. But it is worth remembering that all those who wrote the New Testament wrote in the light of the resurrection and Pentecost experiences.

ACTIVITY: on your own

Who Jesus is in the gospels:

   1 Turn now to one of the gospels, and **read Mark 8.27–33.**
   2 Note down what various people thought Jesus was. It is Peter's own answer that became the first doctrine for Christians about the person of Christ.
   3 Now note down what is said about the work of Christ, in verses 31–33.

   This passage, therefore, sums up briefly the person and work of Christ.

Jesus and the Cross

The crucifixion of Jesus is central to the understanding of the work of Christ. In western Christianity, and Britain is part of the west, great emphasis has been put on the sufferings and death of Jesus as a work of reconciling God and man. **Atonement** is the technical name, because atonement means making people at one, or in harmony.

The **doctrine of Atonement** has over centuries been much discussed in Western Christianity, and several different theories of atonement have been suggested to try and explain how the sufferings and the self–giving of Jesus have brought reconciliation. Some of these theories use the metaphor of a law court. Other theories speak of the crucifixion as a sacrifice, that is that Jesus gave himself willingly in order to save other people, many people, even the whole world. It is in this sense that Jesus is called Saviour and Redeemer. It is beyond this course to try and detail various theories of atonement.

In the Catholic tradition, the sacrifice of Christ is thought of as eternal, and something in which Christians can share in the Mass. People speak of the Mass as a sacrifice which repeats, or more properly relives, the sacrifice of Christ. The Protestant tradition, on the other hand, stresses that the sacrifice of Jesus was made once only and once for all, and therefore cannot be repeated in the Mass, Lord's Supper or Eucharist. At most this service recalls or remembers the sacrifice of Christ. More is said about this problem in Part Two Chapter 4 on Holy Communion.

In Catholic churches it is usual to find a crucifix, and the figure of Jesus is often carved with great realism to emphasise his sufferings as if they are happening now. Protestant churches usually have a plain cross. This is the empty cross from which the body of Christ has gone because his work of atonement is now complete.

There is a chapel in Germany where both Catholics and Protestants worship, but at different times. There is a big cross hanging on the wall. Turned one way round it is a plain cross, but the other side has a figure of Jesus, in fact a crucifix. Which tradition turns it which way round?

Eastern Christians see the work of Christ somewhat less in terms of the sufferings on the cross, important though this is for all Christians. Emphasis instead comes in three other places: first in the incarnation; second in the triumph of Christ over crucifixion in his resurrection; and third in his future coming to judge the world. Therefore the Orthodox often have a crucifix or icon with a figure of Jesus Christ in kingly robes, reigning from the wood of the cross.

Again, Jesus Christ as almighty, both in creation and in his return as judge at the end of time, often dominates Greek churches in the solemn figure painted (or in mosaic) in the central dome, the Pantocrator.

Pantocrator, a 14th century mosaic

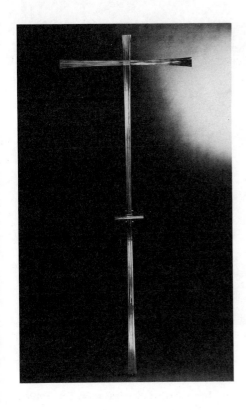

The empty cross is a symbol of resurrection. Neither cross nor grave can hold Jesus who has risen to new life.

The crucifix symbolises the sufferings of Jesus which continue as long as there is any suffering anywhere in the world. Through his self–giving, Christ has redeemed the whole of creation. When someone holds a crucifix, therefore, this may be a kind of prayer to God, asking for mercy, and showing the lengths of suffering to which Jesus has gone to save the world.

5 Judgement

At Advent Christians are preparing for Christmas, but there is another theme there as well. This is the return of Christ at the end of the world to judge the living and the dead. The creed affirms this Christian belief in the **Last Judgement**.

God is able to judge fairly, according to this belief, because he sees everything and is aware of the innermost thoughts and plans in people's hearts and minds.

Some Christians are glad to think that God is present with them in everything they do. For others, however, this feels like a threat because they would rather keep their activities hidden from God. This picture of God's eye (see page 200) could therefore be either a warning or a source of strength and comfort. In either case the all–seeing eye reminds people that God is both judge and witness at the great Day of Judgement.

Christianity teaches that God is the final judge. This can often be represented as a great Day of Judgement at the end of the world, or the end of time, known as Doomsday. Early Christians expected Christ to return very soon to bring judgement in the form of justice to the oppressed and badly treated, and to begin his kingdom with a very positive and dynamic kind of justice. With the passing centuries this idea has become less prominent, but it is definitely still there for Christians, and they are urged to be always on the alert.

A Dutch painting of the 'All seeing Eye of God'. Can you find out what the words on the picture mean?

We usually think of judges as those who administer laws which have been laid down by someone else, kings and parliaments. According to the Bible God has given out explicit laws, and in addition to this, everyone, whether religious or not, seems to have some inborn sense of right and wrong. So God appears as both lawmaker and judge.

One of the difficulties connected with Christian belief is the following problem: Does God make his laws because they are right, or do we only call them 'right' because God has made them and they could in fact be quite arbitrary?

People think that good behaviour ought to be rewarded and bad behaviour punished. But God does not seem to work like that, and we find people who have got rich by cheating others, and at the same time other people who suffer terrible misfortunes through no fault of their own.

Many Christians have believed and still believe in heaven and hell. Some preachers go into great detail about the punishments to be expected in hell, in order, it seems, to frighten people into coming to church and leading peaceable and moral lives.

Heaven and Hell stand for the judgement of God, or rather for the consequences. There are colourful descriptions of what is imagined to go on, both in the Bible and in later writing (e.g. Dante) much of which is allegorical (i.e. a tale with a hidden message), but some of it is meant quite literally. Thus a revivalist preacher from Britain or the U.S. can have a smile as he speaks on '*Millions perish in Hell!*' — not a very Christian thought by some standards.

There is a story of a hell–fire preacher who wanted to spare his hearers no detail: '*There will be weeping and wailing and gnashing of teeth*'. One old biddy interrupted, '*But I ain't got no teeth*'. In righteous indignation the preacher glared at her: '*Teeth will be provided!*'

Ideas of heaven and hell, punishment and reward, have been affected by our longing for justice, the kind of justice which by giving rewards and punishments will meet with our ideas of what we and other people deserve.

Those condemned at the Last Judgement, a drawing from a 12th century psalter

ACTIVITY: on your own

1 **Write brief answers to the following:**
   (a) What is meant by a hell–fire precher?
   (b) Why do you think he (or she) wants to preach like this?
   (c) Do thoughts of heaven and hell affect how Christians behave?

2 **Read the parable of the sheep and the goats in Matthew 25.35−46.**
   (a) List the things that the people had done (or not done).
   (b) Why do you think they seemed surprised?
   (c) Why does the judge bring himself into the case? (mention of '*me*')
   (d) Do you think that the judgement given is fair to all concerned? Give reasons for your view.
   (e) Are '*sheep*' and '*goats*' a good description of the two sets of people? Why do you think so?
   (f) Do the Judge's words give us much idea of Heaven and Hell? Do you think it is meant to tell us much about them, or is the point of the parable something quite different?

The parable of the sheep and goats raises the question whether God is forced to give judgement in strict proportion to each person's actions and motives. The whole idea of God's mercy can have no meaning if strict justice must always take its course. Christians feel sure that all who are sorry for their sins can appeal to God's love already shown in Jesus Christ.

A shepherd with his sheep and goats. Which are the sheep and which are the goats?

A second very important question is to ask how far human beings are really free to make choices and therefore solely responsible for what they do. No religion which is centred on faith in a personal God can ever have a fully reasoned answer to this problem, and Christianity is no exception. On the one hand we think that people, either as individuals or as groups in society, are in some way able to choose what they do, say and think. On the other hand the power of God can direct the wills and hearts of men and women and everyone, and this takes away from the sense of human responsibility. If I do something dreadful, can I not just blame God? In addition to this, the belief that God knows everything in advance, the future as well as the past, suggests that my choices are not really open options, and that in some way I am destined or fated to choose X and not Y before I start.

The idea of God's loving mercy is very important for Christians. According to Christian belief Jesus saves people in spite of their sins. In the picture language of judgement those who are saved will be rewarded in heaven. So judgement is not a mechanical matter of weighing up how people have behaved, nor can the justice of God be thought of as blind. The idea of God's mercy is central here. No–one deserves to be saved, but God gives favourable judgement as a gift, and this is an act of pure **grace**. Christians believe in being saved by grace, all the more so because of the person and work of Christ, his incarnation, crucifixion and resurrection. But grace does not make salvation automatic. How far the final verdict actually depends on man and how much on God's decision has been the subject of debate.

It may be helpful to imagine a kind of scale, on which God's power to ordain or predetermine our actions is at one end, and complete human freedom is at the other. In the first case everything is arbitrary and humankind has no responsibility or choice, and nothing makes sense. In the other there is only cold morality with unavoidable consequences to catch up with all of us, and God cannot be the kind of God whom Christians (and others) have experienced. If we think about this, every religious group has got to take some compromise between these two extremes. Most Christians today take a position rather nearer to the free will end than for instance the followers of Calvin after the Protestant Reformation. The tension between freedom of choice and the belief that your actions are completely determined or predestined is one for which again no completely satisfactory solution can be agreed.

You may find it helpful for the next exercise if you have a case history to focus your minds on. Imagine therefore that a teenager finds a chance to 'borrow' his mother's car without her knowing. But he has an accident, and so the whole thing comes out. How far is the accident his choice, and how far was it really caused by factors outside his control? If you prefer, however, you can do this exercise in general terms, without using a story.

ACTIVITY

As a whole class, if you have got room, **you could try out the game called '*Value Continuum*'**. This is what you do:

- Clear floor space for people to be able to sit in a long line, perhaps diagonally across the room.
- Call one end '*Free will*' (this might be one corner) and the other end '*I have no choice*'. These are the two extreme positions mentioned above, but naturally there are all sorts of compromise positions in between.

1 To play the game, each member of the class in turn takes up a position on the line, either at one end, or in the middle, or rather nearer one end than the other.
   - You can stand or sit on the floor, but sitting is better.
   - When taking up this place each of you must say, '*I am taking up this position because I think . . .*' giving obviously a reason along the lines suggested in this section.
2 When all have taken up their places and given their reasons, everyone should be given the chance to think again and change if they want to.
   - You might feel persuaded by reasons which someone else gave.
   - If you want to change, you make your move (again in turn) and at the same time say why you have decided to change your position.

A Value Continuum

The parable of the sheep and the goats suggests a much more dynamic idea of justice than just keeping out of trouble. It seems to imply that if people are hungry, justice demands that they be given food. Christians do not think of life as simply a chain of cause and effect. The whole idea of prayer requires the belief that God can intervene, and that praying makes a difference. This is the point of praying for people (intercessory prayer). Of course it is only too obvious that God does not intervene in a lot of things that go wrong, and this is taken as an illustration of God's humility in respecting the choices that people have made for good or ill. But the belief in final judgement overhangs and overarches all this.

6 The Working of the Spirit

The ways in which the Spirit works are impossible to define. This is because he has more to do with movement, ways of doing things and relationship than with specific kinds of activity.

In Part One, the sections on Pentecost pages 41–48 stress this by saying that the spirit is felt as a force which makes people able to do things they could not do or never thought of doing before. Also in Chapter 7 of Part One you can find some description of the ways that Pentecostal Christians celebrate through worship the effects of the spirit in their lives as Christians.

But the spirit is free and unpredictable. Just as there are no special rituals for celebrating the festival of Pentecost in most Christian churches, so God seems in the spirit to make impossible demands on his followers. An incident in John's Gospel illustrates this, when Jesus talked to a learned elder of the Jews, a Pharisee, on exactly this subject.

Wind blowing through trees. How does this relate to the Working of the Spirit?

ACTIVITY: on your own

Read John 3.1–10. Look at the following questions and think about them before writing answers to each.

1 What do modern Christians mean by being born again or being born from above?
2 Do Christians have any special ceremonies for marking this?
3 Why is the spirit compared to the wind (verse 8)?
4 Do you think this is a good way to describe his activity?

Now write about a page on the spirit, suggesting if you can other ways of describing him. (You could look back to the section on Pentecost in Part One, if you are short of ideas).

Jesus left his disciples after his resurrection and ascension. Instead of being around daily, as described in the gospel stories, Jesus promised to send the spirit as a means of communicating God to them. But communication works both ways. The spirit represents the strength and guidance of God to the Christians, and at the same time the spirit presents Christians to God. This last must seem very strange, and so it is, but according to the way Christians understand these things it is only in the spirit of God that people are able to pray and praise God. Anyway this notion is found both in the Bible and in Christian experience.

When you were studying the Trinity (pages 185–189) it was said that St Augustine of Hippo (Tunisia) described the Spirit in the Trinity as the mutual love between the Father and the Son. This same bond is now believed to operate between God and the community of Christians. Naturally they feel this is a very great privilege. Some Christians go further than this and can say that the spirit is the cement which binds God's divine life not just to recognised Christians, but to the whole of creation. Some things in the New Testament, notably Paul in his letter to the Romans, suggest this too.

THE FRUITS OF THE SPIRIT

ACTIVITY: on your own

1 Read about the fruits of the Spirit in Galatians 5.22.
2 Get a large piece of plain paper, and in the middle draw an imaginative picture of the spirit of God.
   - Leave plenty of room round it.
   - Next draw nine lines radiating out from your sketch, and about a third of the way along write on each line one of the fruits of the spirit you have read about in Galatians 5.22.
   - Now continue the lines outwards, and at about two thirds of the way along write a brief account of some particular act you know of which might be said to be an example or illustration of what you wrote before on this line. You will almost certainly be stuck for something, so start with the ones you find easiest to do.

ACTIVITY: as a group

1 **Now bring the individual drawings and diagrams together.** Each one say a few words about your own, and see if you can help each other to complete theirs.
2 By now you will be able to make a new and bigger diagram as a joint effort for the whole group.
   If you leave room at the outside you can add pictures at the end of each line, appropriate to the quality which that radiating line represents. These pictures can be cut from illustrated papers, or drawn by members of the group.

ACTIVITY: on your own

Write a page on '**What Christians mean by fruits of the spirit**'.

7 The Church

No-one should have reached Part Four in this book still thinking that the word church means only, or even mainly, a grey stone building at the corner of the street.

ACTIVITY: on your own

1 Write down as many different meanings of the word 'church' as you can think of.
2 How many churches are there in your town? List them.
3 Did you list buildings, or congregations, or denominations in 2 or something else?
4 What have they got in common which makes you call them all 'church'?

The creeds which Christians use in services of worship affirm that they believe in one church. Yet Christians can disagree about what this means. Two of these differences of Christian opinion need to be explored further.

Called Out from the World

In the New Testament, the word used for 'church' is the Greek word 'ecclesia', and it means called out or called to be separate. This idea is still important, but it can be understood in different ways, giving different meanings of the word church.

If we look at the phrase 'called to be separate', we can either stress the word 'called', or we can stress the word 'separate'. Calling, that is vocation, is basic to being a Christian (see the section on Baptism, which opens Part Three), but once you add the idea that it is God who does the calling, and not bishops or church leaders, then the church appears to be an enormous community of people brought together by God, instead of being a local congregation which individuals have of their own accord chosen to join.

But if you stress the idea of being separate, you now emphasise what the Christians have been called away from, instead of the church which they are called to join. The thought is that individuals are saved by leaving behind their wrongdoing and other problems, which they feel are degrading or unworthy. They often feel that their new relationship with God has taken them out of the ordinary world with its problems of money and politics.

These points illustrate that there can be two opposite views on what it means to be a member of the church, and at the same time there is room for all positions in between.

The doctrine of the church is therefore not one doctrine on which all Christians agree. In practice a lot of the differences between groups of Christians are due to their different ideas of the church. The doctrine of the church affects what people think about holy communion, about religious officials (priests and bishops), and also to some extent it affects their attitude to working in the here and now for God's kingdom. All Christians use the Lord's Prayer with its words 'Your kingdom come' (see Part Two, Chapter 7), but while some Christians think they are praying for God to come and begin his reign as king for all to see, others feel that they have a Christian duty to help bring in God's kingdom by trying to make the world a better place.

Preaching a sermon, in a Methodist church

To try and make things easier to grasp, it is often helpful to simplify. The two outlines that follow should be thought of as two types or models at opposite extremes of a scale, but you must realise that in fact many Christians hold views somewhere in between.

A Christian group who emphasise their being separate from the world and other people are called a **gathered church**. They see themselves as men and women who have either made a decision to commit themselves to Christ, or who have been saved by faith from a world which they see as fundamentally hostile to God. They are likely to be in small congregations, most of whose members know each other well. It is not unusual in such groups for the elders to look carefully at anyone who wants to join them to see if they are suitable. This of course means that only adults would be accepted for baptism, once each candidate has been approved. Because these Christians think of the world as sinful and condemned, they are trying to save individuals out of it by conversion, instead of making any attempt to change the world or its social and economic structures. They are waiting for God to come in judgement to destroy the world and punish the ungodly. They see themselves as chosen people and saved by God's grace. They usually have strict standards of behaviour which they enforce with their children, even though the children are not yet baptised.

At the other extreme are Christians who think that God is still at work in the world, even though people are sinful and lots of things are wrong in both public and private life. But because they regard the world as created by God and redeemed by Christ, they reckon that God has not abandoned it. Somehow he is still at work among people and within the structures of the world. These structures may be political, social and economic. This means that they feel that as Christians they ought to be working together with God to make the world a better place. Of course they welcome converts like the other group, but deep down they believe that the whole world can be redeemed. They are not therefore just waiting for God to come in final judgement. They feel themselves called to be active in private and public life because they think that God's kingdom is in some way related to the world of ordinary people that exists here and now. So by working to improve it they believe they are helping to bring God's kingdom in.

207

Typically these Christians do not see themselves as a community which is already gathered out of the world. They do not expect to know all their members, and they think of themselves as spread world–wide, often regardless of denomination, that all Christians there have ever been belong to the one church whose founder is Jesus Christ. This means that death is just a small dividing line and they can talk of the communion of saints (see next section) as including all Christians, past, present and future.

ACTIVITY: on your own

Make two lists and head one '*The Waiting Church*' and the other '*The Working Church*'. These refer to the two types in the paragraphs above.

Write the following characteristics in one or other list as you think appropriate.

- Faith is more important than any amount of work
- Everything in the world is doomed to destruction
- Christ is already ahead of us at work in the world
- The elders must decide whether you are ready for baptism
- Christians ought not to take part in politics
- The church is a community of saints past, present and future
- God alone knows exactly who is or is not a Christian
- There can be no salvation outside the church of the saved
- Christians have got to help to bring God's kingdom in
- The kingdom of God is totally different from anything here
- As a Christian I ought to think how I vote and spend my money

ACTIVITY

For the whole class

This is another '*Value Continuum*' game, like that outlined in the section on Judgement, page 203. Look back to remind yourselves how to set it up.

The two extremes are '*The Waiting Church*' and '*The Working Church*'.

Each of you must think what it might mean to belong to a Christian group, and then place yourself somewhere along the line, stating your reason for choosing the position you have chosen.

As before, there is a second part to this, when each person is invited to change, but should again of course give a reason.

If you belong to a church, it is almost certainly somewhere between these two extremes.

ACTIVITY: on your own

This is an optional extra exercise if you would like to compare how this works out in practice.

Visit a local priest or minister and members of the congregation. Try to find out about the beliefs and activities of this particular Christian group, and describe what they are like, using some of the ideas you have just been studying.

If (as is likely) you find that in some ways they are like the working church and in others like the waiting church, describe these points carefully.

Write one or two pages about what you have found out.

There is a third type of church which is emerging in the Basic Christian Communities in Central and South America. This looks a very exciting and a very new development, and you will be able to study them in Part Five (Chapter 3). The movement for house churches in Britain is in some ways like this because small groups of Christians really get to know and care for each other, while still recognising that they are all part of a world–wide Christian community.

One Holy Church

The creed speaks of 'one holy church' or 'one holy, catholic and apostolic church'. The word *catholic* means universal, and *apostolic* stresses that the tradition of the apostles is handed on in every generation. These words seem to suggest that the visible church in which Christians worship has been specially created by God and will exist for ever. Some people have identified this with their own denomination and said that people of other denominations are not really church members or even Christians. But this need not be so. Many Christians believe that the *one holy church* can be known only to God and is not any particular denomination. It is something much bigger and exists either in the future or in a completely otherworldly sense, i.e. it has no obvious relation to any church congregations we can see.

The earliest Christians had no political or governmental power. They were often persecuted. Hence the idea of the church as hidden and not yet revealed goes back to the beginning. On the other hand, Christians met for worship, prayer, common meals and holy communion from the first, and so there was always some stress on the visible group, and St Paul, for one, was keen to prevent Christian groups from disagreeing and splitting. The first generation of Christians too had had the Pentecost experience, so it seemed natural to regard the church as God's creation and gift in the Holy Spirit.

The idea of the Church as God's new creation is found in the Bible and in Christian thinking and writing. St Augustine's famous book *The City of God* (which he wrote sometime after the fall of Rome in 410) uses this, and so do a number of spiritual songs, such as 'O what a beautiful city'. Ezekiel in the Old Testament had a vision of a new Jerusalem at the time when the earthly Jerusalem was in ruins. Ezekiel described the city in symbolic terms with the Temple in the middle. The new Jerusalem stands for the ideal and sacred city which God creates for those who are being saved. The last book of the Bible, the Revelation of St John, describes the new Jerusalem in the last but one chapter.

These exercises draw on biblical imagery

ACTIVITY: on your own

Find the following models for the church in the New Testament:

(a) As Christ's body (I Corinthians 12.12–27)
(b) As God's temple (I Corinthians 3.10–17)
(c) As a vine (John 15.1–6)
(d) As a bride (Ephesians 5.25–33)
(e) As the city (Revelation 21)

What do these five models have in common?

ACTIVITY: as a group

Discuss in the group whether any of these models for the church fit with what you know about Christians today.

·If you talked to a minister and congregation as a part of the exercise on page 209 you should have a lot of information. Note down points of similarity and difference.

ACTIVITY: on your own

Write about a page or two on a modern view of the church.

Christian tradition has a great deal to say about the church. The church can be described as the body of Christ, the bride of Christ, his temple, the new Jerusalem, and the mother of us all. Of course all these word pictures are in some sense mystical. Whatever reality they hide remains a mystery. What people disagree about is how far the mystical church exists here and now, and how far it is hidden and not to be revealed in any form until Christ returns in judgement.

ACTIVITY: on your own

For an exercise that draws on a well–known christian hymn:
Read the following three verses from S.J. Stone's hymn, written in the nineteenth century.

1

The Church's one foundation
    Is Jesus Christ her Lord;
She is his new creation
    By water and the word:
From heaven he came and sought her
    To be his holy Bride;
With his own Blood he bought her,
    And for her life he died.

2

Elect from every nation,
    Yet one o'er all the earth,
Her charter of salvation
    One Lord, one faith, one birth;
One holy name she blesses,
    Partakes one holy food,
And to one hope she presses
    With every grace endued.

3

Yet she on earth hath union
    With God the Three in One,
And mystic sweet communion
    With those whose rest is won:
O happy ones and holy!
    Lord, give us grace that we,
Like them the meek and lowly,
    On high may dwell with thee.

Find, and copy out, words or phrases which are connected with the following ideas about the church:

(a) Like a building (temple)
(b) Like a bride
(c) World–wide
(d) On earth and in heaven
(e) Sense of unity
(f) Entered by new birth in baptism
(g) Strengthened by Holy Communion
(h) Redeemed by the death of Jesus on the cross
(i) United with the Trinity

The love imagery in the example of the Bride of Christ is very striking. There is no reason why this should not be used by Christians, because in spite of the male dominance of the church inherited from the Old Testament, God is to be thought of as infinite and therefore beyond male and female, just as he (she) is beyond number.

The communion of saints is another way of talking about the church, although, as explained in the previous section, not all Christians would think it natural to speak of the church like this. But after some thought few would deny it. Nonetheless the doctrine of the communion of saints is more prominent for some kinds of Christian than it is for others.

St Francis of Assisi, on a stained glass window in a church in the Scilly Isles

ACTIVITY: as a group

Do a brainstorming exercise on the words communion and community. Try to explore the points where what these words mean or refer to seem to overlap, and also the ways in which they are different.

When Christians maintain that the church has been founded by God for all eternity and is the community of all Christian people, then it becomes important to believe in the communion of saints. This belief is simply that the end of mortal life does not make any difference to one's status as a Christian. What Christ has sanctified, however unworthy or even unlikely, is sanctified for ever. So the community or communion of saints includes all Christians living and departed, and it goes almost without saying that the vast majority of these are not at present known personally to the Christians who are living in the world today.

In the New Testament, the word saints simply means people made holy. That is, they are sanctified (made holy) by the Holy Spirit, who (as noted on pages 204–205) continues the work of Christ. If we take it in this way, '*saints*' simply means '*Christians*'. All Christians are sanctified in Christ. But in addition to this meaning, however, some groups have felt the need to mark special people as heroes, and they call them saints in a special sense. It is this special sense which since the earliest centuries has become the most common.

There are plenty of popular heroes about. They can be found in almost any walk of life from the banners with pictures of Marx and Lenin to the pop posters in people's bedrooms. Fans who are really keen go in for hero–worship, that is they talk frequently about their idols, collect pictures, records, programmes, and press cuttings about them. Often what the hero does can influence the life of the fans, what they wear, their catch phrases, the food they like, the kind of decisions and personal relationships they have, their songs and their likes and dislikes. Some of this can be found also among Christians, from the catholic practice of wearing a saint's medallion image on a chain round their necks, to Pentecostals who in some instances pray aloud or speak using the phrases of their popular preacher.

The Roman Catholic church has for centuries had a centrally controlled process for naming people as saints in this special sense. For these Christians, new '*saints*' have to be examined, proclaimed and defined by the church hierarchy. In Eastern and Orthodox countries, however, the choosing of saints depends to a greater extent on local people. It seems likely that the very first saints in the sense of special heroes were named in this way because Christians felt that these particular people were close to God, and so they valued their advice and

Small pictures of saints which people can carry with them

their prayers. This would have been especially true of the apostles who had seen Jesus.

Christians today pray for each other (among other things) and often ask friends to pray for them. Many Christians think that those who have left this life are specially close to God, and therefore their prayers are thought to be specially effective. The belief lies behind two common practices through the centuries. One is that a group of Christians may dedicate a new church building to a particular saint, in the expectation that they will have the help of his or her prayers. The other is the practice of praying to saints to ask for their prayers, or less commonly for their material help in times of trouble. A further extension of this is that some Christians either as individuals or as groups adopt a particular saint as their patron.

The veneration of saints in the sense of heroes and heroines often includes festivals during which pictures of the saint or their relics are carried about in a public procession. This is not done by protestant churches. Many protestants instead encourage individual members of their groups to stand up and tell everyone what God has done for them and how they have been saved. This practice is known as **testifying**, and is quite logical if you hold that all Christians are saints. Carrying relics and pictures in procession (which these groups do not do) is essentially the same thing except that it calls on the witness or testimony of departed saints instead of those who are to be seen and lived with every day.

Named saints in the hero sense can and do include all kinds of people, from children to extremely old men and women, servants, soldiers, kings and bishops, housewives, shopkeepers, nurses and nuns, mothers and fathers. There seems to be no limit. These are just the saints who have been publicly recognised. The communion of saints must include many millions who are unknown or forgotten: of these Christians say that '*their faith is known to God alone*'.

St Thomas of Canterbury

ACTIVITY

On your own or as a group

If you work as a group the results can be made into an informative wall display.

1 **Choose a local saint (in the hero sense) who either has lived in your area or is connected in some way,** perhaps by a church dedication or something else.
2 **Find out what you can about her or him.** The information you collect will probably include some historical data (however vague) and maybe also some stories which have been widely believed at some time or other. Collect these stories too, often in praise of a saint and often about miraculous powers, and any other points of interest such as symbols and attributes, and note also who if anyone specially remembers them today.
3 **Write about two pages on the saint you have chosen,** and include sketches or pictures as you think fit.
4 This is an optional extra: **If you have found out some legends which you do not think are very historical, how important do you think this is for today's Christians?**

9 *Forgiveness of Sins*

Have you ever had to choose a team of people, perhaps to play in a football match, or select a group to come with you on a long school journey? Probably you have not, but this kind of situation can present special problems. What do you do about the brilliant player who is a pain in the neck? Or the clever linguist (useful if you are going abroad) who makes you all feel inferior and depressed? You might try having a serious talk with the person concerned to explain that the group would value her or his expertise but that you cannot afford to damage the spirit or morale of the whole party if she or he is not going to behave considerately.

If you can agree, this is rather like forgiveness because you have given him or her another chance. But of course you are also taking a risk. There is no absolutely right or wrong answer, because forgiveness is never free and usually involves a risk on both sides. Ideally you would want to trust a person and give him or her another chance in circumstances in which you think he or she is likely to do all right and not let you down. This is good for both of you.

What Christians mean by the forgiveness of sins includes all these aspects, and one more as well. The extra is the involvement of God. This makes a difference, not because by forgiving God is not taking any risk — the life of Jesus certainly suggests to Christians that he does — but because forgiveness is intended to be an aspect of love which is to be passed on. If you never forgive other people then you are not the sort of person who is likely to be able to accept being forgiven yourself. Forgiveness is a two-sided relationship. Christians pray *'forgive us our sins as we forgive those who sin against us'* (from the Lord's Prayer, see Part Two, Chapter 7).

In order to accept forgiveness by someone else, you should ideally intend to do better next time (i.e. not let them down again), and also attempt to put right the damage done last time. These are not, however, absolute pre-conditions of Christian forgiveness. Forgiveness is thought of as a gift, not a bargain.

ACTIVITY: on your own

What forgiveness is like.

1 Read from Matthew 18.23—35 the most famous parable on forgiveness.
2 Read the section on forgiveness through once again, and then compare this with the parable.
3 Now write your own parable on forgiveness.
4 Read again what you have written. Have you covered the main points mentioned in this section?

10 Resurrection and the Life of the World to Come

Belief in the resurrection of Jesus is fundamental for Christians. From this follows belief in life after death for all Christians, because Jesus is the first of the Christians and he includes or incorporates all who believe in him. This idea is put into words when people speak of Christians as the body of Christ. Perhaps non–Christians are to be included as well, but this is disputed.

When St Paul wrote his first letter to the Corinthians, most Christians thought that Jesus was going to return very soon to judge the world, and that the end of the world was very near. People began to get worried as brother and sister Christians died, because they thought that they would miss the judgement and resurrection. St Paul had to put them right, and what he wrote in I Corinthians 15 is an important part of Christian doctrine on the subject.

Various models are used to try and describe how after the body has decayed people can be resurrected or raised to a new kind of life. The caterpillar, the chrysallis and the butterfly can be used as one model, with the note that the caterpillar does not know what is about to happen to it: in the same way people do not know how they could be changed after death.

Some models or word pictures in the New Testament have become traditional for Christian thought and belief. A grain of wheat must fall into the ground and die before it can grow into something much better, a new plant which bears many new grains. This description comes both in the Gospel of John and in Paul's letters. It is symbolic and in the last resort an example of picture language, and official Christian teaching is short on hard information about the afterlife.

When studying this section you should also refer back to Part Three, Chapter 6 on Funerals. One of the following exercises is referred to there.

ACTIVITY

On your own — selecting key words

1 Bearing in mind the background (as just explained), read carefully I Corinthians 15.35—44.
2 Imagine that you have been asked to store this passage in a retrieval system, and select up to six key words which you think will guide searchers to the main points.
3 Now write about a page to explain why you chose these key words, why they are important and what they link up with.

ACTIVITY

As a group or on your own — gravestones

1 Either as a group or individually, go to a local churchyard where people have been buried for a long time.
2 Make a collection in a notebook of texts carved on some of the tombstones.
3 How many of these, or what proportion of them, refer to the resurrection and the life hereafter?
4 You may like to take photographs or make sketches of inscriptions and stone monuments if they seem related to this theme.
5 Write this up in two pages, or more if you have got pictures. 6 and 7 are optional extras — otherwise, go on to 8.
6 Do the inscriptions seem to go in fashions? Were some texts more popular in the 1880s and 1890s than today? How about in the 1930s?

7 Do any of the gravestones refer to the Day of Judgement? Why do you think this is so? (compare the section on Judgement)

8 Take a plain piece of paper and draw the outline of a tombstone. This is going to be a gravestone for yourself! Write your name carefully on it, followed by the year of your birth, dash, question marks as you do not know the year of your death, like this: 'FRANCIS ANYONE 19..−???? '.

Underneath add an epitaph (inscription on a grave). Would you like a text from the Bible? If so, what?

A number of graves show a plain cross. The cross is the most commonly found Christian symbol. But in addition, the empty cross represents the resurrection of Jesus, and so expresses the hope that Christians too may rise from the dead. More rarely a crucifix may be seen on a grave. As explained on page 199, this represents a prayer for help and mercy through the sufferings of Jesus Christ.

Chapter Four

HOW CREEDS ARE USED

A creed is a statement of beliefs, in this case religious beliefs, which can be referred to, but most commonly the Christian creed is used in the course of church services, that is in the liturgy. The group of people who take part in these services or liturgies are the people who broadly speaking subscribe to these beliefs. This fact illustrates the view that the real purpose of a set of beliefs is to define a community rather than to begin an argument.

This becomes clear when we find that creeds were first used with candidates for baptism who were joining the community of the church. The various statements of the creed formed the basis of their instruction in what Christians believe. They were then required to say the whole thing during the baptism service as a sign that they were true believers. This still holds true in theory, but in many churches today this is shortened to three or four statements or affirmations. As was explained in the section on Baptism (Part Three, Chapter 1), when babies are being baptised their parents and godparents, and often the whole congregation, make the affirmations on their behalf. This is supposed to mean that they promise to bring up the children in the Christian faith.

Of course there is a lot of teaching besides the creed. This would include prayer, services, especially sacraments, Bible teaching and reading, and more generally Christian activities and behaviour. But when the creed is used at Baptism it reminds people that if you cannot agree to it and affirm it (if necessary by proxy in the case of infants) you will not be allowed to join the Christian community.

The first few words of the Creed – on a mediaeval German manuscript

It is because the creed was first used like this that it begins with such a strong affirmation: '*I believe*'. In some modern versions, this has been changed to '*We believe*'. in order to stress the community aspect. This idea too fits in with what is believed to happen at baptism.

For many centuries creeds have been used also in other church services. A short version, sometimes (inaccurately) called the **Apostles Creed**, is used at Morning and Evening Prayer in many denominations, and in some of the daily offices (services) used by religious orders (monks and nuns). At the Eucharist a slightly longer version called the **Nicene Creed** is used.

ACTIVITY: in pairs

Find one or other of these creeds in a church service book. This could be either the order of service for the Eucharist or Mass, or it could be Morning or Evening Prayer. In both cases the creed comes well into the service, so you will have to look carefully till you find it.

1 When you have found it copy the creed out tidily on a piece of paper, beginning each statement on a new line. Number the lines on your paper.

2 Then helping each other, look back through Part Four of this book which you have just been studying and note down the sections which seem particularly to apply to each line of the creed. Use the line numbers you put in when you wrote it out as reference points, and note the page numbers in this book.

3 For follow-up work, choose two of the points you found for 2, and write half a page to a page on each of these points about what you understand by the relevant statement in the creed, that is what you think the phrase should mean for Christians.

Including and Excluding

It is a sad truth that Christians today are divided into many denominations. Some of these divisions are fairly recent. Some of them seem to have come about through a clash of personalities between leaders, or because a church with political power tried to stop a group of Christians who began to look like a threat to them. But not all divisions started like this, and some of them are very ancient.

Some of the divisions are in fact rooted in differences about belief, or rather differences of opinion about how a belief is to be put into words. The most well–known of these concerns the nature of Jesus Christ during the thirty or so years he was incarnate and a man in Judaea and Galilee.

That he was both divine and human at the same time all Christians can agree. But did this mean one nature or two? This is such an involved and confusing psychological question that it cannot be examined here, but the result of this argument is still with us. The Orthodox and Western churches decided on two, i.e. that Christ had both a human nature and a divine nature at the same time. Defining this in a creed brought a split in the church, and the minority group are known as Monophysites (means ('*one nature only*'). They are found today in the Near and Middle East.

This dispute is not very much alive today, and Christians of many denominations work together. But old traditions die hard, and the symbols last for many hundreds of years.

This picture shows an Orthodox bishop (Greek, Russian, etc.) using his right hand to bless the people. The three fingers raised represent the three persons of the Holy Trinity. The other two, that is the finger and thumb which are touching, represent the two natures of Jesus Christ incarnate, that is the human nature and the divine nature.

One Line Answers

(Write answers to these questions in one line or two)

1 What is a creed?
2 Name one church service at which the creed is usually said by all present.

3 Give the usual name for one of the creeds commonly used in church services.

4 What does the word Trinity mean for Christians?

5 Name the three persons of the Holy Trinity.

6 What is meant by the 'image of God' in mankind?

7 Give one reason why Christians might think that human beings are responsible for their environment.

8 What is meant in the creed by the words 'all things visible and invisible'?

9 What is the special name for the belief that in Jesus God became a man?

10 What importance do Christians attach to the phrase 'born of the Virgin Mary'?

11 What do Christians mean by calling Jesus 'the Word of God'?

12 How are the sufferings of Christ represented in many churches?

13 What does the word Atonement mean for Christians?

14 Why do Protestant churches prefer to have a plain cross (no figure on it)?

15 What is the significance of a picture of the Eye of God?

16 What is meant by a 'hell-fire preacher'?

17 What do Christians mean by 'the Last Judgement' and who is the Judge?

18 What is meant by the 'fruits of the Spirit'? Name two of them.

19 Give one reason why Christians should forgive other people.

20 Give two different meanings for the word 'church'.

21 What do the words 'catholic and apostolic' mean in the phrase 'I believe in one holy catholic and apostolic church'?

22 What is normally meant by the Bride of Christ?

23 Why do some Christians direct prayers to certain saints?

24 What is a patron saint?

25 What might resurrection mean for Christians who have been burned or eaten by lions?

26 Why might a plain cross be a suitable symbol to put over a Christian's grave?

Part Five

CHRISTIANITY IN A NON–CHRISTIAN WORLD

Chapter One

CHRISTIANS IN THE WORLD

You have been studying the things that Christians do and believe, and trying to understand why. The reasons are mostly hard to express so are put into symbols instead. Some of these symbols are pictures and carvings and other forms of art, and some are phrases or words, including picture language. Yet Christians live in the world, just as you do, and have to make choices which affect their families, their jobs and their freedoms. This is the context in which we all live, work and enjoy other people's company.

ACTIVITY: as a class

Here is a Value–Continuum game to help you decide how the world relates to Christianity.
Is the world basically friendly to the Christian religion? Or is it hostile? Or is it neither, i.e. quite indifferent?

Clear a space in the room long enough for the whole class to stand in a line, or to sit on chairs in a line if there is room for them. Put enough chairs (if you're using them) out first, roughly in line. This line represents '**the world**': one end is labelled '**hostile to Christianity**', and the other '**friendly to Christianity**'.

It would help to write these words on two big sheets of card, or on blackboards if there are two of them.

To go half way along the line means that you think the world is neither hostile nor friendly to Christianity, perhaps doesn't relate to it in any way, or it could be the world relates to it in different ways with no definite result. Each member of the class, one by one, takes up a position on this line — you will need to sort out an order for people to take turns — and as he or she does so, tells the rest of the class why this particular position has been chosen.

It is possible that several people want to be in the same place, and in that case you can move chairs to be alongside each other.

When everyone has taken up a position, the person at one end is asked if he or she would like to try and persuade other members of the class to join her or him. Everyone is then given a turn to persuade others (words only, no pulling!) if they want to. In this way everyone has the chance to take up a new position in the '*Value–Continuum*'.

Before you leave this, each one of you should make a note on paper of where you have ended up, at the '*hostile*' end, at the '*friendly*' end, in the middle, or a bit nearer one end or the other. Try to add a reason for your choice.

Keep this piece of paper for use later on.

A discussion between members of various religious groups

When you did the exercise, you will have seen that there was a range of opinion about the church and the world. That is why this activity is called a value–continuum. Among Christians also there can be a range of opinions and feelings. It is important to notice that not all Christians make the same choices. In politics, as in matters of riches and poverty, war and peace, and other issues, Christians can be found on opposite sides arguing against each other, voting differently, and even fighting. This does not mean that their faith is superficial. Christians can quite genuinely and sincerely take different lines, and for any study of Christianity it is important to try and see why this is so.

If you have just finished studying Christian beliefs in Part Four, you might think that Christianity means applying beliefs to life–situations. In fact Part Four should have made it clear that Christian beliefs and doctrine grew up because Christians had certain experiences which they wanted to talk about and put into words. Christians today still have experiences, and they act and react in the world today in ways which still express what they stand for.

As students of *Christianity for GCSE* you too have had many kinds of experiences in your life. These are probably very different from those of the first Christians. But your own experiences can help you to understand something about Christianity in the world today, as you think about the situations which are described in this Part. Some, perhaps most of these situations may seem to you to be very unusual, but you are asked to try and imagine what it would be like if you were faced with these pressures and had to make decisions about them. Would you give up and go with the crowd? Would you try and hide, keeping quiet and out of people's way? Or would you want to stand up for your friends and what you think is important, in a word, your values?

Yet life in the contemporary world cannot be the whole story. When you studied Part Two on Christian Worship, it must have become clear that learning about worship is a bit like learning about swimming. Talking and reading is not a lot of good unless you actually go into the water, and so get the chance of learning to swim by doing it. But this is a study course for GCSE, and for that reason it was suggested in the sections on Prayer, for example, that you needed to decide whether you wanted to go beyond learning about prayer, and learn actually to pray. In a book like this, the choice must be left open. Worship is at the heart of Christianity because worship, derived from *worth–ship*, expresses the worth or value

This Part Five is about how Christians live in the world today. It is an essential part of the course to look at and investigate the ways in which modern Christians experience the world in which they live, the choices they make and their reasons for these choices. So this Part is in a way a summing up of the whole book.

of God. This means that Christians have got somewhere a sense or system of values, even if they are a bit hazy when it comes to trying to put it into words.

Christian Values

You could try as an experiment asking twenty different Christians what they think the main principle or value is for Christians. You might be surprised at the answers you get, and it is likely that you will get several different ones.

ACTIVITY: on your own

Here are a number of possible answers to the question, '*What do you think is the most important thing for a Christian?*'

live in peace with other people
not take things that don't belong to you
treat people as you'd like them to treat you
go to church on Sundays
say your prayers
be good
read the Bible
give money and clothes to aid agencies
not to eat or drink too much or spoil yourself
look after your family and friends
help people when they are in trouble
give money to the church
do what the church or priest or pastor tells you
be a good citizen
always tell the truth, never tell lies
keep the Ten Commandments
join or start a Christian political party
wanting to go to heaven
being like Jesus
healing the sick, feeding the hungry
give things up, especially if they are not good for you
not going to discos or films or parties
always thinking about God and Jesus
hoping for the end of the world
being baptised, receiving holy communion fairly often
going regularly to confession
try to convert non–Christians by talking to them
being active in youth club, Sunday school, church choir etc
getting ordained to the ministry
being sorry for sins (repenting)

Look through all these answers on your own. Never mind if some of them look a bit silly. You should know enough about Christianity by now to know that some of them do not really relate to Christian values at all.

Now arrange these answers as far as you can into two columns: Column A is headed '*Things related to the way people live in the world*'; and Column B is headed, '*Things which have little to do with the world and ordinary life*'. If you like, you could frame your two columns to make rectangles.

Now take a new piece of paper and go back to the full list again and arrange the same answers in three groups: call Group 1 'Things which are exclusively Christian'; Group 2 'Things which non–Christians do as well as Christians'; and Group 3 'Things which do not seem to be Christian at all'. Some items may come into more than one Group, so you will need to draw circles which overlap. You will know how this is done from Venn diagrams.

When you have got these three new groups clear, compare the two pieces of paper.

- Do any of the circles on the second piece of paper contain the same list as one of the columns on the first?
- Do either of the columns A or B contain all the entries of circle 1, 2 or 3? If not all, then nearly all? If so, why do you think this is?

ACTIVITY: as a group

Now get your small group together, and **compare notes with other members**.

Are they any big differences? Talk about these, and see if you really disagree, or whether there has just been a misunderstanding.

Pages 143–144 in Part Three are also about salvation, and what it mean for Christians to be saved. It was explained there that baptism into Jesus Christ could be a very personal matter. Christians feel that in spite of everything that is wrong with them and with the world, God has shown his love in Jesus. This is what Christians mean by *grace*, love freely given, although quite undeserved. That is why Christians speak of being saved by God's grace.

But there is a future dimension to salvation also. This world is not perfect, and Christians have an idea of a better state of affairs, of an ideal city or a better world. This is the future dimension of Christianity. It is hard to put it into words, but it is focussed very often on the person of Jesus, and the kingdom of Jesus or kingdom of God.

Your Kingdom Come

All Christians learn to pray, '*Your kingdom come, your will be done, on earth as in heaven*'. Many Christians say the Lord's Prayer at least every day (see Part Two, Chapter 7). God's kingdom is clearly important, and it is one of the ways in which Christians talk about salvation. Many Christians say that God's kingdom is another way of saying '*heaven*'. Many people think of heaven as an ideal state which can only be reached after death. Yet at the same time many Christians feel sure that God's kingdom also applies to the present life, all the good things and relationships in the world which they claim God has created — a good world which has been spoilt by human selfishness and sin, but not yet beyond all recognition. Therefore they believe that it is God's will that they should bring out the good things of this world, by spreading, encouraging, and sharing them; and at the same time they should work to push back the opposite, that is everything which spoils or damages the world, like greed, exploitation, pollution, disease and war. Of course they believe that God's kingdom is also the after life: but the important thing for them is that the way they live now in this world in some way continues into the life to come.

It is possible to find Christians who take extreme views on this. Christians at one extreme feel that God's kingdom is quite distinct from anything in this present life, and even opposed to it. They believe the world is basically evil and condemned to suffer the anger of God, so the only thing here that counts is an act of faith and commitment to Christ on the part of individuals. But those at the opposite extreme say that God's kingdom is already in being and that Christians are called to work in it together with the spirit of Christ. This position is bound to involve social, economic and political relationships as well as how individuals behave to each other.

This is the time to find again the piece of paper on which you noted down your position in the Value–Continuum at the start of this Part. How does your position there relate to the attitude of different Christians to the world as just described?

And yet the world in which we all live is obviously a non–Christian world.

Chapter Two

RICH AND POOR

Is she a rich or poor person?

Would a Christian society allow big differences between rich and poor? This question is easily answered at a factual level because many deeply Christian societies have and still do include both very rich and extremely poor people.

Early Christianity spread in a society where it was quite usual to own slaves if you were even moderately well–off. Those who became Christians included both slaves and slave owners. In the New Testament there is a letter in which St Paul asks a Christian slave owner to forgive his Christian slave for running away.

It was only in the nineteenth century that Christian conscience was raised against the whole institution of slavery. Christian reformers eventually got slavery abolished by law, first in the British Empire and later throughout the world. The point to stress here is not simply that slavery is wrong: people of all religions and none would agree to that now. What has happened is that the Christian attitude to slavery has gone through a social change. Formerly Christians believed they ought to be kind to slaves whom they met, and if they owned slaves, to treat them fairly and with consideration. This was between individuals, people you

Are these people rich or poor?

knew and could talk to. Later, however, Christian understanding changed, and by the nineteenth century Christians believed that the whole institution was wrong and should be abolished by political action and social reform. This obviously affected tens of thousands of individuals whom the Christians at the heart of the campaign would never know or meet.

But do the differences between rich and poor, which are still very obvious in the world today, represent a similar case? Is it possible to abolish poverty like abolishing slavery by law? Or should Christians gradually try to reduce extremes by curbing the very rich and raising the living standards of the very poor? These are hard questions to which many Christians have not got any answers. Social history tells us that in almost every Christian society there have been big differences between rich and poor. People did not think that money or the lack of it had anything to do with being a Christian, but was just a fact of life like being tall, or having dark brown hair, or inheriting a prosperous business. It is possible to see countries in which today or until very recently the poorest were the most loyal church members — for instance the rural poor in Ireland. You can also think of countries where church members are almost exclusively middle–class, not always very rich but comfortably off, while people near the poverty line are hardly ever to be seen at a church: most of England and Scotland provides an example of this.

ACTIVITY: as a group

Get your small group together to discuss the following question:
'Should Christians try to help the poor become better off even though it means making the rich less rich than they were?'

1 Notice that the question is about Christians, and is not asking for your own views on the subject. You can consider this question either in terms of our society in this country, or in terms of the world as a whole. Try to discuss these as two separate issues if you decide to tackle both of them.

   Notice also that Christians do not in fact agree about the answers to this question, so if you find more than one view in the group this is quite reasonable! In any case, work out the reasons for the answers which group members give, remembering of course that these are supposed to be answers Christians would give, so the reasons too must have something to do with Christian religion!

2 Write these answers down with clear reasons for each one.

3 Now discuss the problems of extreme differences in wealth and possessions from your own point of view. What do members of the group themselves feel about this? In home society, or on a world scale? Your reasons this time need not be anything to do with Christianity, although it is possible that some of them may be.

What it is Like to be Rich

There are many different ways of being well–off but being rich usually means money. Money in our society means being able to spend when you want, no matter whether you use cash, cheques or credit cards. But being rich need not always imply ready money. Instead, people possess power and influence, because they either own or control the land, the resources and the means of production. The rich have other people dependent on them. By comparison the poor are the have–nots. In Britain today there are large numbers of people somewhere in between, that is neither very obviously rich nor yet very poor. But in some countries there is almost no–one in the middle. There are only very rich and very poor. A lot of Europe was like this in the Middle Ages.

ACTIVITY: as a group

To help you think about this, get your small group together to **discuss the question, what you would do with half a million pounds**. You may suggest or argue about a number of possible ideas: some of these may involve other people and make changes in the way you live and the kind of things you do and think are worth doing.

Note down what you decide to do, and how this would affect your life and the lives of other people.

Keep this piece of paper for reference later.

The incomes and life–styles of most people in Western Europe and North America look very rich in comparison with those of more than half the world's population. For instance, western visitors to Sri Lanka or Thailand are surprised to hear that the very simple living standard of many professional people like teachers and civil servants is considered good in comparison with most of the population.

For decades industrialised Europe and North America have bought raw materials cheaply from South America, Asia and Africa, and sold them manufactured goods, especially cars, trains and machinery, at prices which were fixed by the industrialised countries themselves. This kind of trading is usually described as a 'free market economy', but it is not a healthy one, because free trade gives the advantage in bargaining to the strong, and the less strong have just got to accept the terms of trade or not trade at all. Either way they get the worst of it. In spite of changes like factories starting in Third World countries, the differences between rich nations and poor are as obvious today as ever.

Many Christians are deeply worried about the differences between rich and poor nations, but it is not exclusively a Christian concern. If you want to follow this up, you can get lots of materials from aid and development agencies, one of which is Christian Aid. Your group might enjoy playing one of the many *Development* or *Trade and Aid* games which are available. You would learn a lot about this topic by doing so.

ACTIVITY: as a group

This exercise calls on your small group to get together and use your imagination. The rich have problems too.

You are all very rich people who live fairly near each other, and you are meeting to exchange ideas on what to do about certain difficulties.

Almost every day you get letters from people asking you to give them money for themselves or for causes which they want you to support. Worse still, a lot of poor people live around your homes who would very much like to get their hands on some of your wealth. They would like to walk or camp in your parks and gardens, eat your food, and even sell your valuables to raise cash for themselves.

- Discuss how you feel and what you could do as a group of very rich people in this threatening situation.
- Write on a piece of paper how you feel and what you could do about it all.
- If within your group you have serious differences of opinion, this is also important and should be noted on paper.
- Keep this piece of paper for future reference.

Christians and Poverty

Christians today are sharply divided in their attitude to poor people and poverty in the world. Perhaps this has always been so, but Christians today are more aware than ever before of poverty both in our own society and around the world because of reports on television and in other mass media.

There have probably always been Christians who say that being saved in the religious sense is much more important than having enough to eat,

Mother Teresa with the Pope when he visited Calcutta

and that anyway it is God who makes people rich or poor. Some of them also think that the rich must have worked hard to earn their money, and that while of course better off people should help the poor, poverty, they say, is a combination of bad luck and laziness: so if the poor die sooner than the rich that is nothing for them to worry about. This kind of thinking puts great emphasis on religion at a personal and individual level, and compared to this, almost nothing else matters. At death all distinctions of status and wealth will disappear, so in the long run the poor need have nothing to worry about.

In an extreme form, when the threat of nuclear war is being discussed, such people would claim that the end of the world would be quite a good thing as it would bring in God's kingdom all the sooner. (See also Chapter 7)

Some Christians appear to think that religious activities, like church services, Bible reading and prayer meetings, need have nothing to do with practical hardships. The story comes from a city slum somewhere in South America where the priest came along every Sunday to celebrate Mass and give a short sermon. A woman related afterwards: *'He told us that God loves the poor. But I always wonder why it is, if God loves the poor, that his minister only spends half an hour a week with us'*.

But the situation in much of South and Central America is changing as we shall see. There have been Christians in all ages who have felt that they ought to do something when people are extremely poor. Mother Teresa of Calcutta said on a television broadcast in December 1987, *'Poverty is not made by God. Poverty is made by me and by you'*. Someone like St Francis of Assisi (1181–1226) gave up his family wealth to become poor voluntarily in order to serve the poor and to serve God through and with them.

ACTIVITY: as a group

Find those notes your group made during the two earlier exercises on wealth, one on what you would do with half a million pounds, and the other when you were a group of very rich people with a problem.

As a group discuss these two sets of notes side by side.

- Compare them and what they seem to say about making changes of any kind.
- What sort of people want to make changes and what sort of people do not want changes to be made?

Of course your discussion may take a variety of directions, but it is likely that you will suddenly come on the answer to an important question: *'Why does God love the poor?'* This does not exactly fit the South American lady's question, but it will become clear that it is particularly relevant to her situation.

From a Christian point of view the world is very far from perfect, the way mankind has got it today. The poor are especially keen to make changes, while the rich mostly want to resist change, because they think change means revolution, or that change will require them to lose some of their wealth. This means that the poor have hopes for a future, while it would seem that the rich mostly want to look back to the past and to protect themselves against the poor because they are in some way afraid of them.

This means for many Christians that they must be ready for change and look for the leading of God's spirit. Being alert and being awake is an important aspect of Christianity and not just something to do with preparing for Christmas, as in the Advent themes discussed in Part One.

Many Christians of all denominations believe that their religion has a lot to do with riches and poverty. Jim Wallis is a good example. He is a modern–day American preacher, who comes from the Plymouth Brethren (a strict protestant and evangelical church). He tells the story of 'the Bible full of holes'. He says a friend of his took a Bible, and with a pair of scissors cut out all those verses which made mention of poverty and what Christians (New Testament) or Jews (Old Testament) should do about it. The result was that a surprisingly high percentage of the text was cut out, and he was left with 'a Bible full of holes'. Jim Wallis is telling Christians that if they take no notice of poverty in the world around them they are in effect relying on a Bible full of holes, that is to say their religion is missing quite a lot of what is essential.

Working for the Poor

Helping the poor is very much part of the Christian tradition, and not only in the Bible. You only have to think of St Martin (fourth century, France) when he was a Roman soldier giving half his cloak to a beggar, or of good king Wenceslas (of Bohemia, now part of Czechoslovakia, tenth century) in the Christmas carol. But there is a difference between helping individual poor people in an emergency and trying to change the overall economic conditions which make them poor. Christian attitudes to the poor include both these approaches.

In the early thirteenth century, Elisabeth (1207–1231) was a daughter of the king of Hungary and was betrothed to (this means promised in marriage arranged by the parents) and later married Count Ludwig of Thüringen, a very powerful nobleman in what is now Germany. Even as a young girl she was deeply concerned about the poor, and used to eat sitting with the serving maids, telling them that they must call her 'Elisabeth' instead of 'Milady'. In church on Sundays she would take off her golden coronet and put it on the seat beside her, although her future mother–in–law told her off and said that she must wear it even in church like all the nobility, otherwise people would laugh at them. 'I cannot sit here,' replied Elisabeth, 'and see my Lord crowned with thorns, while I wear a crown of gold'. There was of course a life–like crucifix prominently displayed in the church.

After her marriage she was an influential person and had to be present at many state banquets and important occasions. But she would not eat unless she could be assured that all the food had been properly paid for and fairly acquired: it was not unusual for the servants of powerful nobles to terrorise peasants and farmers to give them food, furs and wood as presents or as a kind of taxation. We read that Elisabeth sat through many a banquet of good food eating nothing at all. Her husband loved her very much and supported her, but could hardly invite guests to a feast and then eat nothing himself. Yet he could not always control the activities of his servants and supporters.

Every winter many poor people starved in the intense cold of central Europe, and Elisabeth went out in the town and villages with baskets of food to distribute. It seems that she did not ask why it was that so many

A poor family receiving food. When was this picture drawn?

St Elisabeth helping the poor, from a stained glass window in the Elisabethkirche, Marburg, Germany

people were desperately hungry. This is in a way a modern question, and would perhaps not have occurred to anyone in the thirteenth century because poverty was so common and so widespread.

Just as Christians seem to have tolerated eighteen centuries of slavery because it seemed to them quite natural like an ordinary fact of life, so until very recently Christians did not think about changing economic systems. It is really only since the end of the nineteenth century that some Christians have begun to feel that it is possible to abolish extremes of poverty, and further, that because they are Christians they ought to do so. This is to go well beyond simple acts of helping individual poor people whom you happen to meet.

Try to think out why this change has begun to take place about this time: has it got anything to do with the more exact study of Economics? Or with the growth of mass communications? Or better transport systems?

In this respect Elisabeth contrasts with Helder Camara, the present–day Archbishop of Recife in Brazil, who said: '*If I give food to the poor, people call me a saint. But if I ask why the poor have no food then they call me a Communist*'. Seven hundred and fifty years lie between them. Christians can claim to have learnt something in that time.

What kind of people do you think would want to call Archbishop Helder Camara a communist?

Elisabeth's husband Ludwig died very young on his way to the Crusades. They had ridden together to the borders of his territory, but when the time came to part they could not separate and she rode on with him for another day. Again they could not say Goodbye. After the third day they kissed and embraced fondly once more, and this was for the last time. She went home. When news of his death came and was confirmed by showing his ring, she said: '*Is he dead? Then for me the world is dead and anything it can offer!*' She quickly made arrangements for her three children to be brought up, and then devoted herself to service of the poor and sick.

It is easy to understand that quite a lot of the poor were sick too, and quite a lot of the sick were poor. The same happens today in those countries of the Third World where very many people are badly undernourished. Elisabeth realised that to serve the poor she must herself become poor. So that is what she did.

It all sounds very good, but the fact is that the poor often do not appreciate it when someone who was rich becomes poor voluntarily. The poor people round Marburg in Germany where she worked did not know what to make of her. They thought she must be very foolish to give up a life of ease. Some of them made fun of her, like an old woman who pushed her into a muddy pool when Elisabeth stood aside on a stepping stone to let her pass. Working among the sick and having not much to eat herself, she died in four years. She was only twenty–four.

As soon as she was dead, everyone began to understand what she was really trying to do and her motivation of Christian love. She was suddenly enormously popular. She was declared a saint in three and a half years from her death — virtually a record for speed under the Roman system — and twelve thousand people of every sort poured into the little town for the church service. Frederick the Second, Emperor of the Holy Roman Empire, could scarcely be got into the church because the crowd was so thick. He came to Marburg barefoot, wearing a single coarsely woven garment like a penitent, but on his head he had the Imperial Crown. Such was life in the Middle Ages.

Chapter Three

BASIC CHRISTIAN COMMUNITIES

In the late twentieth century, that is today, many people of all religions or none, think that poverty can be changed, and that already enough food is produced in the world as a whole for everyone to get enough. The problem is distribution. In a sudden emergency people want to get the food to the hungry as soon as possible and usually do not mind giving it away. A famine or other emergency somewhere overseas can be an exciting challenge as well as making good television, but it does nothing for human dignity or intelligence. It ought to be possible to avoid sudden emergencies, or at any rate most of them.

Instead of making the poor depend on the rich for handouts, it should be possible for the poor to help themselves. Because the rich are also strong and mostly control the world's resources, it is often necessary to give the poor a start. Basic communities are about this.

What is a basic community? It consists of a group of people who live near each other and share the same aims and ideals, usually religious ideals. By talking and doing things together they develop a spirit of co–operation which in turn becomes essential to the way they understand Christian living.

How big it is depends on what its members do and their relationship with each other. For instance, in a family who live together in the same house, up to twelve or maybe slightly more members is small enough for all of them to know each other well and get on well together. If the basic community is formed in a factory or department of work, however, it may be quite a bit bigger. The people in it have different jobs and different gifts and can help each other in many different ways, all the time feeling a sense of belonging and sharing. Although one works with a smaller group, it is possible to feel a good sense of belonging to a much larger workforce.

Basic Christian communities are found all over the world, in Europe and Africa and Asia, but the most striking examples are those of Central and South America. To belong to a basic community feels good because you really know the other members and you learn to trust and help each other.

ACTIVITY: on your own

This exercise is a problem–solving system which is designed to help you think through the kind of difficulties which every day face the very poor in Central America. And most of the population are by European standards extremely poor.

You are a fit young man of about thirty called Paulo, with a wife and four children, and you have got a job as a city street cleaner.

1 **The pay is so little that you have to choose between either paying rent for a small two–room house in the city or feeding your family.**
   What do you do?
   (a) Keep the house and send your family out to beg in the streets like many others, or
   (b) move to the edge of the city where you can build your own shack?
   If you choose (a), your friends will never talk to you again, so you choose (b).

2 **Your eldest child ought to go to school,** but schools are hard to get into, and you have got to pay fees (no free schooling here!).
   What do you do?
   (a) Try asking your relations to lend you some money, or
   (b) keep the child at home to help mother in the house?
(a) is no good, because all your relatives are as poor as you are, and some have not even got work, so (b) is unavoidable.

3 **Your two middle children become very weak and ill.** Things are so bad that neighbours take your wife with the two little kids to the doctor and say that they will between them somehow manage to raise the fee (no free doctors here!). The doctor says they are suffering from malnutrition and pre-scribes some medicine (which must be bought) and says they must have plenty of milk and eggs, and a bit of meat every day.
   What do you do?
   (a) persuade your wife to earn some extra money by buying and selling vegetables in the market, or
   (b) buy a ticket in the government lottery in hopes of winning the big prize?

4 **Your wife persuades you that (b) is unrealistic, and mean-while the children will die, so you both choose (a).** But she has got to buy and pay for the vegetables in the morning before she can sell them to anyone.
   What do you do?
   (a) Tell her to ask the other market women to lend her some cash for a day, or
   (b) go to the regular money lender as all the other market women do?
   She tells you that (a) is out of the question, so you choose (b).

5 **The moneylender** (who is also a woman incidentally) **tells her that she must borrow ten pounds,** and that she must

pay back two pounds every day, one pound interest and one pound in capital, until it is all paid back.

What does she do?

(a) accept the offer gratefully, or

(b) work out how much interest this comes to per day, and for how many days till it is all paid back, or

(c) refuse absolutely to have anything to do with the moneylender?

There is really no choice here: (b) does not really help, although if you do this it will bring home to you the size of the problem, and (c) would be the end of the chance to make anything in the market.

You can go on with this exercise by inventing more possible choices, but the point is that there really are no choices for the very poor.

A basic community begins with the belief that it is possible to help yourselves. But it is very hard for those who have been really poor all their lives, and have only had experiences like the exercise you did above, ever to believe that it is worth trying to do anything. That is why help has got to come from somewhere, and it is usually in South and Central America the priest or a teacher (some of whom are nuns or other religious) who gets a small group of people together in the first place. Their faith in Christ and in the church is thus a fundamental part of their faith in themselves. After all they have got to realise that they themselves actually are the church in that place.

Latin American society can present strong differences between the roles of men and women. However poor in terms of money, jobs or opportunities, a lot of men like to appear strong. It has been known for a man to beat his wife and terrify his children. For those who are miserable, alcohol is a constant temptation, so too is the chance to run off for a few days with another man or woman.

Being a Christian does not automatically cut one off from these influences nor prevent one from committing these sins and others. But a basic community is small enough for every member, men and women and children, to know each other and to trust each other and to help each other. Some people have written about the need to drive out the 'demons' of drink and male chauvinism from the Christian communities, the need to help those individuals who fail and encourage them to try again. In addition to all this, there is for the first time the real possibility of making things better in ordinary life, at home, at work, in the marketplace.

A shanty town on the edge of a city in South America

All hard at work!

ACTIVITY: as a group

The following activity will help you to see how this is done. You need to get together your small group of five or six, because the work is about just such a group.

1 **Imagine that your school or college will not teach you any more, but you are all still determined to pass your examinations.** Just why you have had to leave college does not matter for this exercise, but feelings are bad: maybe they threw you all out, or they decided to charge high fees which you could not pay, or the government simply decided to shut the place down in order to save money. In spite of your resentment, you want to do this exam, and need to think what you can do about it.

2 You know how much time you have got in hand, and you know what the exam syllabus is (or syllabuses). The first decision: can you do this alone by private study? Or would it be better to work as a group?

3 You decide to work as a group. Do you need any outside help? If so, who can you turn to? Do you need help with books and other resources? What about visits and so on? Libraries, museums?

4 Can you divide up the work between you? Would it help to assign individual tasks and then to come together to share your insights and findings?

5 What can you do about practice in writing answers for examination papers and under examination conditions? What can you do about marking or assessing them?

ACTIVITY: on your own

For follow-up work, write about two pages on working for the GCSE Christianity paper out of school–time and in the holidays.

What you have just been thinking about should give you some clues about basic communities in Central America. Instead of having to borrow money at high interest rates from the moneylender, the group can form a small credit union and pool their cash. To do this, everyone pays in so much a week (a small sum), then members are allowed to borrow at low rates of interest, and are on trust to pay it back. Because a lot of members want to borrow at the same time, there has got to be a rota system for taking turns.

Similar sharing may apply when there is a shortage of paid work (which there is). Jobs too can be shared out, instead of one family household having two or three incomes when others maybe have none. There is no unemployment benefit (dole) in most of these countries.

Employers are often big firms controlled from overseas (mostly U.S.A.) and they often try to push down wages or demand difficult and dangerous working conditions. Previously the only people who dared go on strike were the unmarried young people who had no family responsibilities, but these are the less skilled and the less experienced workers whom the firms can most easily fire and replace. But the basic community makes all the difference, because the basic community can really support the family of someone on strike, or in prison (which is often the result of going on strike or of attending a political meeting).

Other 'miracles' happen too. The basic community is usually small enough for every member to have a say, and of course this includes women as well as men. Sometimes, therefore, you can see a group of women keeping the men in order, and this is a real wonder and miracle in Latin America! Another example can arise when some of the men are called away to a week–end conference which is being held for members of several communities together. They kiss their wives goodbye, and when they come back their children are pleased to see them again, and wives too are specially welcoming and eager to hear how things went. This is all quite different from old times when a man only went off for the week–end to mess with another woman.

Basic Christian communities are like the building blocks for today's church, at any rate in the countries where they are springing up. But the men and women who form them are in the main poor and humble people who are used to being pushed around by the powerful. In this respect they are very like some of the earliest Christian congregations in the time of the apostles. It feels as if something which is very important to Christianity is being rediscovered. Meanwhile, the military leaders and the powerful families in many countries of Latin America call themselves Christian too. The basic communities seem to be saying to them: 'You too are just as much prisoners to riches as we are to poverty. No–one is perfect, but if you join and help us you will get something of the vision of the working of Jesus Christ in the world today'.

It may not be obvious at first why these basic communities are important for the study of Christianity.

ACTIVITY: as a group

Get your small group together to talk over these questions, but each of you should have your own pencil and paper ready to take some notes (see below).

(a) How are the basic communities in Central America related to Christianity? Is it because they are almost always started by a priest or Christian teacher, or is there any other reason?

(b) Can you think of anything in the Bible, especially the teachings of Jesus, which says anything about changing people's lives and the ways in which these particular people are trying to change their own lives?

(c) In what ways are these basic communities like the experience of other Christian groups you know or have learnt about?

(d) How might they become important for the world–wide church if they really begin spreading in other parts of the world, Asia and Africa for instance?

Each of you should make notes during this discussion.

ACTIVITY: on your own

Write about two pages on basic Christian communities.
Say first what they are, and then whether you think they can improve the life of their members.

Chapter Four

PERSECUTION

Persecution means that a strong government with at least some popular support tries to suppress or punish a group of people who think and act differently from themselves. Christian history is full of persecutions. During the first three centuries, the pagan Roman Empire had campaigns from time to time against Christians because they seemed to pose a political threat.

Why did they seem to pose a threat to the rulers? Probably the main reason was that Christians professed loyalty to Jesus (whom the Romans had officially executed) instead of to the Emperor; and secondly, the Roman authorities could be almost paranoiac about any group which looked like a secret society, possibly plotting disobedience and revolution. We know that the citizens of Nicomedea in Asia Minor (modern Turkey) were even forbidden to form a voluntary fire brigade (nothing to do with religion or politics). In addition to all this, some people stirred up popular hatred by saying that Christians held secret meetings when they ate human flesh and blood, so they were also murderers and cannibals.

The Christians at that time wanted to react by living peacefully and being good neighbours to each other, and to Jews and pagans alike. But it was hard. They thought that in their sufferings, which often led to fines, imprisonment and death, they were sharing in the sufferings of Jesus

Christ. In extreme cases, some Christians actually looked forward to death as release from a wicked world.

Usually, persecution is part of a campaign led by the ruling authorities and carried out by army or police, using force and public propaganda. But persecution can also be unofficial. There is always the idea of a strong group bullying a weaker or smaller one, and trying to stir up public hate against them by any means in their power. The persecution of Christians did not end in the fourth century when the Emperor Constantine made Christianity legal. As we shall see, sometimes Christians are the persecutors too, either against another sort of Christian, or against Jews, or a group of 'different' people whom they think of as undesirable.

Persecution always has political implications. In the first three centuries the Romans said that Christians were disloyal to the Roman Emperor; Catholic France at one time wanted to be rid of Protestants; and the Protestant English for some generations after Queen Mary (died 1557) thought that all Catholics must be agents of Spain or France and traitors to England. Today persecution is still for political reasons, and Christians are sometimes still involved.

For and Against the Police

Persecution normally uses authority and force, and typical persecutors would be a government with the help of police. In the two very different stories of persecution which follow, the police are involved. This is not because policemen and women are particularly bad or good — they are much like other people — but because the police force is always on the side of law and public order and is expected to carry out the policy decisions of the ruling government. If the government is oppressive, then the police cannot help being part of this, however much individual police officers may dislike it, and may be able to do individual acts of humanity, sometimes at personal risk to themselves.

Many schools in Britian invite the police in to deal with topics like road safety. This is both valuable in itself and also serves to build confidence in the community, and policemen and women are also part of the community in which they work. The exact opposite happens when the police are used to arrest and persecute members of any group who are thought to pose a threat to the state. This is what has happened in the two cases in this section, one from communist Russia and the other from apartheid–run South Africa.

ACTIVITY: as a group

Consider the following case. It is an example which has been used many times, and this is because it is a real one.

Get your group together — as usual, five or six is the best number — and talk through this problem from one point of view.

Each imagine that you are Jo (male or female, it doesn't matter), **and that you are known to be an extremely open and honest person.** In fact you cannot tell a lie without it showing in your face. One evening there is a knock at your door: it is George, an old friend whom you like a lot, but he is obviously very upset. He says, '*There's been trouble in the city centre: the police were out; people throwing* *bricks. I've got out; I just want to lie down and keep out of trouble'.*

You let him in. You don't know what he's done, or even if he's done anything, except that he is a student at a poly which has a reputation for community action. He goes upstairs.

Twenty minutes later a car draws up. A knock at the door, and it is a police squad car: *'We're looking for someone called George and we have reason to believe that he has come here'.*

You cannot just stand there with your mouth open.

- What do you do?
- On a piece of paper make a note of what seem to be the best ideas.

ACTIVITY: on your own

For follow-up work, choose two of the ideas which your group has just thought were 'best ideas'.

Choose two which are likely to produce different results.

Write about page on each, giving reasons you think would count in favour of each or against.

Father Pavel

Father Pavel was a young trainee priest and theologian in Russia a few years before the 1917 revolution. Pavel is the Russian form of Paul. He married a girl student from his religion class called Nina, although it was clear that really Nina had chosen to marry him rather than the other way round. But he loved her, as she was very nice, lively and intelligent and also very pretty. Nina was a transparently honest person, the sort who could not deceive people, and Father Pavel sometimes called her 'Nathanael', the disciple in John's Gospel, 1.43–51, who was called *'an Israelite worthy of the name, in whom there is no deceit'.*

Nina had a strong social conscience too. When she was a teenage school–girl she had joined in non–violent demonstrations which were part of the first revolution of 1905, when after a general strike the Emperor introduced the first Russian parliament, the Duma. She qualified as a teacher and was very dedicated to her work. In the evenings she often talked things through with her husband, and helped him also with his sermons. Father Pavel became a priest in the city which was to be renamed Leningrad, and was becoming known for his sermons and his writings. They had no children.

After the October Revolution, which was in November 1917, the Communist government had very many troubles. As well as the effects of the war against Germany and the terrible conditions in the army and in industry and in the economy in general, it was clear that a lot of people did not support them. These were not just landowners who had been dispossessed and managers of industries, but many thinking people of all kinds had serious doubts about both the ideals and the methods used by the communists. There was considerable violence and cruelty in practice, which seemed to contradict the teaching and ideals of communism, even if the old regime had been as bad. Others felt that communism could not be made to work without a lot of force, and that it was anyway based on contradictions. Many of those who opposed Lenin and his followers were teachers and university professors, and the government had either to win their support or get them dismissed. Dismissal in practice meant prison and exile.

Nina joined the Communist Party. She understood the benefits to the whole people which the revolution promised and she wanted it to be a success. She had to stop going to church. She even set up a 'godless' corner in her classroom, as was becoming normal in schools where the government wanted to spread antireligious propaganda. She could no longer help Father Pavel with his writing and sermons. In any case she was rarely at home, but often out late at meetings, rallies and school outings.

Although the Communists were closing churches, the cathedral where Father Pavel served was still open till the end of the twenties. (It was later pulled down to make room for the KGB headquarters.) He was sad about his wife, but he did not oppose her, because he respected her as a responsible person with intelligence and a life of her own. Of course he prayed for her, even though he could no longer pray with her.

Nina wanted to bring students and sometimes other teachers home to their flat for planning sessions and other meetings. But anyone who came might meet Father Pavel in his priest's dress, and anyway there were religious icons (pictures of saints) on the wall and many religious books on the bookshelves.

A church in Russia being demolished

ACTIVITY: as a group

There are two questions for discussion here, and it would be good to explore them both before you read on to see what happened. They would be ideal for your small group.

1 What should Nina do?
She might decide never to bring anyone from her work

home, but other teachers did, and she did not want to be different. If she raises the matter with Pavel, what can she say?

2 How do you think Father Pavel should react when he understands the problem?

Even if she has not told him, he is still close to her and so he can sense the difficulty and knows what it is.

The story continues with a compromise. All the religious books are collected together and put into a large bookshelf in the passage which is covered with a curtain when not in use. The icons are also put away, and Father Pavel agrees to sit in the kitchen to read or write whenever school visitors come. This last is no real hardship as he does not want to take part in their meeting anyway.

One beautiful evening in late spring Father Pavel is returning after a glorious evensong in the cathedral. As he gets near the flat, Nina comes out, obviously on her way to a meeting. But she stops. It is such a wonderful evening that they decide to sit on a bench together in the park. She says she can miss her meeting. After some time of sitting and talking together, Nina tells him that the police interviewed her and asked her if her husband knew 'Professor X'. This was a retired professor of history who regularly attended church and made his confession to Father Pavel, not so much a personal friend but someone he knew very well.

'I told them that you did. Was that wrong?'

'No, of course, it is true. You must tell the truth'.

They talk about other things. They do not know that Professor X has already been arrested because some of his earlier writings seem to be sympathetic to those who were in power before the revolution. It is getting dark, and they get up to go home, to spend the evening over a leisurely supper. When they get to the door, neither of their keys will fit. Something is blocking the lock. The door is opened from inside, and a young man who is clearly a policeman in plain clothes tells them to come in. He says that they may have a cup of tea together, but that Father Pavel must put a few things into a case and go along with him.

It is eighteen months before Nina is allowed to visit him in prison. He is in a terrible state. Bad food, illtreatment and a lot of solitary confinement have all taken their toll. He is bent and thin, and he has lost a lot of teeth. Nina is very upset. She is told he is to be sent to Siberia and has a 25 year sentence. In exile one is allowed to live a normal life in a village, do a job, earn money, but not allowed to leave until the sentence is up. But it is only too clear that Father Pavel cannot now live very long, least of all in Siberia, cut off from the Church and everything that he loves.

Nina does not know what to do. An exile is allowed to have a few of his own possessions and may also take a close relative. Should she go to Siberia with him? Although he would not be allowed to work as a priest and would not be fit for manual work on a collective farm or engineering project, she could certainly get work as a teacher. But without anyone to help him, Father Pavel would be dependent on people's kindness and on food parcels.

Nina consults Father Pavel's closest relatives: these are his widowed sister, her daughter of eighteen training to be a pharmacist, and his younger brother who is not married. They are all fond of Father Pavel, especially the girl, who regards him as her spiritual father, and they are all very upset.

ACTIVITY: as a group

There are four characters here. They are Nina who is Father Pavel's wife; his widowed sister Maria; her daughter Alya; and Pavel's younger brother called Arseny.

The group should discuss this situation, and four members could take a part each. The fifth and sixth can either give general advice, or can represent what you think Father Pavel himself would say when he hears about each suggestion, only of course he is really still in the prison. Weigh up the pros and cons of each suggestion.

ACTIVITY: on your own

Afterwards, each of you can write individually what you think would be the best thing from the point of view of one of the participants.

The end of the story is that first Arseny said he'd go, then found he couldn't, so Alya gave up her course of studies — she was partly qualified, enough to get work as a pharmacist's assistant — and followed as far as Irkutsk where she managed to see her uncle in the prison transit camp. But her mother Maria got very ill and sent a telegram, so Alya had to make the hard decision to go back.

On the last part of the journey, first by boat and then overland, Father Pavel was befriended by a young prisoner who found them both lodging with well–off peasants. The system was that anyone with a house larger than normal would have it taken away unless it was filled, so the peasant couple needed to give rooms to Father Pavel and the young man. Strangely, they were glad to have a priest in the village, even though he was now very ill, and they looked after him till he died.

Is the story of Father Pavel in any way typical of Christianity? Perhaps two things are worth noting: first, the villagers in Siberia were glad to have a priest to talk to, as was the young convict (he had murdered his wife and had a life sentence). There was no–one else they felt they could confide in, certainly not the Party official put in charge of them.

A village in Siberia

Secondly, history has shown again and again that Christianity seems to grow under persecution. It is as if when a government favours Christianity, like old Russia under the Czars, people's faith gets weak and their religion lazy and complacent. Certainly the example of Christ and countless saints and martyrs would suggest that the experience of suffering is an important aspect of Christianity in any age.

Oppression Based on Racial Difference

Slavery is a very ancient institution. The classical societies of ancient Greece and Rome used slaves, and slavery is referred to in places in the Bible as quite a normal thing. In the Bible, however, there is some stress on slaves being set free. In the world of the Roman Empire (and the New Testament was written within this cultural world) individual slaves could be set free, either by their masters as a mark of gratitude for something, or because a slave could buy his own freedom. After they had been freed, they suffered no special disadvantage and could rise to riches and to the most important political posts in the Empire.

The more modern experience of slavery is very different. The slaves in America and the Caribbean were all imported to work on the plantations, mainly cotton and sugar. Ships from countries in Europe, including England, went to West Africa to buy slaves from local chiefs, and then shipped them over the Atlantic to sell them at a good profit. This trade was enormous and millions were taken.

In the New World (the Americas), it was indeed possible for slaves to get their freedom. They could do this either by running away, so long as they were not caught and severely punished, or they could be set free by a grateful master or mistress. But even after freedom they could never (until this century) be equal. This was because the difference between masters and slaves was racial and not cultural and economic. They looked different, and this could be seen by anyone even from far away. So this kind of slavery was on a different footing from the older forms, as in the Roman Empire, where slaves could be of any tribe or race, and might not look at all different from their owners. In fact many wealthy Romans had educated Greek slaves as tutors for their children.

Christians and Oppression

When a group of Christians are oppressed or persecuted or feel very poor, they usually adopt one or other of the following possibilities. Either they try to improve things, working in faith and with prayer, but also actively resisting the oppressors. Sometimes they use force, but more usually non–violent means. They work to make their conditions better, form a credit union, a housing trust, or they work in health or education. The other possibility usually goes with a feeling of utter hopelessness, the feeling that the forces of evil are just too strong, and that there is nothing left but to pray for and wait for God's direct intervention, even if this means the end of the world. This second stance has been widespread also in non–Christian or semi–Christian groups and is typical among religions of the oppressed.

This same kind of hopelessness was felt by many of those who were slaves in America too. The once–famous book 'Uncle Tom's Cabin' written in 1851–2 by Harriet Beecher Stowe (1811–1896), includes some of the songs which slaves sang to express their longing for freedom. This freedom, some felt, could only be realised after death. In the book there are lines from the famous Latin hymn 'Dies irae, dies illa' about God's judgement at the end of the world. A longing for death as the end to suffering is also expressed in *'Swing low, sweet chariot, coming for to carry me home'*, a reference not to Moses but to the death of the prophet Elijah in the valley of the Jordan, as described in 2 Kings 2.7–14. You perhaps read this when you were studying the passage on the Ascension in Part One.

ACTIVITY

A useful exercise to do either alone or as a group would be to **get hold of a book of hymns as used commonly in black churches** (songs which a generation ago were called Negro Spirituals) — *'Lift Every Voice'* is suggested as an example — and **pick out those hymns which seem to be looking forward or longing for freedom and release.** Divide them into two groups:

Group A, those that look for release after death and through God's judgement

Group B, those that call for or expect changes to made in this life, here and now.

Steve Biko

Steve Biko belongs to South Africa, but his influence is felt far more widely. He was born in December 1946 and died in prison from exposure, beatings and serious brain damage in September 1977. He was only thirty when he died, but in his short life he founded the South African Students' Organisation, the Black People's Convention, and worked for the Black Community Projects in spite of banning and restriction orders. His entire philosophy and the aim of his work lay in his belief in what it means to be a human being.

It will be obvious that Biko believed people should help themselves. He considered that it was most important not to give in to the oppressors, that is the white government and their police force, by adopting and using their methods of violence. Therefore he stressed the importance of achieving his aims by non–violent means, even if it seemed to take much longer. In this he was much inspired by the example of Gandhi (who, incidentally, also originated from South Africa).

ACTIVITY: as a group

As long as Apartheid exists in South Africa, it will be a useful exercise for you to undertake as a group, if you can **collect over the period of a month, say, newspaper reports and articles about South Africa.**

You must decide whether you will confine your interest to the Republic of South Africa itself, or will include the activities of South African forces in neighbouring countries. This will depend on the amount of news available.

As you build up your collection, meet together to try and assess the standpoints of the people involved. The following categories should be helpful in this, but are only suggestions. These are not just 'either/or' but in threes:

Christian/communist/other non–Christian

use violent methods/reject the use of force/use force only in self–defence

revolutionary (want sudden changes)/reformist (i.e. think change should come gradually and by consent/do not want any social change

oppose Apartheid on human grounds/oppose Apartheid on business grounds/in favour of Apartheid

want peace imposed by a strong police force/peace at any price/peace only with justice

Many cases will need careful discussion.

This might be because the newspaper report does not really give you enough information of the sort you want, or because the people involved themselves are changing their position. You can be very committed to non–violent action, but suddenly when your home is burnt, your family attacked, and all you have worked for is destroyed, something snaps inside you and you react in hot anger. This of course applies to Christians as well as anyone else. Or you simply come to feel that 'they' do not understand anything else.

Here are further questions for your discussion:
When South African schoolchildren protest, is this passive resistance or is it anti–government violence?
Does a crowd always become violent?
What happens when people get suddenly afraid?

STEVE BIKO AND CHRISTIANITY

Steve Biko, painted as an icon by an American, Robert Lenz

Steve Biko was brought up as a Christian, but was not a regular church attender in later years. He remained very close to church people, however, (some individuals especially) and he came to holy communion in the eucharist from time to time, but not on any regular basis.

Some Christian groups take the view that either an individual is a member or he or she must be a non–member. They stress commitment, and say that it must be total and public. These Christians would say, therefore, that Biko should not be counted as a Christian.

Other Christians, however, would maintain that once a person has become a Christian, either by baptism or other public sign, then that person belongs to the Christian community unless he or she positively leaves, either by public statement, by actions which are opposed to Christianity, or by giving up all links. This view is inclusive rather than exclusive.

Steve Biko belongs to the second group. There can be little doubt that he considered himself a member of the wider Christian community, but like so many people overseas he had little time for the differences between the various denominations (all imported from Europe) or for certain aspects of church discipline.

Christians as Oppressors

It is easy to say that the Christian churches should be on the side of the poor and the oppressed, and therefore against the others. But this would not be entirely true. In South Africa, members of the government and police force, probably in fact most of them, also call themselves Christians. They regard themselves as the heirs of the promises of God to Moses and the Israelites that God has given them a land. Their land is South Africa.

They look back to the Old Testament story of Noah and his three sons, Shem, Ham and Japheth. After the Flood was over, Ham did something wrong, and was cursed. The Boers (South Africans of Dutch descent) say that all Africans are the descendants of Ham and therefore they are cursed for ever, to be the servants of the chosen race. Without approving of murder and violence, they believe that God has appointed two levels within human society, and they themselves happen to be the top one. According to them, racialism is ordained by God.

The 'non–Christian world' was hostile to Father Pavel. The Communist powers in Russia were openly atheist–materialist, and were closing churches and arresting clergy as fast as they thought they could get away with it. But the government responsible for the arrest and death of Steve Biko does not call itself atheist. Many of them say they are Christian, but they think that 'Christian' means the same as anti–communist, and then they call a 'communist' anyone who disagrees with them on any grounds. It seems also that they consider 'Christian' government to mean a strong government which uses force to silence all kinds of opposition or disagreement with what they are doing.

A white South African preacher, who felt he had a world–wide mission especially in Pentecostalist churches, was clearly shocked that students and workers in Britain and North America were allowed to hold demonstrations and take part in social protests which were widely reported in the press. He did not want to know whether some of these protests were Christian, or even what they were about. When he returned to South Africa, he sent a duplicated letter to his friends, and said, '*What a relief it is to come back to an orderly and civilised country*'. (It is necessary to understand that there is strict press censorship in South Africa and internal protests and disturbances may not be reported).

Chapter Five

WEAKNESS AND STRENGTH

Two pictures of Christ are particularly significant for Christians. One is Christ the King, who after his resurrection sits at the right hand of God (picture language obviously for the majesty of God as the Trinity). He will come again, according to Christian teaching, at the end of time to judge the living and the dead. This is the Pantocrator (Greek for Almighty) whose picture in mosaic or painted dominates the central part of many Orthodox churches, looking down from the dome.

Which of these pictures is the Pantocrator?

The other picture is an image of weakness. This is the head crowned with thorns, as Jesus was taken, though innocent, and nailed to a cross. This image as the crucifix is seen in many churches of all denominations. Another favourite picture is Jesus as the baby at Bethlehem. This is also a picture of God as weak and helpless, at the mercy of ordinary people who come in contact with him and his family.

We may add to this figure of helplessness the famous parable of the sheep and goats found in Matthew 25.31–46. There is an exercise based on this passage in Part Four, Chapter 3 on Judgement. In this parable Jesus identifies himself with the poor, the sick, the wretched of the earth, those whom many of us would rather not know, and if possible not even know about. So it is plain that weakness and strength in ordinary human terms can be very important for Christians and the way they live in their day to day life.

Russia before the revolution was in many ways a deeply Christian society, and perhaps it still is. There was a tradition in the villages that everyone looked after the handicapped, particularly the mentally handicapped. Such a person, in the days before they were collected into large residential homes, might like to wander about in the open air, visiting farms and smallholdings and appearing at the houses and cottages of the villagers. However inconvenient these visits might sometimes be, the general feeling was that it was a privilege to give food and shelter to this person, who in his (or her) simplicity and helplessness seemed to represent Christ to them. It was almost a sacramental experience.

Christians today who work with the handicapped have said that so far from them trying to teach the handicapped to do things (though they do this too), they have actually learnt far more from the handicapped about naturalness and simplicity, cheerfulness and honesty in personal relations. Of course such work can be tiring and frustrating too, but there are certainly Christians who regard it as a privilege to work with the very young or very old or physically and mentally handicapped. This sense of the presence of Christ, they claim, helps them to pray and teaches them to worship too.

People We Call Handicapped

We all know handicapped people, and we think we know what we mean when we say that someone is handicapped.

ACTIVITY: as a group

It would be a good idea just to **test this out by getting a small group together for a brainstorming session on 'handicap'.**

As usual with this method, when you have got a lot of suggestions try and sort them out into groups, for instance:

- mental handicap and physical
- permanent handicap and temporary
- congenital handicap (ones people are born with) and handicaps due to age or accident
- any other sorts of handicap?

Most schools at some stage have a practical social studies programme which gets the pupils out into the community visiting nursery schools, old people's homes, and homes or day centres for the handicapped. Some groups of pupils have taken on quite ambitious work projects, for instance starting up and running a radio station inside a hospital which meets special requests from patients, entertains, and maybe has its own news desk. One or two who have done this, have begun after leaving school a professional career on local radio or television.

Obviously people of all religions (or none) say you ought to be kind to people in need, help those less fortunate than yourself, and so on — all quite true. In a section of this book about Christians and the handicapped, however, there is much more to think about. At the same time the ideas to be discussed are not exclusively Christian. Christians who are active in this kind of work do not claim to be doing something

Children often take harvest festival gifts to old and needy people

that no–one else is doing. Yet their attitudes tie in with the way in which Christians understand what it means to be a human being in a world created by God and redeemed by Christ, for this is the Christian starting–point. In its effects, however, there cannot always be a distinction between '*Christian*' work and the same work done by non–Christians.

An Exercise in Caring, and What It Teaches

You have probably at some time done an exercise where one person is blindfolded and a companion who is not leads him or her about the room, or even outside, using hand pressure to steer and to negotiate problems. Contact is maintained through the fingers of one hand, that is the person wearing the blindfold holds out a hand and the one who is to guide just holds the fingers lightly in hers (or his), enough to give directions like turn, stop, forward and so on through gentle finger pressure. This is really designed to be an exercise in trust: the 'blind' person has got to trust the other implicitly, and the one who is leading must make efforts to deserve this trust and live up to it. Then they change places, and the one who was blindfold before now leads the other.

But of course at the same time, you also get an idea of how much you rely on your eyes, and what a shock it would be suddenly to go blind.

If you have never done this exercise before, you might like to find a partner and do it, either in the room or outside, but it is important to have a peaceful environment which is safe from obvious dangers.

Yet this is not exactly an exercise to tell us what it would be like to be blind. You could think about a visit to an art gallery, or to a film for that. It is, as has been said, an exercise in trust. One of the most impressive things arising from this exercise is what it feels like to be trusted when you are the guide. It is quite a responsibility.

But there is something else too. The exercise depends on one person being blind and the other being sighted. The partners in each pair have got clearly defined roles. Modern society tries to do this with the handicapped, and for the purposes of social and health care officials want to be able to define exactly who is to count as handicapped and who is not.

Look back now to the brainstorming you did at the start of this chapter. Did you count people in prison as handicapped? Or refugees? Or people with social disadvantages? Perhaps in the end everyone is handicapped in some way, but some are easier to cope with than others. But at the same time it is obvious that if the social services department (or any other group) are going to do things for 'the handicapped' they need to decide exactly who comes into this category. Thus defining some people as handicapped is a purely practical matter, and should not mean that the rest of us are all perfectly normal and all right.

Giving Sight to the Blind

This whole subject is a very important one for Christians. It is easy to see that throughout the Bible the 'disadvantaged' figure very largely. Some of the stories in the gospels relate occasions when Jesus healed a blind person. Some people say that these stories are symbolic, and that the blind person stand for people who do not understand who Jesus is and what he is doing. As they come to him, he gets them to 'see' in the sense of understand. Yet it is also clear that physically blind people were cured too.

People who feel depressed or worried or guilty also need to be touched in the way that doctors and modern psychiatrists try to free them from their burdens and their problems. This can be a long and difficult business. Christians, however, have always seen this as part of the Christian ministry of healing.

Getting people to 'see'

ACTIVITY: on your own

Look in Luke's gospel, chapter 4.16–21, and read about the sermon which we are told Jesus spoke at Nazareth, his home town, at the very start of his ministry. Notice that he read out a passage from the Old Testament, from the prophetic book of Isaiah.

1 **Read this quotation from Isaiah carefully**, and note down each specific thing that Jesus says is about to be done.
2 **Now find in a modern hymn book, the famous hymn by Charles Wesley** (1707–1788) **which begins** '*O for a thousand tongues to sing my dear Redeemer's praise*'. This hymn is still very popular today. Read this hymn through, and note especially in verses 3 and 4 anything which links in with the passage in Luke you just read.
3 **Now go back to Luke's gospel, and read about the question John the Baptist asked when he was locked up in prison.** This is in Luke 7.18–22.
   - Note down on a piece of paper first of all any things which are to be found in *all* three passages you have just read (the two passages in Luke, and the hymn by Charles Wesley), then anything that is in only *two* of them, then anything which is only in *one*.

Count Your Blessings

ACTIVITY: as a group

For this exercise you need a piece of paper and a pen or pencil each. It will be most effective if you take each step at a time, and only read on to the next step when you have completed the one before.

1 Collect your small group together, but working alone at first, and without saying anything, each of you **write down three things that you value most in your life as it is**. Take about five minutes for this.
2 When you are all ready, then **in turn tell other members of the group what you have chosen, and say why you appreciate or value this thing or quality or person so much.** Of course you have listed three things so you talk a bit about each of them.
3 When every member of the group has done this, you have to begin part two, but using the same piece of paper. **You have got to give up two of the items on your list, and keep only one.**

   Again you have about five minutes of silence working on your own. Think carefully, and gently cross out two of the items you had.
4 When you have all done this, you have got one item left. **Take turns again to explain to the group why you value this thing more than the other two.**

5 Now comes the crunch. Imagine that this last and most valued thing has been taken from you, not from your own choice, but you have simply been deprived of it.
- Crunch up your piece of paper and throw it away.
- Take turns to tell the rest of the group how you feel now.

BEING DEPRIVED

You will certainly feel deprived after doing the last exercise. In your case you lost something you valued, and how you feel may depend in part on what kind of thing this was: whether it was something you could do, like seeing or singing or swimming; or something you possessed like a music centre or wonderful clothes; or it may have been a relationship with another person or people.

If you had never had this in the first place, perhaps things would not feel so bad. On the other hand you might wish you could do some of the things other people are able to do, such as play the violin or travel.

Some Christians say that God loves the poor because that is what he wants them to stop being. That means, the poor want to see changes, and they have got potential. The same applies to anyone who is suffering from a disability or disadvantage. In the section on Basic Communities it is suggested that Basic Communities provide a way forward because small groups of people can get together and share their abilities as well as their troubles, and generally help each other. They do not have to sit down under conditions as they are.

But a community like this demands sharing and trust. Everyone has something to contribute and everyone is in some way in need of help. Christians working with the handicapped start with this idea.

L'Arche

Arche is the French for Ark, meaning Noah's Ark. So the word suggests a place of safety from the floods and disasters going on outside. The story of Noah includes a promise made after the flood that God would not destroy mankind by a universal flood again, and the sign of God's promise was of course the rainbow in the sky, and this in French is *Arc–en–ciel*. *Arc* and *Arche* are not so far apart, and the sign of promise and of hope is suggested by the very name of the home which a French–speaking Canadian called Jean Vanier started with two mentally handicapped men at Trosly in France in 1964.

Noah's ark and the rainbow, on a modern stained glass window in France

Jean Vanier (left) and Raphael

Jean Vanier left the Royal Canadian Navy in the 1950s. His Christian vocation led him eventually to work with the handicapped, and he started this house with two men, called Raphael and Philippe. Both were mentally handicapped. He quickly found that he was not there to do things for them, but to do things together and with them. This was brought home to him because of their history and the nature of their handicap.

These two men had been born into a family, and like most people had grown up with brothers and sisters. But a mentally handicapped person can be difficult to live with for many reasons, and both these men had been rejected by their families. They found this experience deeply wounding. They could not understand it and both of them were psychologically damaged by what happened. So in starting a household with Raphael and Philippe, Jean Vanier was not just trying to make the best of life with two people who had mental problems: they were also people who had been deeply hurt. You could say that because of their history, Vanier was not just starting at square one, but well behind the starting line.

ACTIVITY: as a group

To try and visualise this, get the group together to discuss the following problem:

Imagine that someone like Jean Vanier has bought a house in your street or in your village, at any rate not far from where you live, and is going to set up house with two or three mentally handicapped men. The men have had a bad time in the past, and Jean Vanier wants to build up their confidence and their trust. This means that the doors of the house are not going to be locked, and they will be free to come and go at any time.

- Talk over in the group how you will feel about having this little group as near neighbours?
- How might other people feel?
- Sort out the reasons for these feelings and reactions.
- Are they based on faith or fear, or worries about your own family, or what other people in the neighbourhood might say?

ACTIVITY: as a group

Local residents form a committee to discuss Jean Vanier's application for Planning Permission. Your group is that committee.

Sort out the arguments in favour of allowing this home to be set up near you, and the arguments against.

ACTIVITY: on your own

For follow—up work, each of you **write two pages saying why you either do or do not support this project in your street.**

Go on to say what you intend to do either to help it (if you are in favour) or to stop it (if you are against).

FAMILIES AND NEIGHBOURS

L'Arche has now got fifty houses in different countries around the world. The majority of the staff are Christians, from a variety of churches and denominations, but the homes also try to keep a local atmosphere. In Calcutta, for instance, many of those who live at the house are Hindus, plus a few from Muslim families, and their background is respected without trying to make them conform to Christianity. It is true that the home works closely with the Missionaries of Charity: this is the order founded by Mother Teresa. The link with the sisters provides both practical help and also religious and emotional support for both sides, but on a completely voluntary and unofficial basis.

In this kind of work, three levels of relationship need to be explored. The first level is within each community house itself, the relationship between those who live there, whether as handicapped or as people who have come to care for them. The second level which must be handled very carefully is the relationship between each person and the family from which they came, if it can be traced. Thirdly, there are the neighbours, those who live nearby, and it should be clear from the exercises you did in the previous section that there can be very mixed reactions to having a house full of 'non—normal' people living in your street.

First, think how people feel about each other in the house itself. Many young men and women who hear about this work want to come and work with the handicapped, because they feel a sense of vocation, usually religious vocation, and because they want to do something worthwhile with their abilities and their lives. They want to give. And if they are going to give, then there must be someone to receive. But life in *l'Arche* is not quite like that. The helper who wants to be active all the time meets endless frustration. Other people may think differently, or may be naturally slow or obstinate or simply fail to understand. Quite a lot of people do not actually like having 'good' done to them all the time. The handicapped are no exception.

This means that the young helper has much to learn, and from the handicapped themselves. These are qualities like patience, simplicity and cheerfulness, and the whole business of taking time just to treat people

255

as human beings. Like anyone else, handicapped men and women and children can be cross and frustrated, especially frustrated when they cannot do things. What would it be like if you urgently wanted to say something but found you were unable to speak? So giving and taking has to be mutual. Further, Jean Vanier is very much aware that 'carers' also need to be cared for, and *l'Arche* has got networks set up to cope with this need.

Perhaps this is another way of saying that everyone is '*handicapped*' in some way.

It was mentioned in the cases of Raphael and Philippe that they had been deeply wounded. Often a family ask for a seriously handicapped child or other relative to be taken into a special community because they can no longer care for her or him full–time at home. The family can then come on visits, send clothes and other presents, and welcome their child home at week–ends or festivals like Christmas.

But some families can be very upset and feel ashamed if their child is not 'normal' in some way. They want to put the whole thing out of sight and not have to think about it. Naturally the child feels rejected. Jean Vanier recalls one young man who desperately wanted to telephone his mother. He was able to do this, although everyone knew it would end badly. His mother said to him on the phone, '*You are insane and we don't want you*'. It is not surprising that he was very upset. The communities of *l'Arche* reckon that the families of handicapped people need help too, though not as urgently as the people in their houses, and of course a good relationship with the family helps each individual to feel as normal as possible.

The third relationship has already been discussed in outline. But in addition to all the problems you talked over in the exercise, when a house is set up in a very poor district in a Third World country (as some are), neighbours can feel jealous if food, clothes, money and other resources just come through the post or from the bank, while they themselves are often in great need. It is important here for *l'Arche* also to be poor. Neighbours can be much more friendly when you have to go round to borrow sugar, or can lend them salt and flour. This is an interesting example of Christian sharing within the wider community.

The Hospice Movement

Hospices are homes for the dying. The hospice movement is quite a modern development and nearly all of them were started by Christians. Like the schools and the hospitals, however, the hospices too will probably be handed over to the state when the state is ready for them and perhaps the Christian churches will start something new. Perhaps the best known of the homes for the dying is the one started by Mother Teresa in Calcutta. Mother Teresa's Missionaries of Charity now have homes for the dying in many cities all over the world, and the sisters also do other work among the very poorest of the poor. This work contrasts with older ideas of mission in which the plan was to convert people and encourage them to bring up Christian families. But these homes are not intended to convert those who have simply been brought in to die. They have got no future in human terms. The sisters are simply trying to make real in today's world some of the things you read about in Luke's gospel and in Charles Wesley's hymn.

Chapter Six

WOMEN AND MEN

If there is a row or an argument, people take notice. When it comes to relations between women and men in the Christian community, the news media only seem to get interested if there is either a notable sexual scandal, or a public argument about what work men or women may and may not do, like whether women should be ordained priests in the church. Most denominations already ordain women to the church's ministry, but these denominations do not include the two or three largest. The question of women's ordination is taken up later.

Family Power Social Change

A project called '*Family Power Social Change*' was started in 1973 as a result of the World Council of Churches' conference in Malta. Delegates felt that this project was needed as a response to rapid social change. Social change is particularly destructive in countries of the Third World, when traditional village and family life breaks up because people flock into the industrial cities in search of paid work. European societies went through tremendous social changes within six or seven generations as a result of the industrial revolution and its aftermath (which included two world wars). The process of change has not stopped. In the Third World, however, traditional patterns of society are going through the same sorts of changes in two or three generations, which is much quicker.

A discussion over lunch at the Community of St Francis, Brixton, London

Christians at the World Council of Churches conference in 1973 came up with Family Power because they realised that people naturally had close feelings about their families, and that this could be a power for good, especially if a group of families who lived near each other could pool their skills and resources. In this way the movement is rather like the basic communities (pages 233–238). The difference is that the Family Power project is designed to help people cope with rapid social change, due maybe to education, better health, industrialisation or unemployment. And they reckon that the best way to cope with social change is to train people to look ahead, and by supporting each other to gain the confidence to plan their lives in the light of their Christian experience.

In all traditional societies women and men have different roles in relation to each other, the household and the bringing up of children. The Family Power project started out from this pattern of life and has helped Christians to make decisions together on a basis of equality. Groups are quite small, and members' ages have ranged from 2 to 77. Single people and one–parent families can also be members of such a group. All have a part to play, just as far as they want.

In one group of families with children, the children were asked to choose an adult in their group whom they would like to know better. Of course this was only after the group had been established for some time. The result was a marked improvement in the relationships between parents and their children, and a pattern of life evolved which was closer to the extended family of earlier, pre–industrial times.

ACTIVITY: as a group

At this point it would be helpful to **have a small group discussion on whether people of different ages and sexes can share in making decisions which affect them all.**

Obviously you should produce an answer which says more than 'Yes' or 'No'.

Persuade one of your number of take notes on the points raised in discussion, which can be shared with other groups later, if required. Here are some questions to start you off:

1 Are there some kinds of questions which only men ought to decide, or only women?
2 Have children, even fairly young children, got worthwhile views on family life? Or about how they should be brought up?
3 Is it a good idea for three or four neighbouring families to do things together? For instance, going on a joint holiday?
4 How might being Christian make any difference to any of these questions and their answers?

Christians believe that in responding to social change they have two resources to help them. One of these is the whole Christian tradition with its roots in the scriptures and lived out over the centuries. By going back to their roots, Christians are helped to make decisions which affect their personal life and their social relationships. The other resource is the spirit of God who they feel is leading and guiding them. This may be felt through prayer and meditation, through group discussion, or through public events in the same way that prophets in the Bible saw God's message within world affairs. Social change too might be a means of seeing the way God is leading.

Jobs for the Girls

You probably all know people who have got different views on the subject of women at work. Many people say that women ought to have the same education and career opportunities as men. Some go further and say that because of past disadvantage women actually need some discrimination in their favour. The official line in Britain is defined by the 'equal opportunities' legislation. Against this, some people stress the unique role women have as mothers, and say that at least while the children are small mothers ought to spend time with them. They claim that this view is somehow more 'natural'.

Working women?

Yet in many countries women have traditionally done a great deal of productive work, including agriculture and building work. In West Africa today most of the cloth trade is run by businesswomen, not men, and women also started and financed public transport, popularly known as 'Mammy Buses'. In Britain some people may think that it is wrong for the mother of young children to go out to work, even though good arrangements may have been made for them. In communist countries people think the opposite, that is they think very badly of a woman who gives up her job, even for a short while, in order to be with her young children and bring them up. They say she is lazy.

This was a topic for discussion in a Family Power group in East Germany, while one or two communists were members of the group. East Germany is a communist country where Christians live in a mainly anti–Christian and atheist society. Yet it sometimes happens that communist families join with Christians in a Family Power group. It seems that some communists want to join what is basically a Christian group. Is this because they are in process of changing their allegiance? Possibly, but not necessarily: maybe they feel that the roots of Christian tradition and faith are deeper and more significant than those of communism. This means that what binds families together is deeper than the political party.

Should all jobs be open to men or women without discrimination? This question only needs discussion if there is some disagreement in the group! You must realise, however, that this is not only a religious question, nor is there just one possible answer for religious people. Within any of the world's major religions there is room for different views.

Christians draw on their roots in the Christian tradition, and in particular they look back to Jesus and the New Testament as a pattern for their action and their attitudes. Quite a lot of the people we read about in the New Testament are women. Most notable obviously is the Mother of Jesus who is central to the accounts of the birth of Christ in Matthew and Luke, and is also at the scene of the crucifixion in the gospel of John. There are other references as well. Only Luke's gospel includes the psalm which was given to her when she went to call on her cousin Elisabeth a few months before the birth of Jesus. This is a truly remarkable psalm, and seems to contain the central Christian programme if it is compared with the first sermon of Jesus in the same gospel.

ACTIVITY

On your own or in pairs

Take a bit of time over this exercise, because it seems so surprising that these thoughts should be spoken by a woman. Do this exercise either on your own, or in pairs if you think that will be better.

1 Find the psalm in Luke 1.46–55 (commonly called 'Magnificat') and read it through.
2 Note down the main things in it. Pick out what seems important to you.
3 Now turn to a similar passage in the Old Testament, the song of Hannah, the mother of Samuel, in I Samuel 2.1–10.
4 Compare these two for similarities and differences.
5 Now look at the words of Jesus in the synagogue at Nazareth, as seen in Luke 4.16–21. Note down any links you can spot between this passage and the other two.
6 For follow–up work, write about a page on why you think the Magnificat is important for Christians.
7 Finally, do you think it a good thing that this psalm was spoken by a woman, or does it not make any difference who said it first?

Ordination of Men and Women

The question of women's ordination has arisen in this century with particular force because of social change. Christians are part of world society and are caught up in social changes, even if they decide that the right thing to do is to resist. Yet in some cases social change is actually started by Christians. The abolition of slavery is a clear example.

Many Christian denominations have ordained women pastors and ministers as well as men. The largest, however, do not allow this. These are the Roman Catholic Church and the different Orthodox churches. On the other hand over the centuries Christian women in both east and west have exercised great influence even in religious matters either as mystics, teachers, abbesses (leaders of religious communities for women), and of course always as mothers. It is not difficult to find examples in history.

There are many new books and articles on the ordination of women, putting arguments for and against. Some of these discuss what seems to have been the situation in the Bible, especially in the years when the apostles, including of course Paul, were active.

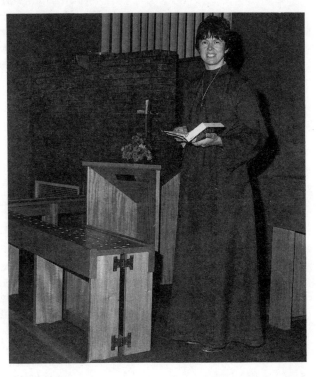

A woman deacon in the Church of England about to take a service

Arguments for the ordination of women to be priests, and bishops too, usually centre on two areas. One is the equality of men and women as suggested by many texts in the Bible, as well as in certain phases of Christian history. This argument boils down to (a) women are just as able as men to be leaders and to preside over the sacred mysteries. Women already preach, and obviously have done so since New Testament times; and (b) Jesus Christ has removed all barriers which separate rich and poor, male and female, Jew and Greek (= non–Jew), so it is actually necessary to put this into practice in modern life in the churches.

The other area is more subtle. It is claimed that there is an important psychological difference between male and female, and this is the contrast between the commanding, decisive role and the gentle, more caring role. It is recognised that both men and women share these characteristics, although caring is more typical of the female, while aggression is more typical of the male. It is obvious that leadership in the church requires both sorts of quality. Perhaps pastoral work actually requires '*female*' qualities rather than the others. This argument then is not just that women ought to be allowed to be priests, but that the job actually requires women as well as men.

The arguments against are mainly based on church tradition and the Bible. Jesus did not appoint any women among his twelve disciples — but there is no denying that it was a man who betrayed him! The apostles were apparently all men, and if the elders (presbyters = priests) and bishops are the successors of the apostles, then they ought to be male too. The argument also draws on the male gender of God as Father, and of Jesus. Can this all be dismissed by saying that in the Bible both Old and New Testaments took shape in male–dominated societies? Of course there are influential women in the Bible and in church history.

The matter is further complicated by practical considerations. The fact is that very many Christians of both sexes are simply opposed to the idea of women priests. To force women priests on these people would simply cause breakaway movements, probably on a massive scale. These factors cannot be ignored.

Every now and then the question of the ordination of women to the priesthood flares up in the newspapers. It is a live issue in parts of the Roman Catholic church, but in the Anglican church it has become especially topical because some Anglican provinces do ordain women to the priesthood and others do not. Women deacons are relatively new for Anglicans.

ACTIVITY: as a group

There may be women pastors and preachers attached to congregations in your area, whom you could meet and talk to. Collect material for an informed debate either in your group or with the whole class, after doing the following:

1 Collect newspaper cuttings on this subject, and try to arrange the arguments for and against.
2 Interview one or two women ministers: these could be from any church or denomination, not only Church of England. Ask them specific questions, which you will need to think out in advance.
3 Find the names of women in the New Testament who were either among the disciples of Jesus, or who were active in mission work at the time of St Paul.
4 Find the names of a few of the women who have been active in Christian history, and a little bit about each of them.

Note: You may find that the people you interview in 2 can give you some help with 3 and 4.

When you have got this information together, organise it for discussion either in the small group, or as a debate in the whole class.

(for more on Women and Men see Part Three, Chapter 3 on Marriage)

ACTIVITY: on your own

For follow–up work, **write in about two sides of paper a speech which could be given by someone who is to open a debate on the subject of women's ordination, either for or against.**

Use material you have collected. This is likely to centre on a particular church or denomination: if it does, simply say which church you are mainly talking about.

Chapter Seven

WORRIED ABOUT THE FUTURE

Many school leavers today say that whether they eventually get married or not, they do not intend to have children. They can point to the rapid growth in world population this century and may feel this planet is already too crowded. As a result of economic and other pressures, many families in Europe both east and west have only one child; one child per family is the official policy in China; the Indian government twenty years ago launched a campaign to persuade parents to limit their family size. But the increase still goes on, mainly in South America, in Africa and a number of other Third World countries.

But overpopulation is not the only anxiety which young people feel today. Different things worry people, all of them important to the people concerned, and some of them are important for everyone. One way to find out what these are is for you to ask each other. But before you do this, do some thinking on your own first, following the stages of this exercise.

ACTIVITY: as a group

Get your small group together, and make sure that everyone has got a piece of paper and something to write with.

1 **Without talking to each other, think about life ten or twenty years into the future.**

Then write down on your paper up to three things which you think will be important to you and your quality of life personally.

What you have in fact come up with may be any one of a number of things. This section is going to concentrate on war and nuclear war, but equally a lot of young people are seriously worried by a range of things. Among the most common are: parents separating (family breakup), pollution of the environment, AIDS, exploitation of animals, unemployment, and the threat of nuclear war (which probably includes serious destruction of the environment for those who survive).

Nuclear Weapons

Almost everyone is opposed to the use of nuclear weapons. Some scientists who are experts in both nuclear physics and environmental studies say that even a few missile explosions would seriously upset the ecology of our planet Earth. The consequences could be biologically disastrous. Others dispute this, and say that a limited nuclear war would be bad, but in the end human life would recover. The effects in any case would be most unpleasant.

Christians react to the threat of nuclear war in the same variety of ways as other people. This does not mean that they are not being Christian, but the fact does invite us to look more closely into the principles behind their decision. What a Christian decides, by the way, ought to take the consequences into consideration as well as the motive: this means that most Christians do not say, '*I will apply this rule* (say one of the Commandments from the Bible) *without any regard for the consequences. Because it is God's order, then if it goes wrong it's not my fault. What God commands he's responsible for, not me.*'

There is no denying that many people feel so threatened by nuclear war that they hardly dare to think about it. They blank it right out of their minds. Christians, like anyone else, are often guilty of blocking out unpleasant thoughts through despair or fear. But in principle the resurrection of Jesus Christ is supposed to be a sign of hope for Christians. Christianity at its best is a faith that looks forward to the future.

So against the threat of nuclear war today's Christians have got values which are important, but they need to be searched for and uncovered. The main reason why they are not on the surface and easy to find is that nuclear war and its accompanying risks form a new threat which has been with us less than fifty years. It is not specifically mentioned in the Bible (see later for a possible mention).

Some Christians are opposed to warfare of any kind. Quakers have taken this position ever since they began in the seventeenth century. In times of war Quakers have refused to use weapons, either facing

A nuclear test explosion in the Nevada desert, USA

punishment for refusing to join the army or serving instead as ambulance drivers and other no less dangerous jobs. Many other Christians as individuals have taken this attitude, and some non–Christians also. It is known as pacifism. For Quakers, the basic Christian principle is reverence for human life as God's creation, as well as the model of Jesus who went to his death on the cross without making any resistance. The Biblical tradition can be summed up for them in the Commandment '*Do not kill*'. These Christians are simply opposed to fighting in any form, and the invention of nuclear weapons does not make any difference in principle.

The traditional attitude of most Christians is that there are circumstances which justify the use of force, fighting, and what they call *a just war*. This applies for instance to fighting in self–defence when your country's life and freedom is in danger, fighting to help a weaker nation, or for the sake of something which you value and think the enemy would destroy. This may sound vague, but each case must be considered on its merits. For these Christians, war can be justified if the aims are good and if the consequences, as far as one can foresee them, are worthwhile.

For some of these Christians, however, the coming of nuclear weapons has made a difference. As a result a considerable number of individuals have effectively become pacifists, but not on the same principle as the Quakers. They would not oppose some kinds of war if they could be sure that nuclear weapons would not be used, but they are not convinced by the argument that nuclear weapons can be used in a controlled way. This is of course debatable and no–one can make a safe prediction about what would or would not happen.

With the views of a fourth group it is easier to see the religious principle once more. Some would call it a very grim and dangerous principle, but at least its roots can be traced. There are towns in America bordering on the Nevada desert whose main industry is the assembly and testing of nuclear weapons. Every Sunday the churches are full, and there is singing, prayer and preaching. The main message is the coming judgement of God and God's kingdom. These Christians do not seem to be concerned whether nuclear war can or cannot be avoided. They believe that if it happens, then it is God's will. Some of them would even welcome the destruction of the entire world as the means, or at least the sign of the establishment of the kingdom and visible rule of God.

The Campaign for Nuclear Disarmament

The Christians who founded CND and those who now support it must disagree very deeply with the outlook of the Nevada churches just mentioned. They feel that because they are Christians they have an even greater responsibility, not just for fellow Christians but for the whole world. CND has many non–Christian members, and there is also a subgroup within the organisation which is called 'Christian CND'. Their main work is to publicise the dangers of nuclear weapons and to act as a pressure group on governments and on public opinion in a number of countries, mainly within NATO, but their influence is more widely felt.

Bruce Kent was a Christian priest with a promising career. He had been promoted to the rank of Monsignor, which is a short step before being made a bishop in the Roman Catholic church. He was a keen supporter of CND, and agreed to help run it as its General Secretary. When he found he could not do two jobs, he gave up his career in the church hierarchy, and devoted himself full–time to CND. This does not of course mean that he has stopped being a Christian, but it was for him a difficult decision to take.

CND is not an exclusively Christian organisation. Some of the members are communists, as well as people of non–Christian religions or of no religion at all. But Christians like Bruce Kent see this work as their Christian vocation, and believe that Christ is already at work within it.

Pacifism and Resistance

The government of countries in Central and South America consider themselves Christian. The same is true for government leaders in South Africa. In communist countries, of course, the governments claim to be anti–religious, but the methods used by the police in Russia and in some right–wing countries seem strangely similar. People often ask when it may be justifiable to resist the police. But Christians must also ask when it may be justifiable to resist police acting in the name of a Christian ruler or government. This is not of course a new problem.

It comes back in the end to the question: How far should Christians get involved in political and social activities? Those in power usually say they should not. According to them (usually anyhow) being a Christian should make one hard–working and obedient, leaving all government and policy decisions to those in authority. No matter how bad things may be in terms of health, money, and exploitation, they say the Christian's reward is in the next life, and on a purely individual basis. The important thing is to join a church and keep quiet.

We have met this argument before. Sometimes it is combined with the teaching that God has already decided who is to be saved and who is not, and so difficult moral decisions are no longer important. Again it is usually the well–off who say this, and it seems to give them the chance to exploit the weak.

They emphasise that peace is a Christian virtue, and then do not want questions about justice to be raised. Yet most Christians say that peace can only come with and through justice. According to this line of thought the government that ought to be obeyed is the government which seeks justice, puts forward and upholds right laws.

Dietrich Bonhoeffer (1906–1945) belonged to the group of Christians in Germany who were strongly opposed to Hitler and to Naziism. He was also a pacifist, and wanted to get rid of Hitler and Nazi rule by non–violent means. The war, however, and what was happening in Europe and in Germany, finally persuaded him that there was no chance of stopping Hitler except by the use of force. For this reason he agreed to take part in one of the many plots to assassinate Hitler. The plot failed, and Bonhoeffer was hanged just a month before the end of the war for his part in this plot.

A young German officer, who was frequently in halls and meeting rooms where Hitler came to consult with generals and other leaders, came to Bonhoeffer one day to ask his advice. The officer was a Christian and secretly a member of the Confessing Church and therefore deeply against all that Hitler was doing. He explained to Bonhoeffer, that all he had to do was to draw his pistol and shoot him. It would not be difficult. There would of course be no escape, but he was quite happy to give his own life for the good of the nation and ultimately the world. He wanted Bonhoeffer to say Yes or No.

Dietrich Bonhoeffer

Bonhoeffer said that even within the fellowship of the Christian church another person could not take such a decision for him. He must think it out for himself with prayer, and decide on his own responsibility. The officer was in great distress: he wanted someone else to tell him what he must do. Bonhoeffer refused, leaving the question quite open, as before. We know, of course, that in the end he did not shoot Hitler. Such decisions are not easier for a Christian than other people, and perhaps actually harder.

ACTIVITY: as a group

You might like to debate exactly this question in your small group.
It is a question of ends and means: the purpose (ends) was to stop Hitler, but the means would mean murder.
Do the ends justify the means in this case?

Chapter Eight

THE FIRE NEXT TIME

The Bible relates in Genesis 6–9 that God was angry with the way the world was going. He therefore made a flood of water cover the whole earth to destroy everything, birds, animals and the human race. Only Noah was to survive, with his family, and God taught him to build a large boat, the Ark, into which he was instructed to load enough animals and birds to repopulate the earth afterwards. The good climax of the story is the convenant or promise which God made, and symbolised for Noah by the rainbow in the sky. According to the story, whenever you see a rainbow, you should be reminded that God will never again send a flood to destroy all life on the earth. The story also has a less good climax, and this is the start of drunkenness and the eating of meat. Obviously there is a threat along with the promise.

Other parts of the Bible suggest coming threats of destruction, to be used if people are cruel to each other and immoral. This thought was put into a rhyme by an unknown American Negro in the Southern states.
God gave Noah the rainbow sign:
No more water — the fire next time.
You may perhaps read the Bible story of the Flood as part of world history, or as a symbolic story which describes the way man relates

psychologically to God, the creator of the universe; or you may understand the story some other way. But you only have to look around or read the papers to see that it now really is possible to destroy our whole environment in a nuclear blast or series of blasts.

The basic principle here which is significant for Christians is the three–way relationship between God, the worlds he has made and goes on making, and thirdly the intelligent beings, i.e. people, who are to be held responsible for wars and accidents. Understood like this, God is both the creator of the universe and also the final judge at the end of time. In addition to this many Christians believe that God is active in world events all the time. On this view, God both creates continually, every new birth, every seed, etc. and also God is working to save the world. '*Save*' means to bring it through its present far–from–perfect state to the ideal condition which Christians call '*the Kingdom of God*'.

The only reason this does not happen immediately is because of the third factor in the relationship, and this is mankind and human responsibility. God, it seems, wants people to decide for themselves and act responsibly. To overrule them and force them to act like machines or puppets would be to deny us our position as intelligent human beings. Thus being human is a privilege, albeit a privilege which includes a burden of responsibility.

It is only in the light of this way of thinking that we get a specifically Christian attitude to the environment, to cruelty to animals, and many other issues. Of course Christians have the same feelings as other people, and can be sad or sentimental in exactly the same ways. So in many cases the way Christians react to environmental questions is not different from many non-Christians. But there is a Christian principle, or principles involved.

Chapter Nine

CHRISTIANS IN THE WORLD TODAY

ACTIVITY: as a group

For a discussion with a difference, **get each member of your small group to choose one of the individuals who has been described or mentioned in earlier sections of this book.**

These would include Steve Biko, Father Pavel, Bruce Kent, Mother Teresa, perhaps the German officer who couldn't decide to shoot Hitler, Jean Vanier, Jim Wallis, Maximilien Kolbe, perhaps St Elisabeth, or maybe other Christians who are fairly well–known, or at any rate known to you.

- When you have each chosen a character, take some time to look back and remind yourselves of the main points about him or her.
- Then you take on the role you have chosen and think yourself into being that person.
- Now introduce yourself to other members of the group and begin to talk to them and with them about who you are.
- Ask each other why you took the decisions you did, even though it led to hardships. How far were these decisions made because they felt themselves Christians who were called by God?

When the exercise is over and everyone has spoken in role to some of the others, go back to being 'yourselves' but sit round again and now ask, **Why do these individuals stand out?** Some of the answers may come from the talk earlier, but you may now have additional ideas.

The various sections in this Part also show that the great majority of Christians do not stand out in this way. Perhaps they do not stand out at all. Lots of people in Europe and America call themselves Christians, but do not seem any different from non–christians. Probably they do, however, take part in some of the life–cycle rituals discussed in Part Three, for instance Baptism, Marriage, and funeral.

A great many Christians also observe the major festivals. These were described in Part One. So if you have to look for Christianity being practised in the modern world, you would need to look at the religious festivals and at the ceremonies which mark stages in life, i.e. look at Parts One and Three.

To assess worship, however, is much more difficult. Obviously worship takes place at the festivals, as well as at other times, but the whole of Part Two should show that worship is in important ways something inward, something which it is not easy to assess from outside.

You can however see how Christians behave and what they do. In Part Five there are notable instances of Christian behaviour, as well as some discussion about Christian choices. Some of them are not very distinctive. In fact Christians may act in confusing and contradictory ways.

How they act depends ultimately on their values and their beliefs. This does not mean for most people the systematic beliefs set out in Part Four. These beliefs are vital for the Christian church and the Christian tradition, but they are not usually uppermost in most people's minds when they make decisions and take action. Instead Christians have general beliefs about the world and about the church and about their individual relationship to both.

Many Christians for instance make a clear division between good and evil. This exists in the Bible and in Christian tradition. Building on the teaching of some of the Protestant reformers it is possible to maintain that Christians form a group of souls who have been saved while everyone else and the world around them has been lost. And by 'lost' they mean that the world is under the control of the powers of evil. This way of thinking has been discussed before, and it sets up a strong contrast between 'Christians' on the one hand and 'non–Christians' on the other. When these people speak about 'Christianity in a non–Christian world' they want to make a definite contrast, because the world is obviously not Christian: in fact they see the world as opposed to Christ.

Other Christians however find such a distinction impossible to make, except in quite general terms. When you get down to detail it becomes less easy. For them the world is not 'lost', not under the control of evil powers. No–one denies that there is a lot of evil and wrong in the world, but they believe that God intends to save many who do not call themselves Christians: God loves the world, because God made it, and the Christian church is a living witness to God's love in Jesus Christ. So when these Christians speak of Christianity in a non–Christian world, they mean a world which is not explicitly Christian, which does not call itself Christian. Anyway, they know there is quite a lot wrong with Christians too: they are not perfect.

These two different world–views affect the way Christians behave in daily life as well as in the big decisions.

Denominations

At the end of the twentieth century it is becoming clear that the two world–views just mentioned are what really separate Christians from each other. This seems to be a much more important difference between Christians than the different denominations. Obviously every denomination has its own history and you can trace how each began. But more people today than ever before are finding these differences less important and less interesting when compared to the major world problems of poverty, weapons and other topics dealt with in this Part. Younger Christians believe that these problems are so urgent that Christians must put differences of denomination behind them and work together for good. They feel themselves called by God out of the past and into the future, to continue the work of Jesus among the world's poor, blind and suffering.

Many Christians go to services run by denominations in which they were not themselves brought up. Yet Christians of the older generation are shy of receiving holy communion or other sacraments in a 'strange' denomination unless invited. Although church leaders and authorities have different rules about going to holy communion within other denominations, some younger Christians ignore these and feel quite at home in each others' churches.

How is Christianity Different?

All religions teach kindness, helping people, honesty and so on. Christianity is not unique in this. What does seem to be special, however, is something else. This is that Christians traditionally have felt they must be ready to give, to suffer loss or persecution, at a personal or community level if need be. It has often been said that Christianity actually grows and thrives when Christians are persecuted.

Behind this outlook is the life and work of Jesus. His death on the cross is seen by most Christians as more than an example. Christians see the crucifixion as making a basic change to the world and how they are to live in it. Christ's death then has created a future, far beyond the events of the resurrection and the first Easter. There are Christians who call themselves 'the Easter people' because they want to live in this future.

Christianity is also a historical religion. Christians believe that they can see God at work and leading them in world events. In the section on Riches and Poverty it was suggested that Christians could have learnt something in the 750 years between St Elisabeth and Archbishop Helder Camara. This means that Christianity is not just a timeless message or philosophy which is to be applied by individuals.
The growth of awareness which led to the abolition of slavery points in the same direction.

Sometimes there are events which symbolise hope. Something special may pull into focus things which people have felt but not been able to put into effective words or deeds. Such events stand out at the time for those who are ready and open for them.

The coronation of Haile Selassie

The name *Haile Selassie* means 'Might of the Trinity'.

One such event was the coronation of Haile Selassie I of Ethiopia in 1930. The blacks of America and the Caribbean had been perhaps the most oppressed and exploited people in the world. By the 1930s they were just beginning to be aware of their past and their potential. Just about all of them were Christians, belonging to a variety of churches, and most of them also regular church–goers. Suddenly the public ceremony in honour of a black emperor flashed on their consciousness from newspaper photographs and cinema newsreels. They saw him as a king and at the same time as one of themselves, a black African, yet one who had never been enslaved (Ethiopia was never a colony of Europe). Yet this man was the centre of a deeply Christian ritual, crowned by Bishops and welcomed by a church that was almost biblical in its antiquity.

This single event gave a boost to the black consciousness movement. Millions who had felt alternately exploited and ignored began to take a pride in themselves, in their past and their traditions. It was significant as a religious event because the coronation took place in an explicitly Christian context. It was a sign of hope. But that was sixty years ago, and Christians are finding new signs of hope in the world today.

ACTIVITY

For a final exercise, find a partner, someone you feel happy with and can talk to easily.

Each of you needs a piece of plain paper and a pencil, and some colours would also be a help.

Working alone at first, use your imagination to draw a picture or shape or shapes which somehow express for you what Christianity as you understand it can offer, or ought to be able to offer as a sign of hope in the world today. You can be as symbolic as you like.

When you have finished, show your picture to your partner.

Take it in turns to talk about your picture, explore the symbolism and the signs of hope (if there are any).

Let your partner ask you about it and make suggestions too.

Then do the same with the other picture.

One Line Answers

(Answer each of these questions in one line or two)

1 What do the words 'Your kingdom come' mean for Christians?
2 What sort of Christians might look forward to the end of the world?
3 Why do some Christians (outside the U.K.) form a specifically Christian political party?
4 Name one Christian who has held strong views on riches and poverty and say briefly what he or she said.
5 Why do some Christians say 'God loves the poor'?
6 Why does the gospel say it is hard for a rich man to enter the kingdom of heaven?
7 What makes a Christian basic community Christian?
8 Name one practical advantage for members of a Christian basic community.
9 Name one Christian in this century who has suffered persecution for his or her faith, and say in which country this was.
10 Name one group of Christians who persecute and imprison another group of Christians.
11 State two things in the gospels which might affect Christian attitudes towards the handicapped.
12 Why might a Christian think it a privilege to help someone who is mentally handicapped?
13 Name one Christian organisation which works with the handicapped.
14 What is the Magnificat, and what might it mean for today's Christians?
15 Name one worldwide Christian denomination or church which does not ordain women to the priesthood.
16 Name one part of a Christian minister's job which you think would be done better by a male minister, and give a reason for your answer.
17 Name one group of Christians who are opposed to war of any kind.
18 What is 'Christian CND'?
19 Do you think the invention of nuclear weapons makes any difference to a Christian's attitude to war?
20 What might be meant by the verse:
   God gave Noah the rainbow sign:
   No more water — the fire next time!
21 Give one reason why Christians should oppose cruelty to animals.
22 Some Christians think that denominational differences are a thing of the past: what do they think is more important?
23 Name one recent world event which you think is a sign of hope for Christians.
24 Name one modern Christian whom you admire, and say briefly what she or he has done.

Absolution, Absolve

Absolution is a ritual (also called a sacrament). The purpose is to assure some one of forgiveness after he or she has confessed a fault or sin. A priest usually speaks the words of absolution in the name of God: '*I absolve you in the Name of the Father, the Son and the Holy Spirit*'.

Adoration

Adoration is combination of feeling and activity which expresses love for God and willingness to serve God in some way. Adoration may be wordless and take the form of concentrated silence, or may include prayer or singing. Working for other people (especially people in need) may also be a form of adoration for those who believe that doing this is serving God or showing one's love for God, because God is seen or felt through and within those in need.

Aisle

Many Western church buildings have one or more aisles inside, which lead like a walkway towards the altar (or a side altar). In a large church there may be three aisles, often with columns or pillars on one or both sides. Together these form the nave of the church.

Altar

The altar, also called the holy table, is part of the furniture or equipment in most church buildings. Typically the altar stands at the East end of the church in a special part called the chancel (Western churches), and may have placed on it a cross or crucifix, candles and or other things, eg flowers. The altar is very important as it is central for celebrating the eucharist. Other ceremonies, especially marriage, are performed in front of it. In Protestant and Anglican churches the altar is almost always a table constructed of wood which usually has a cloth on it and a coloured hanging in front. Roman Catholic churches almost always have a stone altar (or even several stone altars) but many RC churches also use a wooden altar because it can be easily moved and brought down to the congregation.

Atonement

The basic meaning of atonement is the reconciling of man to God (being 'at-one' with God). Christians believe that this was achieved by Jesus Christ, and in particular through his sufferings. There are various theories or doctrines of atonement which try to explain how this was achieved. In Old Testament times (pre-Christian) atonement was a ritual involving an animal's death, and this fact has influenced Christian understanding.

Baptistry

The Baptistry is part of a church building but by no means all churches have one. In churches where they baptise infants or adults by effusion (pouring water on), there is a font instead of a baptistry. Very few churches have both. The baptistry is a kind of pit with steps, several feet deep, which can be filled with water for the ceremony of baptism by total immersion (going right under). Baptists (and some other groups) always practise this kind of baptism and only baptise adults or near-adults. Therefore almost every Baptist church has a baptistry. Orthodox churches also baptise by total immersion, but use a font large enough for the baby to be put right in.

Chalice

A chalice is a cup which is used for holy communion. Most frequently a chalice is made of silver and in the shape of a cup on a stem, like a silver cup sports trophy, but it may be any shape, eg like a large mug. It may be made of china, pottery, wood or horn, in fact anything that will do the job. Because it is used in this sacred ritual, many chalices are ornate.

Chancel

The chancel is part of the church building inside at the East end (usually) and contains the altar and other furniture connected with celebrations, especially the eucharist. In Orthodox churches this area is separated from the rest of the church by a screen (icon screen) and called the sanctuary. In Western churches the chancel is more than the sanctuary, and often includes seats or stalls for a choir, and if there is a screen, this is between the chancel and the nave. Some Western churches and chapels do not have a separate chancel at all.

Church

1 The church is fundamentally people who are Christians, and at its broadest includes millions of people all over the world, dead as well as living (ie ranging through time). When the church is called 'the Body of Christ' Jesus Christ is seen as its head.

2 The word church may mean a smaller group of Christians, such as a denomination ('the Methodist Church') or even a local group such as the church people in a particular place or parish.

3 A church may also be the building in which the local church (=people) meets for worship.

4 The word 'church' occasionally is used to mean the officials of the church or the ministers: so sometimes people say, 'The Church teaches so-and-so,' when they refer to official doctrine; or they say, 'He's going into the church,' meaning he is going for ordination to the ministry. This last is misleading because Christians go into the church through baptism.

Commandments

The Commandments, usually Ten Commandments, are the summary of the law believed to have been given by God to Moses on Mount Sinai. They are listed in the Bible in Exodus 20.1–17 and again in Deuteronomy 5.6–21. All Christians agree that there are ten although not all number them in the same way. Many Christians see the Ten Commandments as the basis for good and moral behaviour, and in many older parish churches in England they are written up and displayed on the wall.

Communion

The word communion basically means sharing or having something in common with other people.

1 Communion or holy communion is the act of receiving the bread and wine (or host, with or without the chalice) at the celebration of the eucharist.

2 A meaning derived from 1 makes 'communion' another name for denomination, eg 'the Anglican Communion': this arose because some denominations would not take holy communion with members of another, and so their communion has been seen as exclusive.

Confess, Confession

To confess or make a confession means to admit to having done something (or failed to do something, or knowing something).

1 Christians make a practice of looking back at their lives and making a confession, confessing sins or faults or failures. They may do this in private prayer, confessing to God alone. Or they may confess to another Christian or group of Christians, either because they have offended or wounded them, or because they value their advice and help.

2 When confession is made in the presence of a priest, the priest usually speaks the words of forgiveness or absolution as from God. People speak of '*confessing to a priest*', but strictly the confession is made to God in the presence of a priest.
3 In times of persecution, one may confess that one is a Christian, and this is quite different from 1 and 2.

Consecrate

To consecrate means to make holy or sacred, usually by a special ritual which sets something or someone apart for a special religious purpose. Thus an individual may be consecrated a bishop, a building may be consecrated as a church, or a piece of land as a churchyard. At the eucharist bread and wine are consecrated for holy communion.

Contemplation

Contemplation in a Christian context is a form of wordless prayer. Contemplation may be focussed on an object like a picture or statue, or on a flower or candle flame or similar. Contemplation may also be concentrated on something less visible like a mood or a feeling. If attention is focussed on an event pictured in the mind, eg a gospel scene, some say that this is meditation, not contemplation, but in any case contemplation presupposes stillness and concentration.

Contrition, Contrite

Being contrite means being sorry for sins or faults or for one particular fault, and at the same time wishing sincerely to make amends and do better in future. In a ritual act of contrition, confessing is the central feature. In general terms, contrition is another name for repentance.

Denomination

A church organisation which is spread across the country, several countries or world-wide is called a denomination if it has a definite identity, system of leadership, ritual practices and doctrines.

Ecclesiastical

Ecclesiastical means having to do with the church organisation or church ritual. A minister or priest may be said to have an ecclesiastical career (possibility of promotion, etc). Activities and ceremonies to do with church order may be called ecclesiastical.

Eucharist

Eucharist is Greek for giving thanks, and is one name for the central service of Christian worship. It is also called the Lord's Supper, the Mass, and Holy Communion, although strictly communion is only one part, although the main part, of the eucharist.

Font

A font is a piece of church furniture which is essentially a large bowl, usually of stone, on a stand. It is used for baptising babies and adults. The baby or the adult's head is held over the font and water poured from a scoop or cupped hand. This form of baptism is alternative to going right under (total immersion) and so not practised by some denominations who have a baptistry instead of a font. Note, however, that in Orthodox churches babies are baptised by total immersion in the font.

Forgiveness

Forgiving and forgiveness in a Christian context means essentially the same as in any other. But forgiveness is associated also with the ritual which involves confession and absolution. This is important for many Christians. In such cases, forgiveness is felt in the first place to come from God (not from the priest who only speaks the words) and in the second place from the person or people who have suffered injury or wrong.

Grace

Among Christians grace is a technical term for the way in which God is thought to relate to individuals and to groups. Grace expresses God's active love and acceptance of people in spite of their unworthiness. This means that grace is always completely undeserved, a free gift.

Hermit

A hermit is a man or woman who lives alone in order to pray. This comes from a sense of vocation. A hermit may be loosely attached to a monastery or church group.

Holy

'Holy' is the basic idea in all religion, and includes purity, goodness and mystery. God is uniquely holy for Christians and therefore totally distinct from and beyond all creation and created things. By association with God and divine actions things can be called holy also, such as holy communion, holy places, holy prayers and people.

Icon

An icon looks like a rather special picture of a saint or gospel scene. Orthodox church buildings usually have many icons on the screen which divides the sanctuary from the main part of the church, hence called the icon screen (iconostasion). Most Orthodox Christians have one or more icons at home as a focus for prayers, and the practice is spreading among individuals of other denominations. For the Orthodox an icon is much more than a picture and indicates the presence of whoever it shows actually with the worshipper. Icon painting is a highly specialised art and icon painting a form of religious devotion.

Incarnation

For Christians, the incarnation is the name for the whole action of God becoming man in Jesus Christ. Christ is thus described as 'God incarnate' – ie in human, flesh and blood form. For some Christians Jesus continues even after his Ascension to be incarnate in the poor, the oppressed and the wretched.

Intercession

Intercession is a way of praying for particular people or situations, asking God to help, save, show pity. Intercession may be almost wordless, simply trying to place the person or situation in God's presence. This makes it different from other forms of prayer, because intercession has a special intention of praying for people etc. Also called 'supplication'.

Lectern

A lectern is a piece of church furniture on which the big Bible is placed at a convenient height for someone to read aloud to the congregation.

Liturgy

Liturgy is Greek for 'service' and means a Christian service in church, especially the eucharist. The eucharist is sometimes called the 'sacred liturgy' and particular forms of it are called 'the liturgy of St Basil', 'the Roman liturgy', etc.

Mass

The mass is a name for the eucharist which is mostly used by Roman Catholics. Its origin is not known, but may derive from the last words of the service in Latin 'Ite, missa est' (depart in peace: the service is over).

Meditate, Meditation

Meditation is a form of prayer which may be silent (but not always) and which is focussed on an event or person, for instance from the gospel or the present. Meditation usually involves the imagination and may use a form of words repeated over and over either as a guide for concentration or as a time check (for instance when used with beads on a rosary). Some people clearly distinguish meditation from contemplation, but for others the difference is less clear.

Messiah

The word Messiah originally meant 'anointed king', for which the Greek word is 'Christ'. Christians see Jesus as the Messiah with two special references: first as the fulfiller of Jewish hopes, the Messiah who is to come, and this role is emphasised by the visit of the wise men to Bethlehem; and secondly as the future king and judge who returns at the end of time.

Monk

A monk is a man who has dedicated himself to the religious life within a community. Usually monks live together in a monastery and follow a rule or pattern of life, which has been drawn up in many cases by the founder of the order.

Moral, Morality

Morality is a general term for good behaviour in accordance with a set of principles. Thus a moral person leads a moral life by having good intentions and producing good results on principle. 'Moral' cannot be applied to good produced by accident. Morality need not be religious in any sense, but Christianity implies and includes a moral outlook. A Christian may see morality as God's will revealed through scripture, tradition, or inspiration, or a combination of these.

Nave

The nave is the main part of the inside of a church building, as distinct from chancel and transepts if there are any. When the church is a simple building without different parts (except the sanctuary), it is not usual to speak of the 'nave' because it is virtually the whole interior space.

Numinous

The word numinous is sometimes used to describe or refer to a mysterious and somewhat uncanny presence which is felt but cannot be clearly distinguished. It is therefore a word and idea which is applicable to all kinds of religion including primal religions. But it is important to realise that the awareness of mysterious presence is vital in Christianity also. This presence can be felt as overwhelming, as frightening, and as attracting or loving.

Nun

A nun is a woman who has dedicated herself to the religious life within a special kind of community. Compare 'Monk' above.

Offertory

The offertory is part of a Christian service, particularly the eucharist, when the offerings of the people are collected and taken up to the altar (usually) to be dedicated. At the eucharist the offertory is the putting ready of bread and wine before consecration. In some celebrations, bread and wine are brought up from the back of the church by members of the congregation, and this is called the offertory procession. Offertory also covers the collection of money from people during the service.

Office, offices

Monks and nuns leading the religious life follow a pattern which includes worship services at certain times of day (and for some, night also). These services are called 'offices'. Clergy who are not in monasteries, and many lay people, may also say offices on a regular basis.

Penance

Penance is an action to demonstrate that the penitent (person who has confessed sins or faults) is really sorry for what she or he has done and intends to do better. Nowadays a penance is a light task, for instance saying a particular prayer or reading a passage from the Bible. It is a token of sorrow, but not in any sense a recompense. Christians believe that God forgives freely those who are sorry and seriously mean to make amends, and that God's grace cannot be earned by severe penance. In earlier times penances were often required to be done in public, and could be very severe and longlasting. Absolution is sometimes called 'the sacrament of penance'.

Penitent

1 A penitent is a Christian who confesses sins, either privately or in front of a priest, more rarely in front of several people.
2 As an extension of 1, a priest may have penitents, meaning people whose confessions he hears (separately) on a regular basis.

Prayer

Prayer is generally personal communication with God, and includes silent prayer, intercession, meditation, contrition, adoration and much else. Group prayer is essentially no less personal, although it can become formal and routine, so almost empty. Prayer is meant to be communication both ways, so should include thought and listening as well as input.

Preach

Preaching is the public proclamation of the gospel or of a theme more or less linked to the gospel. Within a church service, the preacher preaches or delivers the sermon. Preaching can also take place on its own and in public or indeed anywhere.

Pulpit

The pulpit is a piece of furniture inside the church building, or is built into the church as part of it. Typically a pulpit is a raised platform with steps and a reading stand, often a low wall and a door, and it is from the pulpit that the preacher preaches the sermon.

Reconcile, Reconciliation

Reconciliation is the act or process of reconciling two people (perhaps more) who have been angry, suspicious or offended over each other. Christians speak of being reconciled to their neighbours (those they come in contact with) as a preliminary to worshipping God. Reconciliation with people you have upset is a precondition for absolution, unless there is some special reason which makes reconciliation impossible. Christians think of God as the essential partner in all relationships and therefore reconciliation includes being reconciled to God. In global terms, the life and death of Jesus Christ, his incarnation and resurrection, are seen as the means of reconciling God and humanity, or making individual acts of reconciliation possible.

Religious

Apart from the general meaning of 'religious' as describing or to do with religion, there is an additional meaning, as in the phrase 'religious life'.
1 In this sense religious usually means belonging to a religious order or community as a monk or a nun (but there are other possibilities), together with the rule of prayer and so on.
2 From this, 'religious life' may also include spiritual activity generally.

3 'A religious' is an expression used to mean a member of a religious community or order.

Resurrection

1 Jesus Christ's rising from the dead is simply called the resurrection.
2 Christians expect to rise again also, either after death individually (as some believe), or (as more generally believed) all together at the Day of Judgement. This is called the General Resurrection, or the resurrection of the dead.

Revelation

1 If something is revealed by God to human beings, this can be called revelation. The scriptures are said to have been revealed in this sense. But revelation is not exclusively words, or a body of fact, and can include understanding or seeing things in a new light. The key idea is that revelation comes from God.
2 Revelation is the name of the last book of the Bible (New Testament). It is not a prediction of the future, but reveals the relationship of God to man (as Christians believe), drawing on traditional Jewish symbolism, especially suitable for times of persecution.

Rood

A rood is a special name for a carving of Jesus on the cross with the figure of St John (the beloved disciple) standing on one side and the mother of Jesus on the other. These were common inside English church buildings in the Middle Ages, brightly painted, and several survive. When the rood was sited on the top of an openwork screen under the chancel arch (entrance to the chancel), this screen was called the Rood Screen. The purpose is to inspire devotion.

Sacrament

A sacrament is a ritual or ceremony where what is done and the objects used are a sign of the gracious work of God for the Christians taking part. The sacrament represents or enacts the action of God.
1 Sacrament therefore is the name for any of a number of rituals, eg baptism, eucharist.
2 In particular, the eucharist, and people may say 'sacrament' when referring to the eucharist.
3 Further to 2, 'sacrament' can also be used to mean the sacramental presence of God within the bread, and especially when the bread or wafer is put in a special place (reserved sacrament). Thus one can speak of meditating or praying before the sacrament.

Sacred

1 Sacred is a descriptive word with meanings similar to holy.
2 'Sacred mysteries' is a technical term for the celebration of the eucharist.

Sanctify

To sanctify is to make sacred or to make holy, and thus overlaps with 'consecrate', except that sanctify is more general than consecrate. 'Sanctify' is not usually used when speaking of a ritual, ceremony or sacrament, and 'consecrate' is used for these instead.

Sanctuary

1 The sanctuary is that part of the church building where the altar stands. This area is usually marked off by a step or steps and altar rails. The sanctuary is thus only part of the chancel. In Orthodox churches the whole area beyond the icon screen is called the sanctuary.
2 In earlier times certain places were used to offer safety to fugitives, and were called sanctuary. No longer in use.

Sermon

The sermon is the address or preaching which takes place as part of a religious service.

Sin

1 Sin is a technical name for any fault or wrongdoing, and stresses that God is offended, as well as any other people who may be involved. In making confession, a penitent confesses sins.

2 'Original Sin' is rather different and refers to the basic tendency human beings have for going wrong and wanting to make wrong decisions.

Spiritual, Spirtuality

Spirituality is a rather vague term for religious activities of a prayerful, meditative kind, and for exercises or disciplines which someone undertakes to help with these activities. The 'spiritual life' means the practice and development of these activities, and is usually undertaken with the help of a guide, who is called one's 'spiritual director' or counsellor.

Supplication

Supplication means asking or begging for things and is a form of prayer also known as intercession. There is a difference, however, in that intercession means prayer on behalf of other people or situations, but supplication can also include prayer for oneself.

Testimony, Testify

In some kinds of church service, individuals stand up and tell everyone what they feel God has done for them personally. This is called testifying or giving testimony. Sometimes a special time is set aside for testimonies. It is possible to testify at any gathering, not only in church, and even in the street, although the public may not be willing to listen.

Thanksgiving

Thanksgiving is saying 'Thank-you', often in a detailed and appreciative way, and is a form of prayer devoted to thanking God.

Theology

Theology is the reasoned and systematic study of God's dealings with man and man's response, both in the Bible and in other ways. Theology therefore may require the learning of languages, history, doctrine, liturgy and much else. Although the emphasis is mainly on the intellect, it is recognised that God is beyond all human reason, and the attempt to study the being of God is called 'mystical theology'.

Transubstantiation

Sometimes spelt 'transsubstantiation' this is a particular doctrine of the eucharist which was supposed to describe how in the eucharist bread and wine are changed into the body and blood of Christ. According to this doctrine, they are no longer bread and wine. Behind this, however, is the philosophical thought of Aristotle (pre-Christian) which is no longer used. Although transubstantiation is still official doctrine for millions of Christians, mainly Roman Catholics, it is rarely explained in detail today. Instead, most Christians believe that the bread and wine become the body and blood of Christ mysteriously, without being able to say how. The belief that they become Christ's body and blood while still remaining bread and wine, is called consubstantiation. But this is contrary to the strict teaching of transubstantiation.

Vocation

Vocation just means 'calling' and is specially applicable when Christians feel that God is calling them to a particular job, or a particular place. Becoming a Christian at all is seen as a vocation. In particular the word is frequently used to describe being called to the ordained ministry or to the religious life. The means of vocation can be as varied as life itself and it is sometimes difficult for individuals to recognise a vocation.

Worship

Worship means showing love, thanks and devotion to God, praising or thinking about God's supreme worth or value (worship derives from 'worth-ship'). Worship is the basic Christian activity or, as some Christians say, the chief purpose of mankind.